Class, Culture, and Race in American Schools

Class, Culture, and Race in American Schools

A HANDBOOK

Edited by
Stanley William Rothstein

GREENWOOD PRESS
Westport, Connecticut • London

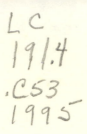

Library of Congress Cataloging-in-Publication Data

Class, culture, and race in American schools : a handbook / edited by
   Stanley William Rothstein.
      p.   cm.
   Includes bibliographical references (p.   ) and index.
   ISBN 0–313–29102–0 (alk. paper)
   1. Educational sociology—United States.   2. Educational
anthropology—United States.   3. Minorities—Education—United
States.   4. Socially handicapped children—Education—United States.
5. Discrimination in education—United States.   6. Multicultural
education—United States.   I. Rothstein, Stanley William.
LC191.4.C53   1995
370.19'0973—dc20   94–38502

British Library Cataloguing in Publication Data is available.

Library of Congress Catalog Card Number: 94–38502
ISBN: 0–313–29102–0

First published in 1995

Greenwood Press, 88 Post Road West, Westport, CT 06881
An imprint of Greenwood Publishing Group, Inc.

Printed in the United States of America

The paper used in this book complies with the
Permanent Paper Standard issued by the National
Information Standards Organization (Z39.48–1984).

10 9 8 7 6 5 4 3 2 1

Contents

Preface

Class, culture, and race have influenced the educational experiences of children for centuries. Yet definitions of these terms and theoretical perspectives have been shrouded in confusion and ideological assertions. With the coming to the United States of another wave of immigration from Latin America and Asia, public schools are faced with a challenge and a crisis: educating children who are from a culture of poverty. Such a culture flourishes in the modern world, where a cash economy, the wage labor system, and production for profit predominate. This culture of poverty generates persistently high levels of unemployment for unskilled labor, making it difficult for families to function effectively in American cities and for students to succeed in public schools. The failure to provide educational, political, and economic organizations for the millions of Hispanics, poor Asians, and African Americans migrating to and living in our inner cities has meant their continued existence in this culture of poverty. The values of American life have stressed that everyone can do better if they try, if they work hard and save their money. Thus poverty, illiteracy, and its culture have been explained as a consequence of the personal inadequacy and inferiority of individuals and groups.

The culture of poverty is an adaptation and a response of the poor and the culturally and racially different to their marginal positions in American society. Its effects on the children are generational, being passed on through the language and value systems of families. The basic values and attitudes of this culture of poverty make it psychologically difficult for children to take advantage of schools. Life experiences on the streets may cut short the childhood of the poor, initiating them into sexual relations, drug addiction, and gang activities. These, in turn, may affect youngsters' abilities to learn in schools that are often not as accepting as they might be.

These children speak languages and come from cultural and racial backgrounds that have been subjected to segregation and discrimination in the American system. The problems associated with educating them echo past failures in the early part of this century and the mythology that covered over these failures. This handbook will provide a systematic look at these problems. Each section of the book begins with an introductory chapter that looks at the categories of class, culture, race, and prospects for the future, and the ways in which they appear to influence the schooling experiences of children. The racial and ethnic groups this book studies are primarily Hispanics, African Americans, and Asians as they struggle to survive and prosper in the United States. The handbook's significance is as a source and starting point for those who wish to know more about the effects of class, culture, and race in American schools. Such information will come into increasing demand as the tens of millions of children from Hispanic America and Asia take their seats in the classrooms of our country.

This reference book is a guide to the effects of poverty, language, and race on the educational experiences of children. Each chapter is written by an authority in the field, emphasizing the key variables of class, culture, and race as they influence the everyday experiences of teachers and students. Together, they provide a comprehensive view of the historical and contemporary forces shaping our modern educational system today.

Chapter 1 presents a historical definition of class, tracing its origins to the estate system in medieval Europe. This is followed by "The Governance of Local Schools as Influenced by Social Class, Race, and Ethnicity," by Frank W. Lutz and Laurance Iannaccone. Using class as a central focus, they show how the variables of race and ethnicity interact with class to influence the way local school boards make their decisions. The reader is made aware that class, culture, and race are deeply entwined in our society and not easily separated in any of these studies. One's class deeply influences one's cultural outlook, one's culture often grows from one's economic and social history, and so on. The third chapter, "The Chicano Educational Experience: Empirical and Theoretical Perspectives," by Daniel G. Solorzano, shows how theory and practice can be used to gain deeper insights into the schooling experiences of Chicano children. Chapter 4, "Class, Race, and Science Education," by David Eli Drew, analyzes the way in which these three variables affect the types and levels of science materials to which children are exposed. Chapter 5, "Diversity and the Institutional Transformation of Public Education," by Joseph G. Weeres and John Rivera, shows how the variable of diversity affects the institutional life of teachers and students.

Part II defines the concept of culture and the way it is used to make sense out of the everyday lives of individuals living in modern society. Chapter 7, "Italian and Mexican Responses to Schooling: Assimilation or Resistance?" is written by Richard J. Altenbaugh. It provides a historical, sociological comparison of two immigrant groups and shows how their cultural heritages influenced their acceptance or rejection of schooling in American schools. This is followed by Chapter 8, "Emerging Educational Structures: The Impact on Leadership 'Culture'," by Andrew E. Dubin, which examines the ways in which change is mandated in educational organizations.

Part III focuses on Race relations and its effect on the schooling experiences of African American, Hispanic, and Asian children. Chapter 9, "Race Relations and Segregation in the United States," by Walter F. Beckman discusses the resegregation of inner-city schools in the United States. Then Mougo Nyaggah and Wacira Gethaiga write about "Race, Class, and the Educational Marginalization of African Americans: A Historical Perspective." This is followed by "Serving Asian American Children in School: An Ecological Perspective" by Mikyong Kim-Goh.

Part IV deals with the Problems and Possibilities in contemporary schools. Chapter 12 examines "Effective Teacher Preparation for Diverse Student Populations: What Works Best?" by Carmen Zuniga-Hill and Carol Barnes. It canvases teacher preparation programs and reports on methods of professional training that are providing the most promising results. Chapter 13, "Ecocultural Context, Cultural Activity, and Emergent Literacy: Sources of Variation in Home Literacy Experiences of Spanish-Speaking Children," by Leslie Reese, Claude Goldenberg, James Loucky, and Ronald Gallimore, examines the problems facing Spanish-speaking children in American schools. Finally, Chapter 13, "Culture, Class, and Race: Three Variables of Decision Making in Schools," by Lenore M. Parker, provides empirical evidence for the influence of culture, class, and race on the schooling experiences of children.

This book differs from others in its systematic approach and its fusion of theory and practice. Using historical, political, sociological, and pedagogical approaches, it provides the reader with an up-to-date compilation and discussion of the social science and educational literature. Then, in the final section, it suggests new ways of thinking and dealing with these problems. Notes or bibliographies are placed at the end of each chapter, directing readers to more specific sources of current research, and a selected bibliography at the end of the volume includes the most important sources for additional information and study.

PART I

CLASS

Chapter 1

From Estate to Social Class: A Historical Perspective and Definition

Stanley William Rothstein

The idea of class in modern society has its beginnings in the feudal period, when an estate system was established to define and control the behavior of the noble vassals and serfs. Oliver Cox has sketched the fundamental role of these estates, citing them as a way of identifying a person's rank and status in the manorial system.[1] Their power resided in their ability to supply objective criteria for a person's social standing, providing a basis for differentiating and legitimating differences in wealth and power in the same moment. Hence those references to a person's position in society, and especially one's seemingly unchangeable social estate.[2] But the greatest significance of the estate system was in its ability to structure the political, economic, and social sectors of feudal society, creating desired behavior in individuals based on their positions in the social order. Following this system's logic, each person was able to see and live by the laws and social mores of masters and peers. Each person was provided with a social schema that could be used in everyday life. Superior and inferior ranks were cast into language and culture by families and the church and translated into social and economic advantages.[3]

The laws of manors and nations also recognized and enforced this separation of the estates, even as they presumed the moral and religious basis upon which they rested. Moreover, the greatest strength of the estate system lay in its traditional values and social cohesion. Those on the bottom, with few exceptions, believed in the efficacy and reasonableness of their status and in the legal and moral right of their betters to live and act as they did.

The ordering of the estate system substituted a tangible idea of land possession in place of other, more imprecise, categories of wealth and standing.[4] These material conditions gave superior rank and privileges to those who owned the land, making it easy for all to know who controlled the basic economic resources and who farmed and lived on them as a matter of largess. If the land was the center of wealth, and it was passed from one generation to the next in an orderly process, those who owned it were of a more superior estate than those who worked it. Sharecroppers and serfs were, by definition then, of lower rank and standing. The family, and individuals in the family, had power, status, and wealth in accordance with their hereditary relationship to landownership. That and that alone determined their social standing in the feudal system. Indeed, possession of the land was the primary characteristic of feudal societies in the West and in Asia.[5]

Nevertheless, the nature and power of the estate system in Europe must be our point of departure: It was there that the conditions of power, authority, and wealth changed sufficiently over time to shake this seemingly eternal order to its foundations, ushering in the class system of commercial society. From the end of the Carolingian Empire to the Renaissance, feudalism reigned supreme in much of the West. But there were important exceptions, and the system developed differently in different countries. As late as the sixteenth and seventeenth centuries in England, France, and Germany, feudalism and the estate system flourished. But industrialism, science, and commerce began to challenge the religious and social assumptions of the estate system after the Reformation.

NEW CHALLENGES

In its strongest periods, the estate system was accepted because individuals were educated into it by families, churches, traditions, and the everyday realities of the people's lives. The language, culture, and values each estate taught its members were passed on to succeeding generations through speech and language, making members of each estate easily recognizable to one another. From the thirteenth century onward, elements of the modern state and class system came into being, challenging feudalism further and influencing the way it responded to the new ventures of commerce, science, and industry.[6] Education in this period still resided in the family and church, but there were rumblings of change in both of these institutions as laborers were forced out of their homes and into mills and factories. The incipient forces of industrialization now made themselves felt and the burgher classes began to grow in real wealth and power. From this time onward, feudalism was increasingly seen as a frozen and archaic society. Its obsession with the land made it impossible for the system to generate sufficient wealth and power to deal with the new realities of an expanding world trade. Its social structures and unchanging hereditary practices were too rigid for the new, fluid situations that were emerging with fresh discoveries in science and technology.

To repeat, then, feudalism was not a conflictual organization of society. Even in its most abusive configurations, the estate system found the traditions and cultural understandings it needed to justify and sustain its existence. Individuals believed that the privileges of the nobility emanated from kings of the realm and moved downward through lords until they reached the lowest serf working the land. All of the soil of England, as one example, was subjected to this method of distribution, which was justified by religious and cultural doctrines of the divine right of kings and lords to rule the land they owned.[7]

But estates did differ in different countries, and the relationships between monarchies and lords did change as situations occurred that challenged the feudal system's economic assumptions. Estates tended to divide themselves into many more levels of status, but essentially they rested upon the three basic divisions of the nobility, the clergy, and the servile peasantry.[8] The first two were the ruling classes of feudal society: they were the aristocracy, and their rights and privileges were formalized in speech and language, in culture, in the mores of the times, and in the laws of the land.

Yet if we look more closely at these estates, they were not homogeneous in their makeup: Within the peasantry, as one example, there were slaves who were household workers, poverty-stricken serfs who were indentured servants for set periods of time, vassals who did not work or live on the land, and free villeins who sharecropped the land along with the free peasantry.[9] Within each estate there was this pyramid of status and wealth, rising level by level until it reached the ruler of the estate or nation.

At the top of the feudal pyramid was the aristocracy, ranked from nobleman to lowly country gentlemen. In the villages and small towns there was still a tiny middle class of tradespeople and townspeople who occupied indeterminate statuses in the social pyramid. Yet these estates were not antagonistic toward one another in the modern sense of the word. Rather they were essentially cooperative social structures that were only separated by theorists and scholars who sought to study them. In the everyday reality of feudal society, their separateness was distinguished by economic and social activities that were augmented by the ideologies and linguistic understandings each estate developed about themselves. The estates had many common interests, and formed mutually supporting systems of ranks and statuses that ordered society and allowed it to create the wealth needed to sustain the social order.

THE CLERGY, THE NOBILITY, AND THE BURGHERS

It is common knowledge that the estate system was initially dominated by the clergy, which organized itself to carry on the work and messages of charismatic leaders and doctrines. It is less commonly known that the ruling groups of the clergy were also united by birth and custom with the landed nobility. It is common knowledge that the clergy developed a powerful political and organizational structure and ethos that allowed it to acquire land, power, and prestige over many centuries; what may be less familiar are the cultural and economic practices that inspired in the nobility and their landless serfs a willing allegiance to the feudal system.[10] Since the power of the church was rooted in religious doctrines and its ability to add to its landed holdings over long periods of time, the Catholic Church became a preeminent international power, often commanding the loyalty and actions of kings and princes in nations far removed from its papal seat in Rome. The church was at the apex of the estate system because of its moral and economic power, and its ability to add to that power across generations. It owned far more land than the nobility, and was the center of all learning and the arts for many centuries. From the ninth century to the eleventh century it was the controlling social, political, and economic organization in European governments and remained powerful for many centuries more. When the nation-states of Europe began to organize themselves, they used the bureaucratic and cultural examples of the church as their guide.

From the beginning, then, one thing seems clear: the clergy was not a religious establishment alone. It was rather a semijudicial institution, an administrative entity that, along with its religious powers, legislated and taxed itself. The rulers of the church sought to provide a stable and continuing organization for its clergy in the midst of a violent and often chaotic period in European history. A quasi-judicial and administrative structure was established by the clerical hierarchy that, along with its already significant economic power, allowed it to function as a shadow government in many European nations. The princes of the church were thus able to preside over their ever-increasing landholdings in an organized manner over many centuries. An absolute clerical sovereignty existed for all titles of ownership of the land, and matters of rank and privilege also needed their assent. The clergy was wealthy, well-organized, and in possession of the only centers of learning and scholarship and able to influence the decisions and behaviors of monarchs across the continent.[11]

In its functioning, or in its recruitment policies, the church sought out individuals from many different countries and stations in life. It was an order that included the nobility as well as those from the aspiring lower estates. It was thought of by the serfs and villein class as a way out of perpetual servitude and bondage, while tradespeople saw it as an avenue to greater wealth and power in an otherwise closed system. But there were ranks and status differences even within this order of priests: those from the most wealthy and powerful families were affiliated through social, political, cultural, and familial ties and assigned to leadership positions in the hierarchy. They were the great princes of the realm whose landholdings entitled them to greater influence and authority in the religious and political affairs of the country.

This structure differed from the nobility itself, which was organized on much more exacting lines. As the warrior class that ruled through the force of arms, it concerned itself more with social distances and standings and the enhancement of its prestige. Nobles tended to compete and war with one another, even as they joined together to exploit the labor of serfs, vassals, and tradespeople. Each nobleman submitted to another in an extended ladder of prestige and power, forming a system within which the specific rights and privileges of each were duly recorded and preserved by the clergy.

This structure had at its base the landed manor or estate within which the nobleman was lord and master over the servile peasantry that lived and worked there. A master-servant or -slave relationship existed with little fellowship about it. Labor on the landed estates was the hard, mandatory toil of the farm tenant system.

The system had continental magnitude during the medieval period. The constitution of a nobility dependent upon the church and monarchies of Europe produced a system in which noblemen were vassals to other noblemen holding fiefdoms and divided lands of still other important noblemen. The greater and lesser nobility were thus bound together through ties of service, fealty, and honor. In many instances an individual might manage many fiefs from several lords so that he could be seen as becoming as powerful or more so than those who claimed his allegiance. This agrarian system was supported by custom and law, but conflicts between lords were common and wars an ongoing concern. As a matter of fact, wars between nobles were a common way of settling disputes, creating an age of conflict and violence that made the nobleman's protection more important to other estates where the means and expertise of war were not known or available.[12] The nobility was fractionalized by these incessant wars and was seldom able to work toward any unifying goal or their own self-interests in feudal society. Nevertheless, they represented a ruling estate that kept lesser orders at a distance so that few were able to aspire to aristocratic status without having been born into it.

In the German states of this period, the children of the nobility were taught to speak and think in ways that set them apart from other segments of society. These princes of the realm possessed rank and privileges superior to those of the lower orders and the burgher class that was beginning to assert itself at this time. Habits of education, social customs, religious beliefs, moral codes, speech, and language—all were placed in the service of differentiating the children and adults of the nobility from individuals in the lesser estates.[13] Their dress also tended to define them further, as did their elaborate etiquette and everyday manners that emphasized their higher status and rank. The lives of these noblemen and -women were segregated as much as possible from the commoners in their midst—eating, sleeping, and playing in situations that kept them separate and apart from others of lower station and rank.

The trade and commerce of later periods did not function in the manorial system, whose chief reason for being was to remain self-sufficient. Before the coming of the mercantile and early capitalist era, most of the common people lived and labored on the manors of lords. Many lived and worked in towns or villages owned by these noblemen, and often they farmed small plots of land on a sharecropping basis. Manors were small communities and civil organizations with their own courts and customs. Independence and self-reliance from outsiders were their goals: churches were provided and presided over by priests nominated and selected by the lord of the manor, as was every other facet of medieval life. Serfs and tenant farmers had no other choice than to sell their produce to their lord at conditions that were arbitrarily set by him. Commoners of all ranks looked to the lord of the manor for physical protection in time of war and benevolent advice during other times. They structured their working and private lives in accordance with his wishes, seeking always to gain his approval. Should they attempt to leave the manor without permission, they could be forcibly apprehended and legally returned to the estate. They were thought of as the lord's property: noblemen were the arbiter of all destinies and all fates when it came to the fortunes of commoners who lived on their estates. During the frequent periods of open warfare, the lord defended the commoners against the enemy, allowing them to seek shelter behind the walls of his castle. This he did to protect them and his own interests as well: his wealth and power depended upon their labor in the fields and villages of the manor. Although these lower orders had their own gradations of status and standing, they remained the least powerful and most poorly organized of all the estates. They were often impoverished and unable to do more than eke out a meager living on their rented lands. They were always subject to the whims and commands of those above them and had little voice in what happened to them and their families while they lived on the manor.

Here a new player began to make itself felt. Rising levels of exploration, science, and commerce expanded trade between different parts of the world, causing the villages and towns of medieval Europe to grow larger and providing commoners and serfs with new avenues of opportunity and freedom. Signaling an end to the agrarian system that had ruled Europe for a millennium, a new burgher class began to rise to prominence and wealth. This was a social revolution that encompassed the political, economic, and social systems of Europe and occurred over many centuries. New towns and villages were built and populated with people who lived by their wits, trading and performing commercial services for an expanding world market. These early towns were able to meet the needs of the new commercialism because there were no precedents for them to follow: the cities and towns of the Roman and Grecian periods had long since disappeared from the face of Europe. These new towns were markets that became permanent as a consequence of their locations and easy accessibility. Still these new ways of living and working were never very extensive in medieval society, and commercial towns and villages remained quite small in their populations. Between the twelfth and fifteenth centuries, the urban populations of feudal society were never more than 10 percent of the population.

From the establishment of the Hanseatic League in the early medieval period, from the later discoveries of the Portuguese and Spanish explorers, and until the introduction of expanded world trade and high-speed machinery, the commercial interests of Europe expanded. They expanded slowly at first, forcing people to leave their farms and come to the cities and towns that were now growing at an ever more rapid pace. And through these demographic changes in agrarian society the cities attracted what was considered to be the trash of medieval order. Men and women who were marginal, expendable members of this agrarian system found themselves with no place else to go: they were landless sons and daughters of tenant farmers who would never inherit the land or its tenancy.

Yet it must not be forgotten that this burgher class became a separate estate distinguishable from that of other members of the agrarian society commanded by the nobility. In the new conditions of trade and commerce that were developing in the world, this new class represented a new and privileged group, whose power lay in their increasing wealth and their ability to exact concessions from the ruling lords. This was more and more true as the economic structures of the feudal system showed themselves to be poorly suited to the needs of the new commercialism. Thenceforth, the burghers were able to receive rights and charters from the nobility in such numbers that they were able to organize themselves legally in ways that facilitated their economic activities. Most of all, these new traders and townspeople desired to be free of the domination and control of the manorial system, to be free to develop their own economic and social institutions.

Feudal vassalage and serfdom constrained men from the trade and commerce of the new age, explicitly disallowing any independent actions by servants of the lord. So it was that in the new urban centers, the townspeople and emerging burgher class called for freedom first: they demanded and were accorded the right to do business, to sign contracts, to own and control property, and to buy and sell commodities. Most of all they required the right to come and go as they pleased, a power that was denied to most commoners during the medieval period. This right to individual liberty was one that the lords of manors sold to burghers operating in their towns and village estates.

In this we can see that the organization of this burgher class was essentially different from the estates almost from its inception. Whereas serfs and commoners were held in bondage, burghers increasingly were granted the freedom and judicial autonomy to initiate new forms of trade, commerce, and government. As their power grew, they provided their own legal and policing agencies and built defenses against the pillaging knights of the countryside.

By the Middle Ages, these burghers were strong enough to build and maintain fortifications for their cities and towns, providing the essential protection they needed against the agrarian estates that constantly sought to rob them. An impressionistic view of rural people developed among these burgher gentlemen with their newly won rights and privileges: country folk were thought of as ignorant persons ripe for exploitation. In the new conditions, the clergy and nobility retired to their castles and manors, leaving the medieval towns more and more to the burghers. The burghers, in turn, created the institutions, economic structures, and military forces they needed to survive and prosper.

As with the older estates, these burghers did not make up a homogeneous class. As they developed, their status remained somewhere below the aristocracy, even as their economic power approached oligarchic proportions. Groups of upper-class tradespeople—unassuming retailers, artisans, and laborers—all formed a part of this expanding bourgeois population. The people of the towns welcomed their rural brethren, but only as new laborers that could be used to keep the price of labor down. If such people tried to purchase land or otherwise engage in trade or commerce, their efforts were discouraged by these same townspeople. Freedom in the new towns was meant to be exercised only by those who had the power and authority to do so. Those who had these rights and privileges became quite wealthy, forming themselves into a closed society that excluded poorer merchants, retailers, and craft workers. But, in the end, these urban centers became the vehicle for a dynamic social mobility that was quite different from the rigid, feudal estate system. The separations in wealth and status between merchants and craftspeople were not as severe as those between knights and yeomen, or between yeomen and serfs. In the new centers of commerce, social standing became, more and more, a mere difference of wealth with the poorest of people in a position to learn a craft and otherwise better their condition by hard work and enterprise. Commoners in the countryside had much less opportunity to improve their fate: they might send their offspring to better schools and universities or send them off to learn a craft or trade. But then these youths were part of the new system of townspeople who believed that anything was possible for them and that any position in society was obtainable. Still social status and prestige in Europe continued to flow from the nobility, even into the twentieth century. Even the wealthiest of merchants and businesspeople were not completely accepted into their inner circles. The great revolutions at the end of the eighteenth century shook aristocratic claims to their foundations. But things took on the shape they had always had once the ideas of the French Revolution were subverted by military adventures. The burghers had the wealth and power that came from world trade and commerce, but they could not break into the schools, clubs, and lifestyles of the nobility. Hence those efforts of wealthy commoners to buy titles for themselves and their families whenever they could. Dominance in European society remained with the nobility, even after the wealth had passed to the burghers. Upper-class fathers and mothers sought to marry their children to knights or lords of great estates, seeking to enter into the highest circles of social and political power.

THE EMERGENCE OF CLASS IN EUROPEAN CIVILIZATION

Trade, commerce, and a capitalist economic order developed alongside the feudal system of Europe, establishing a new dominant class, the bourgeoisie. These newcomers valued trade and profit above all else, giving to money-making a status it had never held before. The new inventions that followed one after another, the factory system that sprang up everywhere, the rush to greater efficiency, individual liberty, competition, ambition—all of these attitudes were part of the ideology that developed around this rising bourgeois class. As they grew in wealth and power, they grew tired of the old restrictions and began to organize European society into a second, parallel social and economic system.

In place of the high nobility that had ruled in the manorial system, they installed the high bourgeoisie. These were men from established and sometimes aristocratic families that had taken up the commercial enterprises that were now dominating Europe. In place of the knights, esquires, and gentry of the old feudal system, there were the lower bourgeoisie and artisans. These men were from the lesser families, sometimes springing from the laboring classes themselves. In place of the yeomen and serfs, laborers made up the base of this economic pyramid. These were men who were nominally free but unable to make the most of their newfound liberty because of their economic conditions. Feudalism still retained its hold on the church through the priesthood, but the new values of commercialism in an increasingly urban culture seemed to make religion less important than it had been in the manorial system. The lords of the manor in the feudal system had no need to create surplus crops because they did not have outlets for such surpluses. Production was localized, meeting the needs of the manor in a self-sufficient way, and money had very little usefulness. A man's word was his bond in this environment and trade and barter predominated.

Now this clear and coherent estate system was never able to assimilate the burghers into its social order. That was because the newer class was not based on landownership and because it was fundamentally opposed to the values and beliefs of feudalism. This became more apparent as the manorial system began to decay, and the emerging bourgeoisie became dominant.

The legal distinctions between the nobility and the bourgeois classes were destroyed, once and for all, by the French Revolution, ending years of struggle between the manorial and commercial interests in European society. The cry for egalitarianism destroyed the political and social basis of the estate system, ushering in the age of individualism. And the triumph of urbanism meant that the wealth and political power of society had shifted to the cities, where people of trade and commerce ruled the day.

People were forced to leave their homes in order to work in the new factories, mills, and offices of the commercial world. Their relations with others were defined by a new status system that saw them as businesspeople or workers and their labor was utilized in new and less overt forms of exploitation. This was because they created greater wealth than they received, with the surpluses being accumulated by those who employed them. Workers found it impossible to know when they had worked long enough to replace their costs to business and when they were producing wealth that employers used for their own purposes. The new processes of accumulated wealth were so intricate in their design that they were usually misunderstood by workers.

In feudal society the labor of tenant farmers and serfs was expropriated by the nobility in an open and easily understood way. The feudal serf worked his rented land to meet his needs and those of his family. But he was also obliged to pay for his right to work the landlord's land by performing extra labor or by paying rent. This was because the serf did not own the land he worked; his only access to it was through the permission and conditions of the property's owners.

In commercial society, workers were taken advantage of only in the factory or mill. Outside of these places of work the workers were relatively autonomous, living a personal life that was separate and apart from their labor. Still, the laborer in feudal society could see when he was working for his own subsistence and when his labor was being appropriated by the landowner. This meant that physical protection of the serfs had to accompany the exploitative aspects of feudalism's economy. Class relations were rigid and tied to military and political power, and the unchanging need to wage war was vested only in the nobility and landowning classes. Political and economic forces were also in the hands of this ruling class, and education was a privilege of the aristocratic classes alone.

In our own times, this has changed significantly. The American educational experience has moved from charity schools for pauper boys, to common schools, to the emergence of the high school as a people's college, and then to the G.I. Bill and the development of higher education throughout the nation. The following chapters in Part I discuss some of the problems that have developed as Americans pursued the dream of an equal educational experience for all children.

NOTES

1. Oliver C. Cox, *Caste, Class and Race: A Study in Social Dynamics* (New York: Modern Reader Paperbacks, 1970), pp. 121–123.

2. William Stubbs, *The Constitutional History of England*, Vol. I (Oxford: Oxford University Press, 1883–1884), pp. 21–24, 45–46. See also his *Cambridge Medieval History*, Vols. I and III (Oxford: Oxford University Press, 1924), pp. 2–15.

3. Frederick L. Mussbaum, *A History of the Economic Institutions of Modern Europe* (New York: Oxford University Press, 1933), pp. 17–28.

4. Stubbs, *The Constitutional History of England*, pp. 273–274; Cox, *Caste, Class and Race*, pp. 124–126.

5. Barrington Moore, Jr., *Social Origins of Dictatorship and Democracy: Lord and Peasant in the Making of the Modern World* (Boston: Beacon Press, 1967), pp. 3–14.

6. Ibid., pp. 23–31.

7. Ibid., pp. 16–17, 22–25, 74–76.

8. Ibid.

9. Cox, *Class, Caste and Race*, pp. 127–129.

10. Stubbs, *The Constitutional History of England*, Vol. III, pp. 298–300.

11. Moore, *Social Origin of Dictatorship and Democracy*, pp. 383–385, 503–504.

12. Cox, *Class, Caste and Race*, pp. 137–140.

13. William H. Bruford, *Germany in the Eighteenth Century* (Cambridge: Cambridge University Press, 1935), pp. 48–51.

Chapter 2

The Governance of Local Schools as Influenced by Social Class, Race, and Ethnicity

Frank W. Lutz and Laurance Iannaccone

The concept of social class has had a long history in American sociology and in American public education.[1] While R. A. Dahl suggests that American democracy is not a matter of equality but of disbursed *inequalities*,[2] those inequalities tend to build up unequally around the concept of social class.

Social class, more than either race or ethnicity, tends to be a better predictor of school success, regardless of the criterion descriptor. This is not to say that in America race and ethnicity are not related to social class, or that people of certain races and ethnic groups are not more likely than others to be found in poverty and with problems in public schools. Unfortunately, they are. But if a child's parents are members of the Negro race, or if that child's parents are Mexican American, and the child's father is an attorney and her or his mother is a physician, that family is not living below the poverty line. The chances of that child being in the public schools may be low but, if he or she is in a public school, the child's chances of school success and life successes are very good.

Additionally, if the parents in this type of family chose to influence the governance of public education in general or some specific decision affecting their child's school experience, their chance of influencing that outcome is high. Not so with the chances of children be they white, black, or Hispanic if their mother is single and a teenager, unemployed, on welfare, without a high school education, and living below the poverty level. The point made is that a student's social class background is a better predictor of his or her school success and more likely to determine the parents' ability to influence the governance structures that define their child's success than is either their race or ethnicity.

One of the useful myths for black and Hispanic upper-middle and upper class Americans is that because they are nonwhite they have no power and, therefore, exercise none. That myth rests of the reality that, on the average, blacks and

Hispanics have less political power than do caucasians. Power is not equal, but it is disbursed. Its unequal dispersion in a capitalistic, free market society is almost always better accounted for by social class origin and its correlates than it is by race or ethnicity. Yet, if one is nonwhite, or female, the likelihood of also being undereducated, underemployed, a single parent, and poor is greatly increased. Under these conditions the political power to influence the public schools, which some hold is the best hope of changing one's socioeconomic condition, is very small. One is not only likely to be "disadvantaged" but one is more likely to remain that way.

TWO CONCEPTS OF SOCIAL CLASS

Without detailing the theory of social class, a job much too space consuming than this chapter permits, it is interesting to note that three major differences distinguish Karl Marx's concept of social class, which drove the former USSR, from W. Lloyd Warner's concept of social class, which continues to drive major aspects of the American democracy.

First, Marx's system has but two classes: an elite, very wealthy, and all-powerful upper class; and the very large lower class proletariat, which has no wealth and no power. Warner posits a three-class system, each divided into two subclasses providing a six-class stratification, with considerable mobility among these classes. In fact, it has been suggested that as many as 85 percent of all Americans think of or identify themselves as being in the "middle class"—a clear empirical unreality. But such a perception is democratically satisfying to the people who believe the myth and useful to the power holders in an egalitarian value of society.

Second, of considerable importance, Marx was philosophically a dialectal materialist, while the philosophy behind the American social class system appears to be some mix of idealism and pragmatism. These different philosophical systems will produce quite different valuing, ideology, and social-political behavior.

Finally, Marx sees production as the driving force in society and violent class conflict as the only means of changing the plight of the otherwise powerless proletariat. American social class also sees production as a prominent, if not the prime, force in society. But it sees the people as "owning" more than only their labor, having endless opportunities to alter their class position, and capable of using the ballot, rather than the bullet, to change their government.

In addition, and extremely important to this argument, the American people have for 200 years viewed their public schools as the "engine" of class mobility. Take away the American public schools and you take away the hope of the American lower-middle and lower classes. Take away the American public school and the American dream becomes a hollow promise, and the American class system becomes the place where the "rich get richer and the poor get poorer." It could quickly become a two-class system, with no more hope to offer the lower class than Marx gave the lower class in his system. Make the governance system elite enough, make it difficult enough for the poor and undereducated to influence government, particularly the politics of public education (where education priorities are determined and where their children might find the means to move out of poverty and the darkness created by generations of hopelessness), and Karl Marx will begin to look a lot smarter than he actually was.

The Role of Public Schooling in American Values

C. E. Sleeter and C. A. Grant link the concept of multiculturalism with social reconstruction.[3] They quote T. Branett, one of the leading social reconstructionists, as noting that reconstructionism is a "critique of modern culture," which illustrates that regardless of how well the past had produced and reformed society, "the preceding centuries of the modern era are not incapable of . . . coping with the problems of today's age."[4] One is reminded of a comment attributed to Abraham Lincoln during the Civil War that the safe solutions of the past would not be sufficient for solving the dangerous problems of the present.

Yet, yesterday's solutions were not necessarily failures. Mostly they succeeded in doing what their leaders had hoped. But yesterday's solutions, having stripped away yesterday's problems, allow new and unsolved problems to become apparent, problems that might have remained invisible if the problems of the past had not been solved. Often these new problems, which might not have been apparent under past circumstances, are not only now visible but may become nearly unbearable. So let us not be too hard on the leaders of the past because they did not solve the problems of today. Rather, let us snatch up the gauntlet of opportunity, and move confidently into the future, but with our own and new solutions, not the retreaded ones of the last century. The continuum of social unrest, social reform, and progress continues. Open a new century and discover new problems, turn another page and find someone trying to solve them. As C. Marshall and P. P. Zodhiates remind us,

> the new politics of race and gender is [generated by] the dissatisfaction with conventional liberal solutions, the search for new alternatives, and the ensuing discussion over means and ends . . . the reason seems clear: the continuing failure of our school system to provide for females and minorities the educational opportunities that lead to successful and productive lives.[5]

The Dynamo of Social Mobility

C. H. Gross, S. P. Wronski, and J. W. Hanson, critiquing the social reconstructionist's movement, note that its total impact was not large, something like the effects of "third parties in American politics."[6] That is probably true. But the influence of third-party politics has not been small in building policy in the

United States. For example, our now-well-accepted social security and medicare system is directly a result of third-party politics.

How does America solve its social problems? Gross, Wronski, and Hanson note that the classic education philosopher and social activist George Counts, in the early 1930s and throughout the next several decades, insisted that the schools must "act as the major agency for revising society in accordance with some grand plan or 'blue print' for the future."[7] Thus may have been born what J. W. Reitman has called the "educational messiah complex."[8]

According to Reitman, Americans have always had a inordinate faith in the ability of public education to move them up the social ladder and to "fix" whatever is wrong in American society. He likens this faith to the Jewish belief in a Messiah and he terms this belief the "educational messiah complex" (EMC). EMC, says Reitman, is the unreasonable belief, held by the vast majority of the American people, that the public schools, by themselves, are capable of transforming the American society into a democratic utopia. That "monumental faith in the redemptive power of schooling" was founded in part, Reitman says, "upon the writings of liberal scholars [like Counts] who were disenchanted . . . with what they considered the excessively gradualistic, individual-centered, and upper middle-class elitist tone of mainstream progressive education."[9]

Reitman is correct that public education is not a magic elixir, making everything right that is wrong in American society.[10] Educators have promised too much and delivered too little, to too few. Yet myths die hard. Like any myth the EMC provides some explanation of reality and, therefore, the ability for society to move forward. The educational messiah complex gave the American lower and middle classes hope. If that hope was unfilled for some it was fulfilled for many. The many who succeeded blamed those who had failed for not succeeding. And those who failed accepted the blame. They also blamed themselves. The myth lived on, and hope continued to burn brightly for another generation, some of whom would, again, not make it. That, of course, would be considered to be their own fault.[11]

As generation followed generation of those who could not make it, as the same racial and ethnic groups remained for the most part outside of "mainstream" America, blaming those who failed became empirically and theoretically untenable. To "blame the victims" of the American society, which while becoming increasingly less de jure often became even more de facto segregated, has become "politically incorrect."

Yet blaming the victims, while politically incorrect, is not dead in the American society. Even the victims continue to blame themselves according to E. A. Brantlinger. In her study *The Politics of Social Class in Secondary Schools* she notes:

> Respondents humanized blame for poverty; that is, they attributed the source as poor people rather than social circumstances (i.e., that society is stratified). They did not depersonalize their observations to conclude that the present class structure

meant that it was inevitable for some people to have comparatively less favorable conditions.[12]

S. E. Tozer, P. C. Violas, and G. Senese point out twentieth-century corporate liberalism grows out of "classical" liberalism and both the Right and Left of that movement are committed to the business ethic and a close working relationship between business and government.[13] Yet there are "significant differences as the politics of the 1980s so clearly demonstrate, including setbacks for the poor and minority rights." As J. G. Cibulka, R. J. Reed and K. K. Wong note, "The Reagan Administration epitomized this attitude of urban neglect . . . [and it was only] . . . [b]usiness concerns about labor shortages [that] renewed attention to the performance of the urban schools."[14] A. G. Wirth provides an excellent and balanced examination of the relationship between education and work in America, which places the influence of American business on America's schools in perspective,[15] and R. E. Callahan describes the influences of American business on public education in the early 1900s.[16]

Still it has become politically incorrect for scholars or the public press to "blame victims." Thus the forces that tend to shape American public opinion have increasingly turned to blaming the public schools for all that is wrong with American society. After all, we promised we could feed the hungry and heal the sick. The inscription on the Statue of Liberty may as well have been affixed to every public school building in America. "Give me your tired, your poor, your huddled masses, yearning to breathe free. . . . I lift my lamp beside the golden door."[17]

Having failed to educate, much less adequately feed, house, and make well these huddled masses for generation after generation, unable to blame the victims any longer, and unwilling to assume the responsibility, the powerful policymakers in America have blamed the public schools. Not only the system itself but the *individuals* who comprise it are blamed. The powerful in that system have pushed the blame as far down the bureaucratic ladder as possible. The teacher is to blame, not as a group, for teacher unions hold power. Individual teachers are at fault. The powerful have adopted slogans, which are cheaper and less threatening than true reform. Those reforms and slogans are supposed to "fix" the system.

The slogan "every child can learn" has been twisted not to mean that every child can learn something but that any child can learn *everything* within the same old school structure that stipulates standard blocks of curriculum (courses of study), to be learned in standard chunks of time (called semesters). If this is not accomplished, who is to blame? Unable to blame the victims of the 200-year-old system any longer, it has become fashionable to blame the teacher because "every child can learn." If it is not the child's fault or the child's family, then of course it is the teacher's fault. This Pavlovian-based "theory" of education drove public schooling in the Soviet Union until its dissolution. And we now call it "reform" in American schools.

More Harmful Reform

Increasingly one of two cries is heard in our national media. One group chooses to "reform" public schooling by doing more of what has been done for 200 years. So far in the last two decades we have seen an acceleration of schooling "reform" toward more days in the school year, more hours in the school day, more credits required to graduate, more control at the state level, more local property taxes (so state politicians will not have to vote to increase taxes). All this reform is directed toward the support of a system run in the same fashion and by the same people and heavily for the good of American business. And the same people, children of those who do not run the system, continue to fail within that system. Is it any wonder that increasingly both the poor and minorities are losing faith in the "educational messiah complex."

Opposed to today's "reformers" are the "disestablishment venders." These individuals would make the schools more like American business, hardly a new idea. They would make the public schools profit oriented; let the people "vote" with their dollars rather than their ballots. They would provide vouchers for the rich and poor alike and let the people choose between competing schools. The best prediction of that future is that today's best private schools will increase their tuition above the price of the voucher, still keeping the poor from their doors. The poor and lower-middle classes will still not be able to afford upper-class schools, and, if they could, the underachievers in the lower class would not be selected by those schools to attend them. The "best" schools in America, and in the world, choose their students—their students do not choose them. J. Moffett recognized this problem and cited the fact that "the Pennsylvania legislature rejected a plan that would have provided a $900 voucher . . . because the amount would discriminate against the poor, $900 being too little to pay tuition at most private schools."[18]

Profit-oriented private schools will emerge as a middle-class option, offering to "resegregate" the youth of America according to race, ethnicity, religion, class, and every other divisive category imaginable. And when the profit is gone, these schools will be taking a "chapter 11." Then the U.S. government may have to bail out the public schools like it did Lockheed and Chrysler when they went broke. Could a parent be left without recourse like you are left when your Chevy truck is vulnerable to explosion and fire from side impact, or the paint on your Ford vehicle deteriorates before it is a year old? Will the slogan of public schooling become *caveat emptor*?

Students who cannot find any voucher-funded private school that will accept them may be left with their voucher and the "old fashioned" public school. It is unlikely these children will be from families better able to provide the family support necessary to succeed in public schools as they are now structured. High school students with poor SAT or ACT scores often fail to obtain admission to any university much less the one of their choice. Many of those end up in "open enrollment" community colleges, whose similarity to the best private universities is slight, at best. Their best hope of securing entry to good universities is being a great athlete, as it had been in high school.

So it will be with children labeled today as "at-risk." They will be left with nothing but the public schools from which those with indicators of probable school success will have fled. These "public" schools will not teach because they will not be able to teach the "unteachable," in spite of slogans. We know of no model of schooling that does not require some type of "family-like" support system for their children. Public schools under these conditions will be little more than warehouses for violence, drugs, poverty, ethnic hatred, and hopelessness.

Where do the unemployed and homeless in the American society go? Under the bridges! And our present system spends its resources protecting their "right" to live there instead of supporting opportunities for them to improve their condition. Where will the children of the "unteachables" go? To the public schools where it will be impossible to teach and it will be impossible to learn. Make the American public schools more like American business? I'm glad I won't be there to see what happens.

Private voucher-supported schools will be free to teach the type of "multiculturalism" demonstrated by the Bosnian-Serbs. Neoethnocentrism is not multiculturalism. The "dis-establishment vendors" who would destroy our public schools had better take a long look at what they might get in return. Those who would destroy the "educational messiah complex" had better understand that myths have meaning and purpose. They are functional, in both manifest and latent ways.[19] When one destroys a myth one had better have something else in which the people can believe.

CLASS, RACE, AND ETHNICITY IN PUBLIC SCHOOLS

D. Easton explains that politics is the "authoritative allocation of values."[20] By this he suggests that in a pluralistic, multicultural society, there is bound to be some fairly wide range of values, aspirations, and customs. As these differences produce differing demands, and there are only so many resources to meet those demands, the politicians decide whose demands will be met and whose will be left unattended. In today's complex school districts, particularly in the largest urban districts, there are an almost infinite set of demands and a very finite set of resources. To a large extent the local school board, a group of generally five to nine people, makes those decisions through the authority vested in them by their communities. They authoritatively allocate values. And whose values do they allocate? Brantlinger reports one board member's answer, "Only the educated vote in school elections and school board members know that. So the board plays to its supporters. The average board member's view is that the way to get along is to go along."[21]

Almost surely school boards allocate the values they believe in and that they themselves hold. How could they do otherwise? Who would deliberately do something that affected childrens' life opportunities if they did not believe it beneficial, if they did not value it? By and large local school boards do what they believe is best for all children. But is there anything that is good for all children, given the diversity of children attending public schools, from the very gifted to the very retarded children, from college-oriented children to at-risk children, from the reasonably affluent to the miserably poor? Which segment of the community will be represented? Might some parents of public school children value what the school board does not? As social class and values are closely related, it should prove instructive to examine the social class of school boards and the social class of the parents who are most likely to send their children to the schools governed by those school boards.

Demographics

For the past three decades the demographics of the public schools have been changing. Yet the American Association of School Boards says "the most notable characteristic of school boards is their stability or lack of [demographic] change."[22] During the decade between 1982 and 1992 there was almost no change in the demographic characteristics of the "typical" school board. Local school boards are still predominately white (94%), male (60%), between 41 and 50 years old (47%), make more than $40,000 (81%), and have held office for six years (that is, they have been reelected once on the average). One interesting change was that only 8.7 percent of reporting board members said they lived in urban areas, down from 10.8 percent ten years earlier. As there are no fewer urban districts, what could be the explanation? Two come to mind. Urban boards could be getting smaller (i.e., Boston went from 15 to 5 following a trend set nearly 100 years ago reforming school boards and making them more elite— "separate from the people."[23] Or perhaps, urban board members tend to live in the upper-class sections of the cities and do not perceive themselves as part of the urban district they govern, comprised as it is of tens of thousands of undereducated and poor, many living below the poverty level.

What part of the school population do these "Dick and Jane" boards govern? From 1960 to 1990 the percent of minorities in public schools increased from 13 percent[24] to approximately 35 percent.[25] These percentages are even higher in urban schools, where nearly 70 percent of the nation's public school children attend. Remembering that the income of the typical board member is between $40,000 and $60,000 per year, M. D. Usand reports: "Indeed, the growing evidence of children's poverty is among the most salient issues facing not only the schools . . . but the society at large . . . 5.6 million children under the age of six were living in poverty in 1991—a 33% increase . . . since 1979."[26] If one lives in the center of our major cities, the chances of poverty increase; and if a child's mother is black and single, the chances of poverty are even greater.

Given that the indicators of social class are income, education, and occupation, it is clear that the social class of school board members is quite different than that of the individuals who send their children to those schools.[27] As social class is closely related to value structure, it is clear that the values of those, presumed to be represented by school boards, is very different than those who presume to represent them.[28] John Stuart Mill wrote in 1859 that

> the people who exercise the power are not always the same people over whom power is exercised; and the self government spoken of is not always the government of each by himself, but of each by all the rest. The will of the people, moreover, practically means the will of the . . . most active part . . . those who succeed in making themselves accepted as the majority.[29]

If politics is the authoritative allocation of values, whose values are likely being allocated, "the people," or the minority who succeed in making themselves the majority and whose values are clearly different from their constituency?

Value Differences

During the "community schools" controversy in New York City during the mid-1960s, the following event took place at a meeting where some 300 black, mostly female citizens attending one of New York City's 32 local school board meetings. The board was composed totally of white males. The situation was tense. The community was angry and demanding major change. The president of the board was explaining all the things the board was doing for the children who attended the schools. A tall, slender woman dressed in an African-type gown and turban rose from the audience and was recognized. She extended her arm, pointing to the board seated on a stage above the audience: "You say you are preparing our men for college. You aren't. You are preparing them for the penitentiary."[30] She was empirically correct. A much higher percentage of black males end up in penitentiaries than on college campuses. But the point was lost on a school board whose social class and values were too far apart from those of the community the board members were honestly trying to serve. It is not that the board was malicious and deliberately harming the children of that district. They were nearly as unhappy about the situation as were the citizens attending the meeting. They were simply out of touch with those in the audience whose social class, race, ethnicity, and sex were totally different than was theirs. The board's concept of school board representation was that of the trusteeship in "elite" councils, not of being a delegate of the people in an "arena" council.

The simple act of acquiring wealth does not in itself change one's social class. Ask those who, due to newly acquired wealth, try to move into the upper-upper American social class. Ask those of the lower class who happen to win the lottery. As noted earlier, social class is, most of all, a matter of values. Perhaps obtaining wealth, only one of the symbols of social class, without first acquiring the values of the higher class, is a sure way to block actual upward social class mobility.

Hopelessness

What Oscar Lewis probably misnamed the "culture of poverty" is an excellent example of the fact that money alone does not alter one's social class.[31] It can be contended that America's welfare system pays the lower class to remain undereducated, underemployed, poor, and hopeless. If a minority, poor, undereducated, single mother gets some education and a job paying more than the minimum wage, her aid to dependent children, subsidized housing, and food stamps are lost or reduced so that her actual expendable income is less than it had been before she got the job. What would you do? Under these conditions most have a hard time seeing how they were moving "up the ladder." Those caught in this "culture" are likely to perceive the situation as hopeless and their culture is better named the "culture of hopelessness." The sequence of events described has robbed the lower class of hope. Thus, American public policy has for generations subsidized a class of people to remain poor, undereducated, and, finally, hopeless. What has been produced is a culture of hopelessness composed of people who must remain in the lower classes in order to acquire the symbols of the lower-middle class, which they buy with their welfare benefits. Some may ask who these "benefits" actually benefit—the poor who obtain the TV set and the used car, or the wealthy who can count on a large pool of individuals whose skills and education levels remain at a level commanding only the minimum wage.

That is the tragedy of the last three decades in American society when the rich got richer and the poor got not only poorer, but also *hopeless*. This condition is much more dangerous than a culture of poverty. With the hope of achieving upward mobility through the public schools gone, what is left? Public schools are an element of American politics and perceived by the American people in general as the best hope for upward mobility. If those schools are not democratically governed, if the poor and hopeless have no means of changing the schools so as to better serve their needs, if they have no means to influence the authoritative allocation of values in public schools, what is left to them?

THE GOVERNANCE OF LOCAL SCHOOLS

While some have called the notion of local control of public education "a myth,"[32] and in spite of the legal fact that the governance of public education has always been the province of the "states and their people" (see Tenth Amendment to the U.S. Constitution), historically and in the minds of the American people, schooling of American children should be, and for the most part has been, in the hands of the people at the local level. If a myth, the idea of local control of education is a "cherished myth" in the American culture. During the same year that M. Lieberman called local governance of schools a myth, Gross, Wronski, and Hanson wrote:

America has always cherished a belief that face-to-face democracy, the democracy
of the small town, the democracy of the town meeting, is the cornerstone of the
good life. Nowhere has the social philosophy revealed itself more clearly than in
our faith in the local public school and the local school district.[33]

The debate is therefore at least thirty years old and it continues. As recently
as 1992 F. W. Lutz and C. Merz, set the groundwork for their position in the
history of American education and the classic description of the "American
Democracy" offered by A. de Tocqueville,[34] arguing in their preface that

the grassroots of politics [is] in the local school districts and the local schools of
America. There in public school politics, the American people [can] govern them-
selves, when they choose, as they choose, and about issues of concern to every
American—issues concerning the education of their children.[35]

The Reform of the Early 1900s

There has been an attempt for at least a century by reformers, posing as
"liberals," to take the governance of education out of the hands of the "common people" who send their children to those public schools. This movement
has placed that governance "in trust" for the people, in the hands of upper-
middle- and upper-class socioeconomic elite school board members, and increasingly state legislators and state school boards and agencies. It has assumed
that these trustees will do what is right for those who are unable to do what is
right for their own children.

M. W. Kirst is correct when he asserts that the last real reform of school
politics was in the late 1800s and early 1900s when the number of members on
school boards was greatly reduced, elections were changed from single-member
ward-based elections to at-large, or blue-ribbon appointed boards, in an effort
to get politics out of education, and corruption out of city schools.[36] This urban
reform was in part initiated and led by Woodrow Wilson while he was still
teaching at Princeton University.[37] Briefly, he suggested that the development
of public policy be left to elected politicians but the administration of those
policies be placed in the hands of presumably incorruptible, highly trained professionals, hired to "civil service" positions and, thus, above the corruption of
city politicians.

In 1973 J. M. Cronin noted that by 1920 the reform had been largely accomplished as "the number and kinds of school boards had diminished . . . [but] the
large cities continued to search for a system that would insulate the schools even
further from . . . the sordid side-effects of city politics."[38] And in 1984 F. W.
Lutz reminded us that "there [still] prevails a trend among reformers to move
education governance away from the direct influence of the people. . . . This and
other trends [remain] part of the general trend in education . . . removing public
education from the people [whose children attend the public schools]."[39] L.

Iannaccone and Lutz have called this "achievement" the latent consequence of a successful education reform.[40]

Machine versus Reform Government

The major purpose of the school board and city reform in the early 1900s was the removal of machine corruption from city politics and particularly from the public schools. It was largely successful in that "manifest" intended outcome. What may not have been anticipated was the effect that success would have on the ability of the poor and lower classes, whose children attended the public schools, to influence the education of their children and the ability of those schools to operate as the conduit of upward mobility in the American social class system.

Also, the link between general-purpose government, and the services it provides, and the public schools was destroyed. The machine that had coveted the jobs available in the public schools as "specific rewards" for the party loyal was gone, or at least underground. Without the jobs, city government easily shed itself of the responsibility of providing its services to the children in the public schools. Perhaps it could be suggested that the machine was the "bridge" between the undereducated and poor and the public schools, as well as between the schools and general-purpose government services so badly needed for urban public schools to succeed with the at-risk children of today. That latent and unintended consequence has made it nearly impossible, in spite of the good intentions of reform school boards, to meet the needs of the vast majority of the children at present attending the public schools of our urban cities who are, more often than not, the children of minorities and the underemployed and unemployed poor of America—largely the lower classes and the racially and ethnically "different" in the society.

If we are to improve public education in America in the twenty-first century we must reform the governance of local education. But actually reforming is not as simple a matter as making slogans or even passing laws. Once the power holders understand what must change if true reform is to occur, reforms are likely to encounter some tough resistance. C. Pipho reports: "Once it became clear . . . that all communities, all schools, and all educators would have to change, their opposition became an organized force against change of any kind."[41] Reforming should mean changing, not merely doing more of the same as the reformers of the 1980s and 1990s have tended to demand. Pointing to that fact, D. L. Clark and T. A. Astuto report in the same journal as Pipho has written: "The evidence we discovered . . . convinced us that merely doing more of the same will not be adequate."[42] That is surely correct and the present reform trend in the governance of local education is almost entirely toward more of the same reform initiated and isolated from the people of the lower classes and the minority poor.

SOME VIEWS OF LOCAL SCHOOL GOVERNANCE

Until now a good deal has been said about the nature of social class in America, the composition of school boards, the demographics of the public school population, and the nature of school reform during the last century. It is now time to examine the nature of education governance and the political process that shapes the policy outputs in public education. We have already said that, by virtue of the Tenth Amendment to the U.S. Constitution, the governance of public education is vested in the separate states. The federal government, while it may encourage action, initiate programs, fund any portion of public education it chooses, may not establish a federal education system of education. It may not directly regulate, confine, or interfere with state public education systems, so long as those systems do not abridge the rights of any citizen or in other ways defy constitutional law. When and as they do the federal courts will intervene and change that condition.

It could be said that the two major reforms in American public education in 250 years are due to two Supreme Court decisions. The first was that there "is a wall of separation" between church and state, separating religion from public education. The second was that "separate is not equal," eliminating de jure, if not de facto, segregated schools in America. Both decisions reformed and reversed public school practice constituted during colonial education.

As noted, the individual states establish public education and, if they choose, control it. However, every state but one, Hawaii, chooses to exercise that right through the establishment of some type of decentralized, local school district, governed by some form of local school board. Although the trend for at least a century has been to centralize more power in the state school agency, local school boards remain a major influence in establishing public education policy. Thus, the manner of establishing those boards, a matter of mandate in each state, becomes a concern of considerable importance. As it should be clear by now, the present political arrangements leave something to be desired.

Theoretical Views of Local School Governance

There are three somewhat differing views of local school governance. Yet, while there are considerable differences among them, there are some unifying threads. One view examines the nature of the office of school board member and the voter participation in elections for that office and for public school financial proposals. As school board membership is not usually seen as a stepping stone to higher political office, nor a paid office itself, there is not much competition for the office. School board incumbents often run unopposed and voter turnout is normally very low, between 5 and 25 percent. As the competition/participation theory sees these two elements as the heart of democracy, L. H. Zeigler and M. K. Jennings proclaim local education governance as basically undemocratic.[43]

A second view proclaims the essence of democracy to be the degree to which the people are able to get from the political process the things they want, or demand. The resources and demands of the people are declared inputs to the political process and the policies and programs are the outputs. The degree of democracy within the system is measured by the relationship between those inputs and outputs. Given what has been previously said in this chapter, one can easily conclude that, given this measure, local school governance is not very democratic. That is the conclusion of F. Wirt and M. Kirst, who have formulated this theory of local school politics based on D. Easton's political systems model.[44]

The final view considered here, called the dissatisfaction theory, agrees with the first two theories about the competition, participation, and lack of general output responsiveness to citizen demands. It does not view democracy as an end, however, but as a process. It suggests that in local school districts the voters are generally "apathetic" voters. They are not dissatisfied enough with public policy or its policymakers to bother to vote. Under these conditions participation is low, policymakers become less responsive, and policies are less relevant to the specific demands.

When this situation becomes bad enough, when the voters are sufficiently dissatisfied, they go to the polls and defeat incumbent school board members. Superintendents often are removed by these newly constituted boards. Outsider superintendents are hired, and their new policies look more responsive to the demands. When the voters perceive their demands are better attended they become less dissatisfied, turnout diminishes, and gradually the elected officials tend to again become less responsive. Lutz and Iannaccone say this is the model for the way the American democracy works at every level, in both general-purpose and education governance.[45] It is closest to the people and works in those school districts that have not become so large so as to be impossible to represent. Therefore, Lutz and Iannaccone declare that local school governance in the vast majority of the 15,000 local school districts of America is the grass-roots of American democracy.

The process gets distorted, however, when the minority make themselves the majority and the values of the minority are authoritatively allocated by that minority to the disadvantage of the unrepresented majority. This distortion robs the people of their hope, makes a mockery of the ideal of American democracy, and is turning America's public schools into little more than places where the children of the poor are kept off the streets and out of the labor market. In government when the minority totally dominate the majority the "iron law of oligarchy" is consummated. The very few privileged comprise the elite oligarchy and make the rules and laws for a larger and larger number of people. This is the case in large urban school districts where governance by their oligarchy has become the rule rather than the exception. This situation has not been an untended accident to the cities of America. It was the specific and manifest intent of the school board reform of the early 1900s.[46]

While the reform of the 1990s generally ended corruption in the public schools, it separated school politics from general-purpose politics. It moved ward elected boards that represented the people of the cities, and reduced the number of seats on school boards. As suggested by Lutz, it removed the governance of local education from the people whose children attended those schools.[47] It successfully eliminated machine government of education but at the same time it burned the bridge between the public schools and the people, and the government of those schools and general-purpose government.

In accomplishing these goals the reform also established the myth that politics and education should and could be separate from politics. What it actually did was to change those politics from an arena form of politics to an elite form of politics.[48] It empowered the upper classes in the politics of education and virtually removed the lower classes from that process. As social class in America is related to race, ethnicity, and wealth, it tended to disadvantage nonwhites, non-Anglos, and the poor. That is what social class, race, and ethnicity have to do with the governance of local education.

The last reform of local education governance, 100 years ago, deliberately removed the means the lower classes had to influence public education. In doing so it may also have destroyed their best hope of moving up the social ladder in the American society. It is that reform that must be undone before the condition of education will likely improve for America's poor and the "culture of hopelessness" can be dissolved.

Some Hopeful Signs

Earlier in the chapter the unsuccessful attempt to obtain community control in New York City was reviewed. It was defeated by what D. Rogers called the "professional machine."[49] The effect of that takeover is documented by Iannaccone and Lutz.[50] It can be accurately termed "pernicious." It was ruinous to the control of the public schools by the people of New York City whose children went to those schools and who were being prepared "for the penitentiary."

E. Goffman suggests that all conflict exhibits itself as "two team play."[51] That is to say that regardless of the conflict between subsystems within a political coalition, that coalition will act as a single system and in opposition to another political coalition that is opposing it. The battle for community control in New York City was fought between a coalition of old enemies: the teachers' union, school administrators, and the central board (those who had long battled each other for power within the professional insiders). The sum of the power of these traditional combatants was sufficient to defeat the political coalition of outsiders that threatened to usurp some of the power insiders had previously exercised in some fashion, but shared only among themselves. The fight was a two team play. The powerful and traditional groups in the politics of local education won easily.[52]

About thirty years later in another major American city the effort to decentralize a monolithic professional machine was taking place. Then Secretary of Education William Bennett had called the Chicago School System the worst in the country. That may not have been totally accurate, but it was close. The reasons for that evaluation certainly included the conditions of social class discussed in this chapter and the correlates of being lower class, living in poverty, being undereducated, and without much hope. It also included the moral corruption of the system, if not some illegal form of economic payoffs to the faithful in the professional machine. This time, however, it was not the indigenous poor of the city who demanded change but those who were powerful within the Illinois state legislature.

It is not clear why they chose to act in the manner they did. It is clear that the country was running full steam along the track of educational reform, engineered by the "Nation at Risk" rhetoric. The Illinois state legislature, dominated by downstate representatives, passed a Chicago reform. They decentralized the Chicago schools, cutting almost in half the central office staff, and decentralized decision making to elected school-site boards of parents, teachers, the principal, and a student. Each board was given power not just to advise about policy but to make policy decisions about the school, including budget, curriculum, and personnel.

Two facts may account for the passage of this act. Downstate Illinois is generally as rural, conservative, and antilabor as is the deep South. The powerful labor unions, which had defeated the New York City reform bill thirty years earlier, probably had little influence on downstate Illinois legislators. Additionally, the downstate boys did it to Chicago, not to themselves. In no other school district in the state were the traditional power relationships altered. If Chicago was the nation's worse, surely East St. Louis ran a close second. Why Chicago and not other Illinois school districts?

Illinois has several types of school districts, which allows for some districts to be very small and govern, in some cases, a single school or type of school. Often the governance of these schools was already very close to the people whose children attended the schools. As Iannaccone and Lutz point out, many of such schools are working reasonably well, largely unnoticed by today's education critics, both the traditional reformers and the disestablishment trumpeters and the media that amplifies their recommendations.[53] Perhaps as many as 70 percent to 80 percent of America's school districts work reasonably well for the majority of their students and are governed by boards that reasonably represent their communities. The problem is that even in those schools where governance seems to work reasonably well, it is largely the same group, the poor and the hopeless, that are failing. Still it is in the largest most urban school districts, where the governance is most elite and furthest from the people whose children attend the public schools, that most of the failures cited by the reformers exist.

J. P. Danzberger, M. W. Kirst, and M. D. Usand proclaim the Chicago reform as the most "radical as any promulgated in the history of American education.''[54] Certainly the legislation was radical. But reform suggests that something actually changes. It is unlikely that the professional machine has given up in Chicago. There is at present little empirical data upon which to proclaim a victory and very little to celebrate the Chicago reform bill as a general success. Mostly word-of-mouth description suggests some real power shifts and successes both in community participation and academic achievement. There are also reports of administrative stonewalling, and some failure, including corruption in office, and failure to produce better academic results. What is clear is that the power has shifted toward the people and away from the traditional power holders. If mistakes are to be made in Chicago, the people will now make them. Once made, the people will have to correct them themselves. Perhaps that is what democracy is all about.

New Directions

Danzberger et al. correctly state that the last time school boards were reformed was 100 years ago and that they are long overdue for another reform.[55] They point out that school boards themselves say that their area of poorest performance is that of policy making. As the job of any governing board is the "authoritative allocation of values" through policy making, then school boards are worst at their most important job. Those authors recommend reforming school boards by state legislation, which would make school boards "policy boards." It is an easy trick to do and not unlikely to occur. All that is necessary is for the legislatures of fifty states to rename school boards, calling them policy boards. As ridiculous as that seems, it could happen. At least it would remind school governance boards of their primary task. But it is unlikely that those policy boards will be better at making policy.

Of course Danzberger et al. are well aware of that and they recommend other changes. All the changes they recommend, however, are rooted in the old reform of a century ago. All would make school governing boards more elite, further from the people, more consensual and trustee-like, less diverse, and less likely to act as representatives of the people who might elect them. Apparently they believe that the old diagnosis was correct and the prescription was not wrong, the patient simply has not taken enough castor oil.

Lutz and Iannaccone see the same problem but prescribe a quite different solution:

> We have shown that it is unlikely that urban schools, governed and structured as they have been for more than a half a century, will suddenly begin to succeed. We have further demonstrated that the problems faced by the urban schools— poverty, breakdown of the family, drugs and, violence—are not problems created by the public schools but ones the schools as governed and structured) have been unable to solve. . . . The major focus of urban school reform must be, however,

the political process and the target of that process must be the control and governance of local schools.[56]

Recent research in Texas questions the ability of state-legislated, site-based decision making to effectively change the nature of power within the present structure of school governance.[57] Texas respondents agreed that site-based decision making would increase the participation in school governance, and improve the degree to which school policy would look like citizen demands. They thought, however, that citizens would have little input into budget or curriculum decisions due to the Texas mandate, and that citizen dissatisfaction and school board incumbent defeat would be little affected. In other words the respondents—school board members, administrators, and citizens—thought there would be greater participation, some policy influence, but little power shifts in the important areas of budget or curriculum where the traditional power holders would remain in control. The result would be continued public dissatisfaction and political turmoil at the polls.

CONCLUSION

Why not give the schools back to the people? Why not try democracy? Why do again what was done a century ago and failed, and still call it reform? Even those who think of the people as "a great beast" must admit that, left to their own devices, most of those in the wild know how to and do take good care of their young. Surely humans will do no worse. What if a physician, having told us to "take two aspirin and call in the morning," hearing we were even sicker in the morning, then told us to "take six aspirin and call me tonight"? Which of us would not get a second opinion? Most of the "physicians" of school board reform are prescribing "more of the same."

If we are to change the plight of the children in the lower classes, the minority, the ethnically different, and the hopelessly poor, if their chances in school are to improve, first we must change, actually reform, the governance of local education in the nation's largest school systems. We should consider making the system governable by drastically reducing the size of those districts so as to render them possible to represent. We must give the schools back to the people. We must do a "Chicago Reform" to ourselves and the nation, not just in words but in deed. And, in doing so, we must avoid undoing what has worked well for the majority of the more than 15,000 school districts where the people are represented and the data suggest the "crucible of American democracy" exists.[58]

NOTES

1. For American sociology, see R. S. Lynd and H. M. Lynd, *Middletown: A Study of American Culture* (New York: Harcourt Brace, 1956); W. L. Warner, *Yankee City* (New Haven, CT: Yale University Press, 1963); C. W. Mills, *White Collar: The American*

Middle Class (Oxford: Oxford University Press, 1951). For American public education, see A. B. Hollingshead, *Elmtown's Youth and Elmtown Revisited* (New York: John Wiley, 1975); T. S. Coleman, *The Adolescent Society: The Social Life of Teenagers and Its Effect on Education* (New York: The Free Press, 1971); A. H. Peskin, *Growing Up in America* (Chicago: University of Chicago Press, 1978).

2. R. A. Dahl, *Who Governs? Power in an American City* (New Haven, CT: Yale University Press, 1961).

3. C. E. Sleeter and C. A. Grant, *Making Choices for Multicultural Education* (New York: Macmillan, 1994).

4. T. Branett, *Comprehensive Multicultural Education* (Boston: Allyn and Bacon, 1956), 37–38.

5. C. Marshall and P. P. Zodhiates, "The Politics of Race and Gender," in C. Marshall (Ed.), *The Politics of Race and Gender* (Washington, DC: Falmer Press, 1992), 1.

6. C. H. Gross, S. P. Wronski, and J. W. Hanson, *School and Society* (New York: D.C. Heath, 1962), 498.

7. Ibid.

8. S. W. Reitman, *The Educational Messiah Complex: America's Faith in the Culturally Redemptive Power of Schools* (Sacramento, CA: Caddo Gap Press, 1992).

9. Ibid., p. 14.

10. Ibid.

11. See a discussion of how ideologues of social classes affect schooling in S. W. Rothstein, *Identity and Ideology: Sociocultural Theories of Schooling* (Westport, CT: Greenwood Press, 1991).

12. E. A. Brantlinger, *The Politics of Social Class in Secondary Schools* (New York: Teachers College Press, 1984), 42.

13. S. E. Tozer, P. C. Violas, and G. Senese, *School and Society: Educational Practice as Social Expression* (New York: McGraw-Hill, 1993), 399.

14. J. G. Cilbulka, R. J. Reed, and K. K. Wong, "The Politics of Urban Education: Introduction and Overview," in J. G. Cilbulka, R. J. Reed, and K. K. Wong (Eds.), *The Politics of Urban Education in the United States* (Washington, DC: Falmer Press, 1986), 1.

15. A. G. Wirth, *Education and Work for the Year 2000: Choices We Face* (San Francisco, CA: Jossey-Bass, 1992).

16. R. E. Callahan, *Education and the Cult of Efficiency* (Chicago: University of Chicago Press, 1962).

17. E. Lazarus, "The New Colossus," *Inscription on the Statue of Liberty* (New York, 1883).

18. J. Moffett, "On to the Past: Wrong-Headed School Reform," *Phi Delta Kappan*, 75(8) (1994): 588.

19. For the original discussion of "manifest and latent" functions, see R. K. Merton, *Social Theory and Social Structure* (Glencoe, IL: The Free Press, 1968).

20. D. Easton, *A Framework for Political Analysis* (New York: Prentice Hall, 1965).

21. Brantlinger, *The Politics of Social Class*, 25.

22. American Association of School Boards, Faxed material, February 1994.

23. For a discussion of the concept of elite and arena councils and the decisions they make, see G. F. Bailey, "Decisions by Consensus in Councils and Committees," in Michael Branton (Ed.), *Political Systems and the Distribution of Power* (London: Tavistock Publications, 1969).

24. U.S. Department of Education, *Digest of Education Statistics* (Washington, DC: OERI, 1993).

25. J. P. Danzberger, M. W. Kirst, and M. D. Usand, *Governing Public Schools: New Times, New Requirements* (Washington, DC: Institute for Educational Leadership, 1992).

26. M. D. Usand, "The Relationship Between School Boards and General Purpose Government," *Phi Delta Kappan*, 75(5) (1975): 375.

27. R. E. Herriott and N. H. St. John, *Social Class and the Schools* (New York: John Wiley, 1966), 17.

28. T. Parsons, "A Revised Analytical Approach to the Theory of Social Stratification," in *Class, Status and Power*, R. Bender and S. M. Lipset (Eds.) (New York: The Free Press, 1957).

29. J. S. Mill, "A Classic Statement on Liberty," in Gross, Wronski and Hanson (Eds.), *School and Society*, 176–177.

30. F. W. Lutz, Field notes from the New York Danforth project, 1968.

31. O. Lewis, *Anthropological Essays* (New York: Random House, 1970).

32. M. Lieberman, *The Future of Public Education* (Chicago: University of Chicago Press, 1960).

33. Gross, Wronski, and Hanson, *School and Society*, 78–79.

34. See A. de Tocqueville, *Democracy in America* (New York: Knopf, 1945).

35. F. W. Lutz and C. Merz, *The Politics of School/Community Relations* (New York: Teachers College Press, 1992), xiv.

36. M. W. Kirst, "A Changing Context Means Reform," *Phi Delta Kappan*, 75(5) (1994): 378–381.

37. See W. Wilson, "The Study of Public Administration," *Political Science Quarterly*, 51(4) (1987): 481–506, Reprinted from an 1887 issue.

38. J. M. Cronin, *The Control of Urban Schools* (New York: The Free Press, 1973), 116.

39. F. W. Lutz, "The People, Their Politics and Their Schools," *Issues in Education*, 2(2) (1984): 143.

40. L. Iannaccone and F. W. Lutz, "The Crucible of Democracy: The Local Area," in *The Politics of Education Association 25th Yearbook* (Washington, DC: Falmers Press, 1994).

41. C. Pipho, "Opposition to Reform," *Phi Delta Kappan*, 75(7) (1994): 510.

42. D. L. Clark and T. A. Astuto, "Redirecting Reform," *Phi Delta Kappan*, 75(7) (1994): 513.

43. L. H. Zeigler and M. K. Jennings, *Governing American Schools: Political Interaction in Local School Districts* (North Scituate, MA: Duxbury Press, 1974).

44. F. Wirt and M. Kirst, *Schools in Conflict: The Politics of Education* (Berkeley, CA: McCutchan, 1982); Easton, *A Framework for Political Analysis*.

45. F. W. Lutz and L. Iannaccone, *Public Participation in Local School Districts: The Dissatisfaction Theory of American Democracy* (Lexington, MA: D.C. Heath, 1978).

46. Kirst, "A Changing Context."

47. Lutz, "The People."

48. F. W. Lutz and A. Gresson, "Local School Boards as Political Councils," *Educational Studies*, 11(2) (1980): 125–144.

49. D. Rogers, *110 Livingston Street: Politics and Bureaucracy in the New York City School System* (New York: Random House, 1968).

50. Iannaccone and Lutz, "The Crucible of Democracy."

51. E. Goffman, *Presentation of Self in Everyday Life* (Garden City, NY: Doubleday, 1959).

52. L. Iannaccone, "Norms Governing Urban State Politics of Education," in F. W. Lutz (Ed.), *Toward Improved Urban Education* (Worthington, OH: Charles E. Jones Publishing, 1970).

53. Iannaccone and Lutz, "The Crucible of Democracy."

54. Danzberger, Kirst, and Usand, *Governing Public Schools*, 21.

55. Ibid.

56. F. W. Lutz and L. Iannaccone, "Policymakers and Politics in Urban Education," in S. Rothstein (Ed.), *Handbook of Schooling in Urban America* (Westport, CT: Greenwood Press, 1993), 97–98.

57. R. M. Iden, "A Delphi Study: Forecasting the Future Impact of Site-Based Decision Making of Local School Governance in the State of Texas" an unpublished dissertation (Commerce: East Texas State University, 1994).

58. Iannaccone and Lutz, "The Crucible of Democracy."

Chapter 3

The Chicano Educational Experience: Empirical and Theoretical Perspectives

Daniel G. Solorzano

The lower achievement and underrepresentation of Chicanas and Chicanos in most areas of education is a serious problem for the United States.[1] Indeed, Shirley Malcom has stated that "to understand the reasons for the mere trickle at the end of the . . . pipeline . . . , we must go all the way back to the head-water."[2] Consequently, the underachievement and underrepresentation of Chicanas and Chicanos at each point in the educational pipeline might be better explained by examining the educational conditions at the elementary and secondary "headwater."[3] As educational researchers and policymakers, we need to theoretically understand the cumulative effects of inadequate educational preparation of Chicanos at the precollege level and how that impacts on their educational attainment in college and beyond. This lack of achievement and representation at each point in the pipeline has resulted in both a talent loss to U.S. society and a loss of important role models for the next generation of Chicano students who aspire to educational and professional careers.

This chapter will address these concerns by (1) examining the issues related to defining both the Chicano and Latino populations, (2) placing this population in a demographic context with special emphasis on their educational achievement and attainment, (3) examining the educational conditions of schools in Chicano/Latino communities, (4) positing theoretical models to explain the poor educational outcomes of Chicanos at the elementary and secondary levels, and (5) offering some educational reform models for the Chicano community.

DEFINING AND DEMOGRAPHICALLY DESCRIBING CHICANO/LATINO POPULATIONS

One of the most critical aspects of any research or policy project is to carefully define the population both conceptually and operationally. For Chicanos this

Table 3.1
Selected Characteristics of Latino Groups: March 1992

	Latinos					
	Mexican	Puerto Rican	Cuban	Central South	Other Latino	Non-Latino White
Number-Millions (All Latino=22.1) (Total U.S.=251.4) (Latino=8.8% of Total U.S.)	14.1	2.4	1.0	3.1	1.6	189.2
% of Latino Population	63.8	10.9	4.5	14.0	7.2	NA
Median Age	24.4	26.9	40.4	28.4	32.4	35.2
Mean Size of Family	4.03	3.49	3.16	3.40	3.03	3.03
% 4 Years High School or more (25 yrs +)	45.2	60.5	62.0	61.7	70.9	83.4
% B.A. Degree or more (25 yrs +)	6.1	8.4	18.4	16.0	14.2	23.2
% Manager/Professional Occupation: Female	14.0	20.6	26.6	14.9	23.1	29.7
% Manager/Professional Occupation: Male	9.3	10.9	21.3	13.6	18.3	28.6
Median Family Income	23018	20654	30039	24999	30155	39239
% Families Below Poverty Level*	27.4	35.6	13.9	23.9	19.8	7.1
% Female-Headed Houses Below Poverty Level	47.7	66.3	NA	42.8	45.3	24.6
% Persons Under 18 yrs Below Poverty Level	39.7	57.9	33.3	33.4	33.6	13.1

(*) Poverty is defined as earnings of $13,924 a year (1991) for a family of four.

Source: Adapted from U.S. Bureau of the Census, Current Population Reports, Series P-20, No. 465RV, The Hispanic Population in the United States: March 1992. U.S. Government Printing Office, Washington, D.C. 1993, Tables 1, 2, 3 & 4.

becomes complicated because of the lack of knowledge most researchers, policymakers, and practitioners have about this group. For instance, many people use the terms "Latino" and "Chicano" synonymously, when in fact Latino is an overarching, umbrella, or panethnic term that represents persons of Latin American ancestry who reside in the United States. Chicanas and Chicanos, on the other hand, are defined as female and male persons, respectively, of Mexican ancestry living in the United States.

Another problem emerges when data for Chicanos is required and only information on Latinos is provided. This is especially true for those who are gathering institutional educational data at the school, district, state, or national levels. At most elementary and secondary education sites in the United States, data are not collected for specific subpopulation groups such as Chicanos, Puerto Ricans, or Cubans, but are aggregated into the overall Latino category.

Likewise, it is important to note that the Latino population has significant subgroup differences that should be disentangled. For instance, Table 3.1 identifies at least seven characteristics specific to Chicanos. First, Chicanos are by far the largest of the Latino subgroups at about 64 percent, with Puerto Ricans 11 percent, and Cubans 5 percent. Second, with a median age of 24.4 years, Chicanos are the youngest of these subgroups and in fact one of the youngest population groups in the United States. Moreover, for those planning on becoming teachers in the western United States, there is a good chance that a large percentage of the school-age population in the district will be Chicano or Latino. Third, Chicanos have the largest families. In fact, they have one of the highest fertility rates of any group in the United States.[4] Indeed, from 1980 to 1990, while the white population grew by 5 percent, Chicanos increased by 54 percent, making them one of the fastest growing populations in the United States, and the largest ethnic group in most cities west of the Mississippi River.[5] This growth is in large part due to the high immigration and fertility rates of this population. Fourth, Chicanos have the lowest educational attainment levels of any other group. Whether one uses high school diploma or college degree data, Chicanos are the least formally educated. Fifth, Chicanas and Chicanos are the least likely to be in professional/managerial occupations. Sixth, Chicanos have the second lowest family incomes. Seventh, over one-quarter of all Chicano families live below the poverty line, nearly one-half of all Chicana-headed households live in poverty, and four in ten Chicano children under eighteen live in poverty.

It should also be noted that within the Chicano population there are significant differences by generational status, language usage, social class, and gender that are not captured in Table 3.1.[6] These data are important for those who teach, plan to teach, or train those who teach in Chicano/Latino communities.

THE EDUCATIONAL CONDITIONS AND RELATED OUTCOMES OF CHICANO STUDENTS

At any given point in the educational pipeline—no matter how one goes about measuring educational outcomes—Chicano students have not performed as well as whites.[7] Although not exhaustive of all outcomes and conditions, Table 3.2 visually depicts the Chicano pipeline with the top half focusing on educational outcomes and the bottom half on relative conditions that might affect those outcomes. While this model is an overall visual guide, this section will focus on only a few of the many conditions listed.

Some social scientists implicitly begin from the assumption that the educational experiences and conditions are equal for all students. However, this assumption becomes problematic when examining the educational background of Chicanos. This section will study the comparative educational conditions of

Table 3.2
Chicano Educational Pipeline

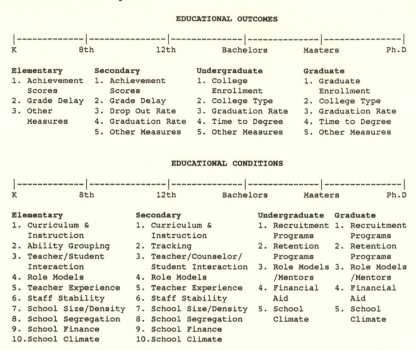

EDUCATIONAL OUTCOMES

```
|-------------|----------------|---------------|---------------|----------------|
K            8th              12th            Bachelors      Masters         Ph.D

Elementary        Secondary           Undergraduate      Graduate
1. Achievement    1. Achievement      1. College         1. Graduate
   Scores            Scores              Enrollment          Enrollment
2. Grade Delay    2. Grade Delay      2. College Type    2. College Type
3. Other          3. Drop Out Rate    3. Graduation Rate 3. Graduation Rate
   Measures       4. Graduation Rate  4. Time to Degree  4. Time to Degree
                  5. Other Measures   5. Other Measures  5. Other Measures
```

EDUCATIONAL CONDITIONS

```
|-------------|----------------|---------------|---------------|----------------|
K            8th              12th            Bachelors      Masters         Ph.D

Elementary              Secondary               Undergraduate  Graduate
1. Curriculum &         1. Curriculum &         1. Recruitment 1. Recruitment
   Instruction             Instruction             Programs       Programs
2. Ability Grouping     2. Tracking             2. Retention   2. Retention
3. Teacher/Student      3. Teacher/Counselor/      Programs       Programs
   Interaction             Student Interaction  3. Role Models 3. Role Models
4. Role Models          4. Role Models             /Mentors       /Mentors
5. Teacher Experience   5. Teacher Experience   4. Financial   4. Financial
6. Staff Stability      6. Staff Stability         Aid            Aid
7. School Size/Density  7. School Size/Density  5. School      5. School
8. School Segregation   8. School Segregation      Climate        Climate
9. School Finance       9. School Finance
10.School Climate       10.School Climate
```

Chicano and white students by examining the educational pipeline in three segments: elementary school, high school, and postsecondary education.

First Segment: Elementary School Conditions

In elementary school, as an important prerequisite to later educational attainment, one would expect to find a high-quality academic curriculum. But research
has shown that, compared to white schools, these high-quality programs are not
available in minority elementary schools.[8] Indeed, Chicano and other predominantly minority elementary schools are more inclined to stress academic remediation and a slowing down of instruction, instead of academic enrichment or
an acceleration of the curriculum.[9] M. Lockheed and others also found that when
quality academic programs were available (e.g., magnet programs), minority
students participated less often than white students.[10] This finding may in part
be due to teachers' low educational expectations for Chicano students, the school
staff assuming less responsibility for educating Chicano students, and these quality programs located outside Chicano/Latino neighborhoods.[11]

There is also a general shortage of teachers servicing minority communities.
The most severe shortages involve Latino teachers, and specifically teachers in

bilingual and special education fields.[12] Indeed, a higher proportion of uncertified and less-experienced teachers, more unfilled teacher vacancies, and high teacher turnover occur in minority schools.[13] In addition, there is more likely to be rigid ability grouping in minority elementary schools and these placements lead to lower academic achievement for minority students.[14] Moreover, there is a shortage of quality programs for limited-English-proficient students.[15] Generally, the curricula and textbooks often exclude the Chicano social and historical experience or, worse, reinforce negative stereotypes.[16] Last, predominantly Chicano/ Latino elementary schools are more likely to be larger, more segregated, and provide fewer educational dollars per pupil than nonminority schools.[17]

Second Segment: Secondary School Conditions

At the secondary school level, students who intend to go to college also need quality academic programs. Again, research shows that college preparatory programs are less likely to be found in predominantly minority schools than in majority schools.[18] When college preparatory programs do exist, Chicano/Latino students are more inclined to be tracked away from them and into the general or vocational tracks.[19] As with elementary schools, researchers have found that high schools in predominantly Chicano communities focused more on academic remediation than academic enrichment.[20] Also, educational programs for limited-English-proficient high school students are almost nonexistent.[21] As in elementary schools, the negative stereotypes associated with Chicanos are often reinforced in the curricula and textbooks.[22] Though research shows that race/ ethnic role models and mentors are important to the development of future professionals, Chicanos are underrepresented in the ranks of high school teachers.[23]

As in elementary schools, research data consistently show that Chicano high school students are disproportionately found in large, overcrowded, ethnically segregated, and lower financed schools.[24]

These elementary and secondary school findings lead to at least two fundamental and related questions: (1) Do these unequal school conditions at the elementary and secondary levels begin to explain the different educational outcomes for Chicano students? and (2) Do these unequal conditions and outcomes also help explain the underrepresentation of Chicanos at the postsecondary levels? The search for answers to these questions leads us to the third segment.

Third Segment: Postsecondary School Conditions

When Chicano students reach the beginning of the college segment of the educational pipeline, they are placed at a distinct disadvantage. While there have been absolute or numerical gains in Chicano college enrollment in the last ten years,[25] upon closer inspection we find three patterns related to these "gains": (1) the increase is not in proportion to the overall growth of the Chicano pop-

Table 3.3
Theoretical Perspectives on Chicano Educational Inequality*

Theoretical Perspectives	Attribution of Responsibility	Primary Policy Solutions
GENETIC DETERMINIST-- The Chicano fails because they are genetically inferior. Traces inequality to the Chicano genes.	The Chicano genetic makeup is responsible.	No solution is possible because nothing can be done to change the Chicano genetic makeup.
CULTURAL DETERMINIST-- The Chicano fails because their culture is viewed as deficient. Traces inequality to Chicano culture.	The Chicano cultural values and related behaviors are responsible.	Acculturate Chicanos to the values and behaviors of the dominant group.
SCHOOL DETERMINIST-- The Chicano fails because of the unequal conditions at the schools they attend. Traces inequality to social institutions.	The unequal conditions at the schools that Chicanos attend.	Change the unequal conditions at the schools that Chicano students attend to that of majority students.
SOCIETAL DETERMINIST-- The Chicano fails because schools reinforce and reproduce societal inequalities. Traces inequality to the overall social system.	The socioeconomic structure is ultimately responsible. Institutions, such as schools, serve primarily to reinforce the unequal social structure.	Change the socioeconomic system to one that is more equitable, then social institutions, such as schools, will reflect that equality.

(*) Within these general theoretical categories are specific hypotheses that focus on specific constructs.

Source: Adapted from Alfred Alschuler, *School Discipline: A Socially Literate Solution* (New York: McGraw-Hill, 1980); and Stanley Sue and Amado Padilla, "Ethnic Minority Issues in the United States: Challenges for the Educational System," in California State Department of Education, *Beyond Language: Social and Cultural Factors in Schooling Language Minority Students* (Los Angeles: Evaluation, Dissemination and Assessment Center, California State University, Los Angeles, 1986).

ulation, (2) the increase is located in two-year community colleges from which the transfer rate to four-year institutions is low, and (3) there are a disproportionate number of part-time community college and four-year college students.[26]

To elaborate, one of the first decisions many Chicano students face is the choice between a two-year community college or a four-year college or university. This decision has important consequences for their academic future, since research shows that the transfer rate of community college students generally, and Chicano students specifically, to four-year colleges is very low.[27] Therefore, many Chicano students terminate their educational careers at the community college level, which is unfortunate, since Chicano students—more often than whites—attend two-year community colleges.[28] Further, when in college, Chicano students are more likely to attend both two- and four-year colleges on a part-time basis.[29] Finally, Chicanos who attend four-year colleges are more likely to drop out before graduation than white students.[30]

The institutional and interpersonal experiences of Chicanos in college can lead to negative school outcomes. For example, in each of the higher education segments, Chicano students are less likely to meet other Chicano students, take a class with a Chicana or Chicano professor, or find the Chicano experience integrated into the curriculum.[31] Adding to this situation is the fact that Chicano and other minority college students are more likely to experience a racially hostile campus environment.[32] In the final analysis, when bachelor, masters, and doctorate degrees are conferred, Chicano students do not receive them in the same proportions as white students.[33]

THEORETICAL MODELS USED TO EXPLAIN LOW EDUCATIONAL ATTAINMENT

How do we explain the low educational achievement and attainment of Chicano students? This question is important because the answer will theoretically guide the policy recommendations and educational reforms needed to solve the educational inequities described above.

There are at least four general theoretical models used to explain the lower educational attainment of Chicano students: genetic deterministic, cultural determinist, school determinist, and societal determinist. Each model focuses on a specific unit of analysis and examines particular concepts for explaining the lower educational attainment of Chicano students. It is important to note that within these general models are more specific models and, indeed, these specific models may bridge two or more general models. Table 3.3 presents, in simplified form, each general model's underlying theoretical perspective, each model's attribution of responsibility for school failure, and each model's primary policy solutions.[34]

Genetic Determinist Model

The genetic determinist model takes the position that the low educational attainment of minorities generally, and Chicanos specifically, can be traced to deficiencies in their genetic structure.[35] In this scenario, there are few social policy options—lacking genetic transformation or total neglect—to raise the educational attainment of Chicano students. While in recent years this model has been out of favor in educational research and policy circles, there could be a resurgence in interest as a consequence of the work of Lloyd Dunn,[36] the Minnesota Twin Studies,[37] and the work of Frederick Goodwin.[38] In fact, in 1988, the *Hispanic Journal of Behavioral Sciences* devoted an entire issue to the general topic of science, ideology, and Latino research, and to the specific work of Lloyd Dunn.[39]

Two points from this Special Issue on Dunn are worth noting. First, the relationship between achievement and IQ tests is likely to be reciprocal. For instance, David Berliner states: "At the very least the evidence about the co-variation of achievement and intelligence tests informs us that the two major competing hypotheses about the direction of influence (i.e., whether IQ causes achievement or whether achievement "causes" IQ) cannot now be answered with any surety."[40]

Second, when addressing non-English-speaking students who come from a different culture, the use of vocabulary as an IQ measure may not be appropriate. Again, Berliner points out:

> Vocabulary, while a strong correlate of the g factor of intelligence, and present as a sub-test in most familiar intelligence tests, is also the best example of a test that easily shifts from a central indicator of intelligence to an almost pure measure of academic achievement. . . . The cultural group one belongs to is the basis of the clarification of the test.[41]

Thus the ambiguity that IQ tests present relative to their role as achievement or intelligence tests for language minority students certainly casts doubt on subsequent interpretations of genetic inferiority for Latinos.

Cultural Determinist Model

The culture determinist model argues that Chicano cultural values are the primary determinant of low achievement and attainment. The model focuses on such deficient cultural values as present versus future time orientation, immediate instead of deferred gratification, an emphasis on cooperation rather than competition, and placing less value on education and upward mobility.[42] For example, former U.S. Secretary of Education Lauro Cavazos stated that Latino parents deserve much of the blame for a high dropout rate among their children because "Hispanics have always valued education . . . but somewhere along the line we've lost that. I really believe that, today, there is not that emphasis."[43] Moreover, Thomas Sowell has claimed that "the goals and values of Mexican Americans have never centered on education."[44]

While John Ogbu's work would fall within a more critical theoretical framework, specific statements in a recent work seem to fall within the cultural determinist model.[45] For instance, he attempts to explain how "involuntary" racial minorities (e.g., blacks, Chicanos, and Native Americans) reinforce their own inequality through a cultural frame of reference that ensures failure. Ogbu claims that "involuntary minorities have not developed a widespread effort of optimism or a strong cultural ethic of hard work and perseverance in the pursuit of education."[46]

These models also examine deficiencies in Chicano family internal social structure, such as large, disorganized, female-headed families; Spanish or nonstandard-accented English spoken in the home; and patriarchal family structures. The deficit models argue that since Chicano parents fail to assimilate and embrace the educational values of the dominant group, and continue to transmit or socialize their children with values that inhibit educational mobility, then the low educational attainment will continue into succeeding generations.

This cultural deficit view of the Chicano has become the social scientific "norm," despite the fact that there is little empirical evidence to support it.[47] On the practical side, the deficit model gets transferred to the classroom and to students by teachers who are professionally trained in colleges, and specifically in a teacher education curriculum that is geared to reflect an individualistic and cultural deficit explanation of low minority educational attainment.[48] The educational policy solutions that emerge from this model focus on the acculturation of Chicano students to the values and behaviors of the culturally proficient dominant group; while criticizing, downplaying, or ignoring the values and behaviors of Chicano culture.

Despite this history, claims that the cultural deficit model has been debunked and is no longer widely used seem premature. In fact, the 1980s have seen a revival of the cultural deficit model, under the rubric of the cultural "underclass," to explain low minority attainment.[49] More recently, Douglas Massey and Nancy Denton introduced a construct called the culture of segregation.[50] They argue that

> residential segregation has been instrumental in creating a culture of segregation that concentrates poverty to build a set of mutually reinforcing and self-feeding spirals of decline. These include oppositional culture that devalues work, schooling, and marriage, and that stresses attitudes and behavior antithetical and often hostile to success in the larger economy.[51]

Once again, the deficit model reemerges in different forms and language.

School/Institutional Determinist Model

School determinist models begin with the premise that educational inequality exists because of the unequal conditions of the schools that Chicano students attend.[52] These models examine—at a minimum—the effects of differential school factors such as ability grouping, tracking, low teacher expectations and behaviors, and differences in educational resources on Chicano educational performance. These models suggest that once programs are established that equalize the conditions and processes in the schools that Chicanos attend, then educational inequities will diminish.[53]

Refocusing on and redefining the school context allows the researcher to continue to challenge the assumption that Chicano and white students attend schools of equal quality. Researchers can then redefine and analyze the effects of differential school opportunities and conditions on the educational achievement and attainment of Chicano students. Some research suggests that these institutional characteristics are related to the educational attainment of minority students.[54]

Societal Determinist Model

The societal determinist position argues that Chicano educational inequality is rooted in the unequal class structure of a capitalist society.[55] One general societal framework used to explain the education of Chicana and Chicano students is critical theory. According to William Tierney, "critical theory is an attempt to understand the oppressive aspects of society in order to generate societal and individual transformation."[56] It appears there are at least three models that would fall under the rubric of critical theory: social reproduction, cultural reproduction, and resistance.

There are at two types of reproduction models, social and cultural reproduction. The social reproduction model starts from the premise that capitalist societies call for a hierarchically structured workforce to provide goods and services, and this workforce needs to be reproduced from one generation to the next. Therefore, society's agents of socialization (e.g., schools, media, and polity) serve (intentionally or not) to reproduce, reinforce, and legitimize this hierarchical workforce by socializing young people to take and accept their place in the workforce.[57] In fact, in 1988, then-presidential candidate George Bush told a crowd of predominantly Chicano students at Garfield High School in East Los Angeles that they "don't have to go to college to be a success . . . we need those people who build our buildings . . . the people who do the hard physical work of our society."[58]

Indeed, Samuel Bowles and Herbert Gintis use the "correspondence principle" to explain the relationship between the school and the workplace.[59] The correspondence principle posits that the hierarchically structured patterns of values, norms, and skills that characterize the U.S. workplace are mirrored, or correspond, to the social dynamics of daily classroom life. For example, through differential classroom social relations and materials based on social class, ethnicity, and gender (i.e., the hidden curriculum), schools function to inculcate students with the attitudes and behaviors necessary to accept and function in their subsequent social and economic roles.[60] An extension of this model would argue that Chicana and Chicano students do not enroll or persist in college because the schools they attend serve as "sorting" machines that function to prepare them to take on certain occupations that do not need a college educa-tion.[61]

The primary focus of the social reproduction model is on the social structural conditions inherent in the societies' institutions (i.e., schools), instead of indi-vidual (i.e., parent or child) or group (i.e., social class, race, or sex) deficits to explain variations in educational attainment. Despite their shifting the educa-tional responsibility to the schools, the social reproduction models appear very pessimistic and offer little hope for changing the low educational attainment of minorities, short of massive social change, and even less hope for developing alternative educational practices where teachers and parents can place their en-ergy. These models seem to take the position that there are critical structural "deficits" or "assets" (depending on your perspective) that inhibit Chicanos from raising their educational attainment and that massive societal change is the answer to the problem.

The second model is the cultural reproduction model, which begins where the social reproduction model ends.[62] The social and cultural reproduction models are similar for they focus on how capitalist societies are able to reproduce them-selves. However, the focus of the cultural model is on how school culture is selected, produced, legitimized, and transferred, and how this school culture helps to reproduce class societies and related inequalities.[63] Pierre Bourdieu and Jean-Claude Passeron have argued that schools are institutions that reproduce existing power relations by producing and distributing a dominant culture that confirms what it means to be educated.[64] The dominant class defines what is valued culturally and linguistically, and disguises this "cultural arbitrariness" in the name of neutrality. These dominant ideologies are transmitted by schools and actively incorporated by students, while the cultural and linguistic traits of subordinate groups are less valued or ignored altogether. Therefore, schools are an important force in the process of class and cultural reproduction. Indeed, by appearing to be an impartial and neutral transmitter of the benefits of a valued culture, schools are able to promote educational inequality in the name of fair-ness and objectivity.

The cultural reproduction model would argue that Chicano students do not perform adequately in school, let alone continue to and persist in college, be-cause the schools that they attend focus on and reward the culture of the dom-inant class and place little, if any, value on the culture of Chicano students. One criticism of this model is that it comes very close to reaching the same conclu-sion as the cultural deficit model, since both models argue that the lack of, mismatch with, and refusal to acquire the cultural capital of the dominant group is viewed as a critical problem for the Chicano. Indeed, the cultural strengths, adaptations, or forms of resistance of Chicanos are either downplayed or ig-nored.[65]

Despite these criticisms, both the social and cultural reproduction theorists would argue that the unequal distribution of attainment among Chicano children in the United States derives from variability in the nature of the schools they attend.[66] Indeed, the data in the previous section has shown that the schools Chicanos and other minority students attend are qualitatively different from the schools that majority students attend.

In the final group are the resistance models. By integrating critical social theory with an ethnographic methodology, resistance theories try to illuminate the dynamics of accommodation and resistance of individuals and groups both inside and outside schools. Hence, these theories focus on the internal workings or day-to-day operations of the schools. Theories of resistance place a central emphasis on the tensions and conflicts that mediate relationships between and within the home, school, community, and workplace. They argue that social and cultural reproduction is never complete and is always faced with elements of opposition from students, teachers, parents, and the community. These oppositional behaviors, or resistance, can take on either a reactionary or a progressive mode. In this model, progressive resistance represents a form of discourse that rejects traditional explanations for lower Chicano attainment and oppositional behavior, and focuses on the empowerment of the individual or group. Resistance models offer valuable choices to the pessimistic social and cultural reproduction models of schooling that find it impossible to challenge or modify the situation. Resistance theorists argue that schools can be both dominating and liberating institutions.[67] When schools dominate, consciously or not, they prepare students for the roles in society that people of their kind have historically occupied. As a liberating force schools, consciously or not, can prepare students to break those dominating patterns and empower them to take on new roles that people from their social condition had not filled.[68]

By reexamining and connecting the societal and institutional (i.e., school) context, researchers can observe how schools reproduce minority social inequality through its various mechanisms. Also, using resistance models, researchers can examine how some minority students resist the schools' mechanisms of social control.[69] In either case, these models must examine and be sensitive to reproduction and resistance within a race/ethnic and gender context.[70]

DISCUSSION

In this chapter we tried to examine the inadequate conditions that exist in Chicano/Latino schools and the resulting low educational achievement and attainment. We also attempted to introduce the theoretical models used to explain these negative educational outcomes. At this point, there is a need to propose some general education reforms that might challenge the existing conditions and outcomes for Chicano students.

At least three reform models offer some hope for minority communities generally and Chicano communities in particular. They are the Effective Schools model, the Accelerated Schools program, and the Cultural Continuities model. Specifically, Ronald Edmonds conducted research on "effective" urban minority (primarily black) schools and found five factors that "are the most tangible and indispensable characteristics of effective schools."[71] The five Edmonds' factors are high expectations and responsibility for student learning, strong instructional leadership, emphasis on basic skill acquisition, frequent monitoring of student progress, and orderly and safe school environment.[72]

Also, Levin's Accelerated model represents an elaboration of certain elements in the Effective Schools model.[73] The Accelerated program is designed to speed up rather than remediate the curriculum and bring at-risk minority students to grade level by the sixth grade.[74] This is accomplished by (1) developing a unity of purpose toward a common set of goals for the school that will be the focal point of every person's effort, (2) making sure that primary responsibility and accountability for educational decisions and results are delegated to the staff at the school site in conjunction with parents and students, and (3) building on the unique assets and strengths of at-risk students, their families, and their cultures.

The Cultural Continuities model begins from the assumption that minority parents and students value educational achievement, and building on this strength and using it as the basis for intervention (as in the Accelerated Schools approach) can improve the achievement of minority students. This model begins by examining the home for cultural activities that are compatible with school achievement. These culturally compatible activities are then adapted for classroom use.[75] Indeed, viewing the student's home culture as a strength complements the Accelerated Schools model, and leads to programs of mutual accommodation in which the teacher and the student modify their behavior toward a common goal.[76] Showing how forms of cultural production displayed by subordinate groups can be analyzed to reveal both their limitations and possibilities has shown some promising research and intervention directions.

These three models offer an opportunity to challenge the genetic and cultural determinist models by shifting the primary responsibility for school failure from the students, their families, and their culture, to the school's structure, resources, and processes. These three models also challenge the pessimism of the school and societal determinist models by identifying educationally effective schools in poor and minority communities that empower disenfranchised parents and students with hope for their educational future.

This chapter has proposed that in the educational and occupational race from elementary school to professional careers, Chicano students are running at a distinct disadvantage since they are forced to run over, around, and through social and educational obstacles not encountered by most majority students. It is to be hoped that through informed educational policies and programs we can better understand and remove some of the obstacles, and make the race to higher education and the professional careers more equitable for Chicana and Chicano students.

NOTES

1. For this study, Chicanas and Chicanos are defined as female and male persons of Mexican origin living in the United States. Latinos are defined as persons of Latin American origin living in the United States. For this chapter, I will follow Denise Segura and

Beatriz Pesquera's ("Beyond Indifference and Antipathy: The Chicana Movement and Chicana Feminist Discourse," *Aztlan*, 19 (1988/90):69–92, lead and treat both Chicanas and Chicanos, and Latinas and Latinos, under the broad term Chicano and Latino, respectively. In most of the literature on Latinos, the term "Hispanic" is used to identify this population. I prefer to use Latino (see David Hayes Bautista and Jorge Chapa, "Latino Terminology: Conceptual Bases for Standardized Terminology," *American Journal of Public Health*, 77 [1987]:61–68).

2. Shirley Malcom, "Who Will Do Science in the Next Century?" *Scientific American*, 262(2) (1990a):112.

3. For an important discussion and critique of the pipeline metaphor, see Michael Olivas, "Trout Fishing in Catfish Ponds," in Jessie Jones, Margaret Goertz, and Charlotte Kuh (Eds.), *Minorities in Graduate Education: Pipeline, Policy, and Practice* (Princeton, NJ: Educational Testing Service, 1993).

4. Frank Bean and Marta Tienda, *The Hispanic Population in the United States* (Ithaca, NY: Russell Sage Foundation, 1988).

5. William O'Hare, "America's Minorities: The Demographics of Diversity," *Population Bulletin*, 47 (1992):2–47.

6. Alejandro Portes and Carol Truelove, "Making Sense of Diversity: Recent Research on Hispanic Minorities in the United States," *Annual Review of Sociology*, 13 (1987):359–385.

7. Beatriz Arias, "The Context of Education for Hispanic Students: An Overview." *American Journal of Education*, 95 (1986): 26–57; Katherine Haycock and Susan Navarro, *Unfinished Business: Fulfilling Our Children's Promise* (Oakland, CA: The Achievement Council, (1988); National Assessment for Educational Progress, *America's Challenge: Accelerating Academic Achievement, A Summary of Findings for 20 Years of NAEP* (Princeton, NJ: Educational Testing Service, 1990; Francois Nielsen and Roberto Fernandez, *Hispanic Students in American High Schools: Background Characteristics and Achievement* (Washington, DC: National Center for Educational Statistics, 1987; J. O'Malley, *Academic Growth of High School Age Hispanic Students in the United States* (Washington, DC: Center for Education Statistics, 1987; Lori Orum, *The Education of Hispanics: Status and Implications* (Washington, DC: National Council of La Raza, 1986); Russell Rumberger, "Chicano Dropouts: A Review of Research and Policy Issues," in Richard Valencia (Ed.), *Chicano School Failure and Success: Research and Policy Agendas for the 1990s* (New York: The Falmer Press, 1991).

8. Jonathan Kozol, *Savage Inequalities: Children in America's Schools* (New York: Crown, 1991).

9. Henry Levin, *Educational Reform for Disadvantaged Students: An Emerging Crisis* (West Haven, CT: National Educational Association, 1986); Henry Levin, "Accelerated Schools for Disadvantaged Students," *Educational Leadership*, 44 (1987):19–21; Henry Levin, "New Schools for the Disadvantaged," *Teacher Education Quarterly*, 14 (1987): 60–83; Henry Levin, "Accelerated Schools: A New Strategy for At-Risk Students," *Policy Bulletin*, No. 6 (1989), 1–6.

10. M. Lockheed, M. Thorpe, J. Brooks-Gunn, P. Casserly, and A. McAloon, *Sex and Ethnic Differences in Mathematics, Science, and Computer Science: What Do We Know?* a report to the Ford Foundation (Princeton, NJ: Educational Testing Service, 1985).

11. R. Baron, D. Tom, and H. Cooper, "Social Class, Race and Teacher Expectations," in Jerome Dusek (Ed.), *Teacher Expectancies* (Hillsdale, NJ: Lawrence Erlbaum, 1985); Jere Brophy, "Research Linking Teacher Behavior to Student Achievement: Po-

tential Implication for Instruction of Chapter 1 Students," in B. Williams, P. Richmond, and B. Mason (Eds.), *Designs for Compensatory Education: Conference Proceedings and Papers* (Washington, DC: Research and Evaluation Associates, 1986); Thomas Good, "Two Decades of Research on Teacher Expectations: Findings and Future Direction," *Journal of Teacher Education*, 38(4) (1987):32–47; Thomas Good and Jere Brophy, *Looking in Classrooms* (New York: Harper and Row, 1987); G. Jackson and C. Cosca, "The Inequality of Educational Opportunity in the Southwest: An Observational Study of Ethnically Mixed Classrooms," *American Educational Research Journal*, 11 (1974):219–229; Caroline Persell, *Education and Inequality: The Roots and Results of Stratification in America's Schools* (New York: Free Press, 1977); Raymond Rist, "Student Social Class and Teacher Expectation: The Self-fulfilling Prophecy in Ghetto Education," *Harvard Educational Review*, 40 (1970):411–451; United States Commission on Civil Rights, "Teachers and Students: Differences in Teacher Interaction with Mexican American and Anglo Students," Report V: Mexican American Education Study (Washington, DC: U.S. Government Printing Office, 1973).

12. California State Department of Education, "Certified Staff in California Public Schools by Ethnicity and Gender," a special table computed from the California Basic Educational Data System (Sacramento: California State Department of Education, 1988); Linda Darling-Hammond, "Teacher Quality and Equality," an unpublished manuscript presented at the Colloquium on Access to Knowledge, Educational Equity Project, College Board, Oakland, CA (1988); Los Angeles County Office of Education, *The Condition of Public Education in Los Angeles County 1990–91: Annual Statistical Review* (Los Angeles: Los Angeles County Office of Education, 1991); Tomas Rivera Center, *Resolving a Crisis in Education: Latino Teachers for Tomorrow's Classrooms* (Claremont, CA: Author, 1993).

13. Edwin Bridges, *The Incompetent Teacher: Managerial Responses* (New York: The Falmer Press, 1992); Darling-Hammond, "Teacher Quality and Equality."

14. Jeanne Oakes, *Keeping Track: How Schools Structure Inequality* (New Haven, CT: Yale University Press, 1985); Jeanne Oakes, "Tracking in Secondary Schools: A Contextual Perspective," *Educational Psychologist*, 22 (1987):129–153; Jeanne Oakes, *Lost Talent: The Underrepresentation of Women, Minorities, and Disabled Students in Science* (Santa Monica, CA: The Rand Corporation, 1990); Jeanne Oakes, *Multiplying Inequalities: The Effects of Race, Social Class, and Tracking on Opportunities to Learn Mathematics and Science* (Santa Monica, CA: The Rand Corporation, 1990).

15. Arias, "The Context of Education for Hispanic Students"; Eugene Garcia, "Effective Schooling for Language Minority Students," National Clearinghouse for Bilingual Education, Occasional Papers in Bilingual Education, Number 1 (1987//88); Ann Willig, "A Meta-Analysis of Selected Studies on Effectiveness of Bilingual Education," *Review of Educational Research*, 55 (1985): 269–317.

16. Council on Interracial Books for Children, *Stereotypes, Distortions and Omissions in U.S. History Textbooks* (New York: Council on Interracial Books for Children, 1977).

17. Ruben Donato, Martha Menchaca, and Richard Valencia, "Segregation, Desegregation, and Integration of Chicano Students: Problems and Prospects," in Valencia, *Chicano School Failure and Success*; Kozol, *Savage Inequalities*; Gary Orfield and Franklin Monfort, *Status of School Desegregation: The Next Generation* (Cambridge, MA: Metropolitan Opportunity Project, Harvard University, 1992); Ronald Solorzano, "School and Student Components and Their Relationship to Hispanic Fifth Grade

Achievement," an unpublished doctoral dissertation, University of California, Los Angeles, 1987.

18. Oakes, *Keeping Track*; Oakes, "Tracking in Secondary Schools"; Oakes, *Lost Talent*; Oakes, *Multiplying Inequalities*.

19. Oakes, *Keeping Track*; Oakes, "Tracking in Secondary Schools."

20. P. Brown and Katherine Haycock, *Education for Whom* (Oakland, CA: The Achievement Council, 1984); Haycock and Navarro, *Unfinished Business*; Orum, *The Education of Hispanics*.

21. Hispanic Development Policy Project, *Make Something Happen: Hispanics and Urban High School Reform*, Volumes 1 & 2 (Washington, DC: Hispanic Development Policy Project, 1984).

22. Council on Interracial Books for Children, *Stereotypes, Distortions and Omissions in U.S. History Textbooks*.

23. James Blackwell, *Mainstreaming Outsiders: The Production of Black Professionals* (Bayside, NY: General Hall, 1981); California State Department of Education, "Certified Staff in California Public Schools by Ethnicity and Gender"; Darling-Hammond, "Teacher Quality and Equality"; Haycock and Navarro, *Unfinished Business*; Los Angeles County Office of Education, *The Condition of Public Education in Los Angeles County 1990–91*; Malcom, "Who Will Do Science in the Next Century?"; Shirley Malcom, "Reclaiming Our Past," *Journal of Negro Education*, 59 (1990):246–259; Irene Rodriguez, "Hispanics in Math and Science: Attracting Student Teachers and Retraining Experienced Teachers," *Mexican American Education Digest*, ERIC/CRESS (Las Cruces: New Mexico State University, 1984).

24. Donato, Menchaca, and Valencia, "Segregation, Desegregation, and Integration of Chicano Students"; Ruben Espinoza, "Fiscal Resources and School Facilities and their Relationship to Ethnicity and Achievement in the Los Angeles Unified School District," a manuscript prepared for the Social Equity Center, San Diego State University, 1985; Ruben Espinoza, "Myths: Educational Myths Regarding Education as the Great Equalizer," an unpublished manuscript prepared for The Tomas Rivera Center for Policy Studies, Claremont, CA, 1986; Ruben Espinoza and Alberto Ochoa, "Concentration of California Hispanic Students in Schools with Low Achievement: A Research Note," *American Journal of Education*, 65 (1986):77–95; Kozol, *Savage Inequalities*; Orfield and Monfort, *Status of School Desegregation*; United States Commission on Civil Rights, "Ethnic Isolation of the Mexican-American in the Public Schools of the Southwest." Report I: Mexican American Education Study (Washington, DC: U.S. Government Printing Office, 1971); United States Commission on Civil Rights, "Education in Texas: A Function of Wealth." Report IV: Mexican American Education Study (Washington, DC: U.S. Government Printing Office, 1972).

25. However, in the three years 1989, 1990, and 1991, the number of Latino students enrolled in the University of California system declined. See L. Gordon, "Black, Latino Enrollment at UC Drops," *Los Angeles Times*, May 16, 1992, p. A30.

26. Alexander Astin, *Minorities in Higher Education* (San Francisco: Jossey-Bass, 1982); Shirley Brown, *Minorities in the Education Pipeline* (Princeton, NJ: The Educational Testing Service, 1987); California Postsecondary Education Commission, *Background for Expanding Equity* (Sacramento: California Postsecondary Commission, 1986); Center for Educational Statistics, *Trends in Minority Enrollment in Higher Education, Fall 1978–Fall 1986* (Washington, DC: Center for Education Statistics, 1988);

Deborah Carter and Reginald Wilson, *Minorities in Higher Education: 1992 Eleventh Annual Status Report* (Washington, DC: American Council on Education, 1993).

27. Astin, *Minorities in Higher Education*; Steven Brint and Jerome Karabel, *The Diverted Dream: Community Colleges and the Promise of Educational Opportunity in America, 1900–1985* (New York: Oxford University Press, 1989); California Community Colleges, *Transfer: A Plan for the Future*, a report (#7) to the California Community Colleges Board of Governors (Sacramento: Author, 1991); Jerome Karabel, "Community Colleges and Social Stratification," *Harvard Educational Review* 42 (1972):521–562.

28. Gail Thomas, *The Access and Success of Blacks and Hispanics in U.S. Graduate and Professional Education* (Washington, DC: National Academy of Science, 1986).

29. Carter and Wilson, *Minorities in Higher Education: 1992*.

30. Astin, *Minorities in Higher Education*.

31. American Association of Community and Junior Colleges, *Minorities in Urban Community Colleges: Tomorrow's Students Today* (Washington, DC: Author, 1988).

32. Alexander Astin, Jesus Trevino, and Tamara Wingard, *The UCLA Campus Climate For Diversity* (Los Angeles: Higher Education Research Institute, 1991); Sylvia Hurtado, "Campus Racial Climates: Contexts of Conflict," *Journal of Higher Education*, 63 (1992): 539–569; Shirley McBay, *The Racial Climate on the MIT Campus* (Cambridge: Massachusetts Institute of Technology, 1986).

33. Brown, *Minorities in the Education Pipeline*; Carter and Wilson, *Minorities in Higher Education*; National Research Council, *Summary Report 1992: Doctorate Recipients from United States Universities* (Washington, DC: National Academy Press, 1993); National Science Foundation, *Women and Minorities in Science and Engineering* (Washington, DC: National Science Foundation, 1990).

34. Adapted from Alfred Alschuler, *School Discipline: A Socially Literate Solution* (New York: McGraw-Hill, 1980); and Stanley Sue and Amado Padilla, "Ethnic Minority Issues in the United States: Challenges for the Educational System," in California State Department of Education, *Beyond Language: Social and Cultural Factors in Schooling Language Minority Students* (Los Angeles: Evaluation, Dissemination and Assessment Center, California State University, Los Angeles, 1986).

35. Lloyd Dunn, *Bilingual Hispanic Children on the Mainland: A Review of Research on their Cognitive, Linguistic, and Scholastic Development* (Circle Pines, MN: American Guidance Service, 1987); Richard Fernandez (Ed.), "Special Issue, Achievement Testing: Science vs Ideology (Response to Lloyd Dunn)," *Hispanic Journal of Behavioral Sciences*, 10 (1988):179–323; Arthur Jensen, "How Much Can We Boost I.Q. and Scholastic Achievement?" *Harvard Educational Review*, 39 (1989):1–123.

36. Dunn, *Bilingual Hispanic Children on the Mainland*.

37. T. Bouchard, D. Lykken, M. McGue, N. Segal, and A. Tellegen, "Sources of Human Psychological Differences: The Minnesota Study of Twins Reared Apart," *Science*, 250 (1990):223–250.

38. Peter Breggin and Ginger Breggin, "The Federal Violence Initiative: Threats to Black Children (and Others)," *Psych Discourse*, 24 (1993):8–11.

39. Fernandez, "Special Issue, Achievement Testing."

40. David Berliner, "Meta Comments: A Discussion of Critiques of L. M. Dunn's Monograph, Bilingual Hispanic Children on the U.S. Mainland." *Hispanic Journal of Behavioral Sciences*, 10 (1988):280.

41. Ibid., p. 282.

42. Thomas Carter and Roberto Segura, *The Mexican Americans in School: A Decade*

of Change (New York: College Entrance Examination Board, 1979); Celia Heller, *Mexican American Youth: Forgotten Youth at the Crossroads* (New York: Random House, 1966); Spencer Kagan, "Social Motives and Behaviors of Mexican-American and Anglo-American Children," in Joe Martinez (Ed.), *Chicano Psychology* (New York: Academic Press, 1977; Florence Kluckholn and Fredrick Strodtbeck, *Variations in Value Orientations* (Evanston, IL: Row, Peterson, 1966); Audrey Schwartz, "A Comparative Study of Values and Achievement: Mexican-American and Anglo-American Youth," *Sociology of Education*, 44 (1971):438–462.

43. William Snider, "Outcry Follows Cavazos Comments on the Values of Hispanic Parents," *Education Week*, April 18, 1990, p. 1.

44. Thomas Sowell, *Ethnic America: A History* (New York: Basic Books, 1981), p. 266.

45. John Ogbu, "Minority Education in Comparative Perspective," *Journal of Negro Education*, 59 (1990):45–57.

46. Ibid., p. 53.

47. Persell, *Education and Inequality*; Daniel Solorzano, "Mobility Aspirations Among Racial Minorities, Controlling For SES," *Sociology and Social Research*, 75 (1991):182–188; Daniel Solorzano, "An Exploratory Analysis of the Effect of Race, Class, and Gender on Student and Parent Mobility Aspirations," *Journal of Negro Education*, 61 (1992):30–44; Daniel Solorzano, "Chicano Mobility Aspirations: A Theoretical and Empirical Note," *Latino Studies Journal*, 3 (1992):48–66; Marta Tienda, "The Mexican Population," in A. Hawley and S. Mazie (Eds.), *Nonmetropolitan America in Transition* (Chapel Hill: University of North Carolina Press, 1981); Charles Valentine, *Culture and Poverty: Critique and Counter-Proposals* (Chicago: University of Chicago Press, 1968).

48. Persell, *Education and Inequality*.

49. Maxine Baca Zinn, "Family, Race, and Poverty in the Eighties," *Signs: Journal of Woman in Culture and Society*, 14 (1989):856–874. In fact, the Los Angeles urban rebellions in the spring of 1992 sparked a resurgence of the cultural deficit and underclass models in the popular literature and press.

50. Douglas Massey and Nancy Denton, "The Forgotten Factor of U.S. Relations," *Los Angeles Times*, May 30, 1993, p. M3.

51. Ibid.

52. Espinoza, "Fiscal Resources and School Facilities"; Espinoza, "Myths"; Espinoza and Ochoa, "Concentration of California Hispanic Students in Schools with Low Achievement"; Oakes, *Keeping Track*; R. Solorzano, "School and Student Components and Their Relationship to Hispanic Fifth Grade Achievement."

53. Wilbur Brookover, "Can We Make Schools Effective for Minority Students?" *Journal of Negro Education* 54 (1985):257–268; Ronald Edmonds, "Effective Schools for the Urban Poor," *Educational Leadership*, 37 (1979):15–24; Ronald Edmonds, "School Effects and Teacher Effects," *Social Policy*, 15 (1984):37–39; Ronald Edmonds, "Characteristics of Effective Schools," in U. Neisser (Ed.), *The School Achievement of Minority Children: New Perspectives* (Hillsdale, NJ: Lawrence Erlbaum Associates, 1986); Pamela Bullard and Barbara Taylor, *Making School Reform Happen* (Boston: Allyn and Bacon, 1993).

54. Baron, Tom, and Cooper, "Social Class, Race and Teacher Expectations"; James Cummins, "Empowering Minority Students: A Framework for Intervention," *Harvard*

Educational Review, 56 (1986):18–36; Oakes, *Keeping Track*; Arthur Pearl, "Systemic and Institutional Factors in Chicano School Failure." In Valencia, *Chicano School Failure and Success.*

55. Samuel Bowles and Herbert Gintis, *Schooling in Capitalist America: Educational Reform and the Contradictions of Economic Life* (New York: Basic Books, 1976).

56. William Tierney, *Building Communities of Difference: Higher Education in the Twenty-First Century* (Westport, CT: Bergin & Garvey, 1993), p. 10.

57. Bowles and Gintis, *Schooling in Capitalist America.*

58. Gerald Boyd, "Signs in Idaho Hint Trouble for Bush," *New York Times*, May 7, 1988, p. 34.

59. Bowles and Gintis, *Schooling in Capitalist America.*

60. Jean Anyon, "Social Class and the Hidden Curriculum of Work," *Journal of Education*, 162 (1980):67–92.

61. Joel Spring, *The Sorting Machine* (New York: David McKay Company, 1976).

62. Stanley Aronowitz and Henry Giroux, *Education Under Siege: The Conservative, Liberal, and Radical Debate Over Schooling* (South Hadley, MA: Bergin & Garvey, 1985); Henry Giroux, *Theory and Resistance in Education: A Pedagogy for the Opposition* (South Hadley, MA: Bergin & Garvey, 1983); Henry Giroux, "Theories of Reproduction and Resistance in the New Sociology of Education: A Critical Analysis," *Harvard Educational Review*, 53 (1983):257–293.

63. Aronowitz and Giroux, *Education Under Siege*; Giroux, *Theory and Resistance in Education*; Giroux, "Theories of Reproduction and Resistance in the New Sociology of Education."

64. Pierre Bourdieu and Jean-Claude Passeron, *Reproduction in Education, Society and Culture* (Beverly Hills, CA: Sage, 1977).

65. Hugh Mehan, "Understanding Inequality in Schools: The Contribution of Interpretive Studies," *Sociology of Education*, 65 (1992):1–20.

66. Edmonds, "Characteristics of Effective Schools."

67. Paulo Freire, *Pedagogy of the Oppressed* (New York: Seabury Press, 1973); Henry Giroux, "Teacher Education and the Politics of Engagement: The Case for Democratic Schooling," *Harvard Educational Review*, 56 (1986):213–238; Paul Willis, *Learning to Labor* (Lexington, MA: D.C. Heath, 1977).

68. Freire, *Pedagogy of the Oppressed.*

69. Douglas Foley, *Learning Capitalist Culture: Deep in the Heart of Tejas* (Philadelphia: University of Pennsylvania Press, 1990); Jay MacLeod, *Ain't No Makin It: Leveled Aspirations in a Low-Income Neighborhood* (Boulder, CO: Westivew, 1987); Peter McLaren, *Life in Schools: An Introduction to Critical Pedagogy in the Foundations of Education* (New York: Longman, 1989); Willis, *Learning to Labor.*

70. Giroux, *Theory and Resistance in Education*; Giroux, "Theories of Reproduction and Resistance in the New Sociology of Education."

71. Edmonds, "Effective Schools for the Urban Poor"; Edmonds, "School Effects and Teacher Effects"; Edmonds, "Characteristics of Effective Schools."

72. Bullard and Taylor, *Making School Reform Happen*; Thomas Carter and Michael Chatfield, "Effective Bilingual Schools: Implications for Policy and Practice," *American Journal of Education*, 95 (1986):200–234; Garcia, "Effective Schooling for Language Minority Students."

73. Wendy Hopfenberg, Henry Levin, Gail Meister, and John Rodgers, *Accelerated*

Schools (Stanford, CA: Center for Educational Research at Stanford, 1990); Levin, *Educational Reform for Disadvantaged Students*; Levin, "Accelerated Schools for Disadvantaged Students"; Levin, "New Schools for the Disadvantaged."

74. Accelerated Schools Project, *Accelerated Schools.* Volume 1, Numbers 1, 2, 3, 4 (1991).

75. Claude Goldenberg, "Low-Income Hispanic Parents' Contributions to Their First-Grade Children's Word-Recognition Skills," *Anthropology and Education Quarterly*, 18 (1987):149–179; Roland Tharp, "Psychocultural Variables and Constants: Effects on Teaching and Learning in the Schools," *American Psychologist*, 44 (1989):1–10; Thomas Weisner, Ronald Gallimore, and C. Jordan, "Unpackaging Cultural Effects on Classroom Learning: Native Hawaiian Peer Assistance and Child-Generated Activity," *Anthropology and Education Quarterly*, 19 (1988):327–353.

76. Mehan, "Understanding Inequality in Schools."

Chapter 4

Class, Race, and Science Education

David Eli Drew

Science education not only is vital for an increasingly technological society but also has become a vehicle through which the inequalities of our society are perpetuated and exacerbated. The poor, the disadvantaged, and people of color are severely underrepresented in classrooms where mathematics and science are taught.[1]

The single most important solution to this problem involves a national consciousness raising. Teachers, parents, and the students themselves must recognize that virtually every child has the capacity to master mathematics and science and should be taught these subjects. This is true for females as well as for males, for poverty-stricken students as well as those from more affluent backgrounds, and for persons of every ethnicity. Beyond consciousness raising, recent research provides guidance as to how the reform of science education can proceed most effectively.

MATHEMATICS, SCIENCE, AND JOBS

Training in technical fields is essential for providing both highly skilled labor for industry and professionals to conduct the research and development that fuel our economic competitiveness.

> In 1988 Motorola conducted a study that showed that a Japanese student can be moved into the workplace at an employer cost of $0.47, while an American student's transition costs the employer $226. This is primarily due, says Motorola, to the emphasis on statistics and applied diagnostics in Japanese schools.[2]

According to John S. Rigden, director of physics programs at the American Institute of Physics (AIP), knowing how to operate a drill press is inadequate. To survive, the new employee has to have a firm grounding in math and science and a range of analytic and problem-solving skills. . . . consider skilled trades such as carpenter, plumber, pipe fitter, electrician, tool-and-die maker and model maker. At General Motors Corp., a carpenter now is required to know algebra and geometry. A GM plumber needs algebra, geometry and physics; an electrician needs algebra, trigonometry and physics; and a tool-and-die maker, model maker or machine repairman needs algebra, geometry, trigonometry and physics. These requirements are a harbinger of things elsewhere.[3]

In his book, *The Work of Nations: Preparing Ourselves for 21st-Century Capitalism*, Robert B. Reich defines and discusses three emerging categories of work.[4] These are routine production services (which include most of the traditional blue-collar, assembly-line jobs as well as repetitive work in today's service and information industries), in-person services (also routine jobs but performed on a person-to-person basis and requiring that the worker interact with others pleasantly and courteously), and symbolic-analytic services. This important category includes "all the problem solving, problem identifying, and strategic brokering activities . . . the manipulation of symbols—data, words, oral and visual representation."

Reich goes on to argue that many American children—he estimates 15 to 20 percent—are being well educated for symbolic analytic work, despite the ills that have befallen the American educational system. As evidence, he cites the excellent American university system, the willingness of affluent, symbolic analytic workers to provide such resources as private schools and educational toys for their children, and the more amorphous, but real, educational experiences acquired through social interaction with other children and adults in the same economic background. He argues that, in contrast, "Japan's greatest educational success has been to assure that even its slowest learners achieve a relatively high level of proficiency."[5] The question, of course, is whether 15 to 20 percent is enough.

HOW WELL PREPARED ARE AMERICAN STUDENTS?

The most widely publicized international student assessment was conducted by the International Association for the Evaluation of Educational Achievement (IAEEA) in 1988.[6] Their preliminary report changed the perceptions of many Americans about the status of our educational system.

A summary of the results: as the age of the student being tested increased, the United States moved from the middle of the pack to close to the bottom or dead last, depending on the subject. The IEA researchers noted that between an earlier survey in 1970 and the 1988 survey, "the United States has dropped from seventh out of seventeen countries to third from bottom." They add

"Grade 9 in the United States has about the same level of achievement as grade 7 in Japan and Korea."[7]

Three years later, the findings from a 1991 IEA Assessment were not encouraging for the United States. In the science assessment for thirteen year olds, the United States scored below every other country that sampled a comprehensive population, except Ireland and Jordan. Among the countries whose scores exceeded that of the United States were Spain and Slovenia. In mathematics, U.S. thirteen-year-old students performed below all other assessed countries except Jordan.

An English translation of the mathematics section of the 1990 University Entrance Center Examination, a test given in Japan that parallels the math Scholastic Aptitude Test, recently was published by the Mathematical Association of America (MAA). Mathematicians in the United States have been staggered by the test's sophistication. Richard Askey, a University of Wisconsin mathematician, stated: "College bound U.S. students given the exams would bomb out completely."[8]

One of my former doctoral students, Dr. Margarita Calderon, now is faculty member at the University of Texas at El Paso. For a number of years she directed the remedial center there. Students who are having trouble in a variety of subjects, including mathematics, come to the center for tutoring. The center hires undergraduate and graduate students as tutors. In reviewing the hiring decisions made by the center over a number of years, Dr. Calderon observed that they rarely hired Americans to tutor in math. Rather, they tended to hire tutors who were from Malaysia, India, and Mexico. Most of the Mexican students at the University of Texas at El Paso come from Juarez, which is El Paso's twin border town across the Rio Grande. While it is possible that those Mexican tutors are from the more affluent sector of Juarez, it appears that a young person who goes through the Juarez school system emerges with a much better knowledge of mathematics than the same young person would if he or she attended school a mile away in the United States! In fact, some of the teachers from Juarez have been providing guidance to the American teachers about mathematics instruction.

Carl Sagan has commented:

Every now and then, I'm lucky enough to teach a class in kindergarten or the first grade. Many of these children are curious, intellectually vigorous, ask provocative and insightful questions and exhibit great enthusiasm for science. When I talk to high school students, I find something different. They memorize "fact." But, by and large, the joy of discovery, the life behind those facts, has gone out of them. They're worried about asking "dumb" questions; they're willing to accept inadequate answers; they don't pose follow-up questions; the room is awash with sidelong glances to judge, second-by-second, the approval of their peers. Something has happened between first and 12th grade, and it's not just puberty.[9]

In summary, the American educational system is delivering a mediocre product to those who study mathematics and science. Furhtermore, young women, the poor, and people of color encounter additional barriers that prevent great numbers of talented students from mastering these vital subjects.

CLASS AND SCIENCE EDUCATION

In nineteenth-century America, quite frequently the railroad tracks literally divided towns into two classes: wealthy and poor. People were ashamed of being from the ''wrong side of the tracks.'' In the twentieth-century, sociologists differentiated more classes. Lloyd Warner, a pioneering researcher, identified six in Newburyport, a sleepy Massachusetts coastal community. Each class had definite characteristics: upper-upper class, the ''old families,'' inherited wealth; lower-upper class, the ''nouveau rich''; upper-middle class, professionals and substantial businessmen; lower-middle class, small businessmen, white-collar workers; upper-lower class, semiskilled workers; lower-lower class, unskilled workers, welfare recipients.

During the past quarter-century, our understanding of social stratification has become more sophisticated and our urbanized, transient society has become more complex. Modern sociologists reject the notion of two, six, or twelve ''classes.'' Rather, they recognize that social status is the result of several other factors: occupation, education, and income. These factors usually coincide, or are correlated; typically, those with the most education have the best jobs and earn more income than those with little education. But there are many exceptions. Sociologist Gerhard Lenski coined the term ''status inconsistency'' to identify those who might be high on one scale but low on another—for example, the wealthy but uneducated gambler and the overeducated but underpaid college professor.

The largest barrier to educational achievement is poverty. It is no exaggeration to argue that if poverty in this country had been eliminated during the past decade while no attempts were made to improve the schools, American education would have improved more than it has from all the educational task forces and reform movements. The level of poverty in a rich, developed country like ours is shocking and the percentage of children in poverty is even higher than that for adults.

Consider a ten-year-old Latino girl from East Los Angeles (or a ten-year-old African American boy from South Central Los Angeles) who aspires to become a scientist. She will face a series of barriers because she is female and because she is Latino. Now add to this equation growing up in an environment where there is inadequate health care for her entire family, including the wage earners; parents working one or two jobs each to earn enough to get by; living in a neighborhood where violence is rampant and random killings are a part of life; and higher levels of alcohol and drug abuse in the neighborhood, and perhaps in the family. These children grow up under an incredible stress level. Under such circumstances, survival becomes the goal for most children and thinking about any career, let alone a technical career, is a luxury.

In a classic article entitled ''Keeping the Poor Poor,'' Paul Jacobs presented compelling evidence about how and why it is more expensive to live in a poor neighborhood than an affluent area.[10] The rent is higher per square foot in poverty-stricken East Los Angeles than in affluent West Lost Angeles. Across this country, banks have withdrawn from violence-ridden inner cities. Consequently, residents of these areas have to pay inordinately high fees to cash checks at special establishments. It is virtually impossible for the people who need financial resources the most to get a loan. Those people and institutions who will loan them money charge unbelievably high interest rates. Since major supermarkets also have withdrawn from these areas, most residents must obtain food and other necessities from convenience stores and other small markets where the prices are higher than elsewhere. Once trapped in poverty, it is much more difficult to climb out than it is for the rest of us to stay out.

Citing studies that repeatedly demonstrate that the amount and quality of schooling experiences can change students' IQ test scores, David Berliner states:

It has become clear that the more schooling you acquire, the smarter you will appear on the test. The corollary is one that our democracy is having difficulty facing, namely, that higher social class standing will make a child intelligent, at least as measured by tests of intelligence. Higher soical class standing allows parents to buy high quality day care, preschool, and K-12 schooling; permits the purchase of instructional toys, encyclopedias and computers; and ensures first-rate health care.[11]

Since discussions of poverty usually conjure up images of inner-city persons of color, it should be noted that the devastating effects of poverty know no ethnic boundaries. According to the 1990 Census, those living in poverty in California included about 1.8 million Anglos, 1.6 million Latinos, and 400,000 blacks. Of course the percentages for Latinos and blacks (approximately 21 percent) are considerably higher than those for Anglos (approximately 9 percent) and the forces of poverty and racism combine in pernicious ways.

PEOPLE OF COLOR

The strength of the American economy increasingly will depend on people of color. Yet minority students still do not have the same educational opportunities as white students. This is particularly true in mathematics and science.

By the year 2000, approximately 85 percent of the new entrants to the U.S. labor force are expected to be minorities, women, handicapped, and immigrants, groups which for the most part have been historically underrepresented in science, mathematics, and engineering. Presently, blacks and Hispanics are 25 percent of the precollege level, and, by the year 2000, they will comprise 47 percent.[12]

Consider these findings about the loss of minorities from the scientific pipeline:

> Most blacks and Hispanics are lost to science much earlier in the schooling process, and other minority losses occur throughout the years of schooling. The underparticipation of minorities thus can be largely attributed to their lower levels of achievement in mathematics during the precollege years. However, even those blacks and Hispanics who remain in the precollege pipeline are less likely than whites to choose quantitative fields of study.[13]

According to Betty Vetter, executive director of the Commission on Professionals in Science and Technology, "we're losing a whole generation of children, and probably their children too."[14]

These differences in schooling are not the result of differences in ability. In rigorous research about possible connections between ethnicity and cognitive ability, H. P. Ginsburg and R. L. Russell studied preschool and kindergarten children. They focused on cognitive abilities that are thought to be associated with later mathematics abilities and achievements—for example, counting, conservation, and enumeration.[15] At no point did whites significantly outperform blacks. There were some differences related to socioeconomic status, but most of those differences had disappeared by the time the children reached kindergarten.

A Rand Corporation study assessed the delivery of educational programs to poor people and persons of color.[16] A special examination was made of the efficacy of tracking and how tracking related to issues of racial equality. These researchers found that small differences exist between the science and mathematics experiences of most white students and those of poor, or minority, or "low-ability" track students in elementary school. They also found that these differences became much larger as the students entered secondary school. Being placed in a lower track greatly reduces students' opportunities to learn science and math; furthermore, persons of color are much more likely to be assigned to lower tracks.

In this context, consider an extraordinary report by Nancy Gray.[17] She studied the impact of an academically rigorous urban high school magnet program on disadvantaged students of color. Despite weak preparation in elementary school, these students achieved at a high level. Furthermore, their SAT scores improved dramatically. Gray concluded:

> Results generally support the premise that what students study in high school, how well they master the concepts presented, and the advanced academic skill levels they achieve during those last years of pre-college schooling are indeed major factors in later SAT performance. Although there were some differences among

sub-groupings within the sample, these were relatively minor. Findings do suggest, however, that although rigorous academic preparation in high school is associated with significant gains in SAT scores, many aspects of students' basic achievement patterns are set earlier, at least by the end of middle school. For maximum impact, therefore, curricular and pedagogical initiatives to improve SAT performance must address the nature and quality of the educational program relatively early in students' school experience.

EQUITY 2000, an intervention project of The College Board, is attempting to bring the success rates of minority students to the same level as that for nonminority students. According to Donald Stewart, president of The College Board, "if we are to make the fundamental changes in our educational system that will allow all students to enter and succeed in college, attitudes and beliefs about the ability of students to learn must change." Stewart reported that at the end of EQUITY 2000's first year, which focused in great part upon educating teachers, the percentage of students that math teachers and guidance counselors believed were capable of passing algebra and geometry increased dramatically. In the project's pilot site of Fort Worth, Texas, there was a concomitant 36 percent increase in the number of students who enrolled in algebra classes in one year.[18]

Historically, dominant cultures have justified their subjugation of minority groups by asserting that the minorities were mentally inferior. For many decades, British intellectuals deprecated the intellectual capabilities of people from India. Against this background, the contributions of East Indians to mathematics and statistics are particularly impressive. For sheer drama, few stories in the history of science and mathematics can match the short, troubled life and extraordinary accomplishments of Srinivasa Ramanujan. Top graduate students in mathematics today will carefully study Ramanujan's theorems. Although he died young and had a short professional life, Ramanujan is recognized as one of the towering figures in the history of mathematics. "How many Ramanujans, his life begs us to ask, dwell in India today, unknown and unrecognized? And how many in America and Britain, locked away in racial or economic ghettos, scarcely aware of worlds outside their own?"[19]

WOMEN IN SCIENCE EDUCATION

Jadwiga S. Sebrechts began an article in the *Journal of NIH Research* with a question:

> What do the inventors of the following have in common?: The cotton gin, the microelectrode, nerve growth factor, nuclear fission, COBOL computer language, apgar score, smallpox inoculation, tetracycline.
> A clue: It's the same thing that is common to the scientists who identified and catalogued more than 300,000 stars, who cofounded the Marine Biological Laboratory at Woods Hole, Mass., who founded ecology, who made the calculations

necessary to split the atom, and who invented the branch of mathematics known today as functional analysis.[20]

The answer is that all these scientists were women.

Contributing to the problem are the attitudes and expectations held by some teachers about the capabilities of girls and people of color. I teach about multivariate statistical analysis in our Ph.D. program at The Claremont Graduate School. I have encountered many students, especially women and students of color, who feared math and were sure they could not do it. (As you may know, most graduate students dread statistics and put it off as long as possible.) Virtually all of these students then discover they are capable of understanding and conducting sophisticated statistical analysis like hierarchical multiple regression. In conversation, I often find that their negative self-image goes back to an elementary school teacher with a sexist or racist attitude, a person who thought that ''Girls can't do math'' and managed to traumatize a student who now must be convinced about her real ability. Sheila Tobias has studied ''math anxiety'' and has shown how and why this affliction is particularly prevalent among women.[21]

It is disturbing that many teachers erroneously believe that certain kinds of students can't do math. This becomes tragic when the students themselves incorporate those devastating myths into their self-concepts and then lower their aspirations, thereby shortchanging what they can accomplish with their lives.

Recently I conducted analyses with national survey data about college students gathered by UCLA's Higher Education Research Institute. I examined mathematical self-concepts, specifically the percentage of students who rated their own mathematical ability as being in the top 10 percent of college students. The results are both fascinating and disturbing. Among Anglos, 24 percent of the men thought they were in the top 10 percent while 10 percent of the females placed themselves there. Among African-Americans, 14 percent of men and 8 percent of women thought they were in the top 10 percent; among Chicanos, 28 percent of men and 8 percent of women. Finally, among Asians 40 percent of the men and 24 percent of the women thought they were in the top 10 percent of college students on mathematical ability.

In a further analysis I examined only those students who actually were in the top 10 percent of this sample in mathematical ability, as measured by their score on the SAT Quantitative test. The cutoff for this sample was a score of 670, which actually is higher than the threshold that marked the top 10 percent of those who took the test during that year (high school seniors in 1984), which was 580. Thus, this is a conservative definition and these students actually may have been in the top 5 percent. Furthermore, each of them would have received a report from the Educational Testing Service indicating their score *and their percentile*. Despite this, only 49 percent of the women freshmen who were in the top 10 percent believed they belonged there. Furthermore, four years later about half of those 49 percent no longer considered themselves to be in the top

10 percent in math ability. Only 23 percent of the women who actually were in the top 10 percent believed that they were in both their freshman and senior years.

In light of these findings, consider this observation by Jeanne Oakes:

> Finally, a greater proportion of female science majors in the sample switched to other fields, even though they had higher overall grades during their first two college years than did the men. . . . When other factors are taken into consideration, then, attitudes may play a critical role in high-achieving women's defection from (or rejection of) science.[22]

A study by the American Association of University Women (*Short-changing Girls, Short-changing America*) observed that the perception of others that girls are less able in math and science correlates, unfortunately, with a general loss of self-esteem among adolescent girls. "Even objective positive evaluations of competence in math and science, such as respectable grades, tend to be dismissed by girls as irrelevant."[23]

In contrast, Etta Falconer, director of science programs at Spelman College, has commented that the school's expectations are that they will succeed and they do. This is what should be happening to both men and women, majority students and students of color, across the United States.

Once again, these differences in schooling are not the result of differences in ability. S. G. Brush has summarized findings from recent research that challenge and contradict the notion of sex differences in cognitive ability.

> Reports of cognitive differences between the sexes received widespread publicity, perhaps in part because of hostility toward the women's movement. The studies that called cognitive sex differences into question, on the other hand, have received comparatively little attention. Thus misconceptions linger. Scientists and journalists have an obligation to correct them.[24]

Lynn Friedman conducted a meta-analysis of recent studies on sex differences in mathematics. Systematic and rigorous analysis and comparison of many studies all suggest that the gender difference in mathematical performance, if it exists, is very small. Furthermore, reported gender differences have been decreasing over time.[25]

> With respect to self-concept [Eccles observes], sex differences began to emerge in junior high school, at which point the females had lower estimates of their math ability than did the males. The size of this sex difference grew as the students moved into high school.[26]

In summary, women, like minority students and poor people, are much less likely to study mathematics and science. To a great degree, they are the victims of unsubstantiated negative expectations and prejudices built into our educational system. How can we change this?

WHAT ARE THE KEYS TO SUCCESS?

Studies of student achievement repeatedly have suggested the need for curriculum reform and revitalization. During the past decade, ambitious, systematic curriculum reform efforts have been launched by the American Association for the Advancement of Science, the National Science Teacher's Association, and such disciplinary groups as the National Council of Teachers of Mathematics. These new curricula could make a major difference in American science education, if they were widely implemented. A persistent theme has been instruction that reveals the relevance of science to everyday life. However, it would be a mistake for whose who recognize the need to improve science education to rely solely on new curricula.

Educators have learned that there is a huge gap between the development of new instructional concepts or technologies and their successful implementation in the classroom. Also, in a recent article, Sheila Tobias has observed:

> Materials development remains the darling of the science education community. Why the nearly exclusive focus on instructional materials? Is it because these are products that give educational reformers and their paymasters something to show? Or is it that science education reformers, with some notable exceptions, don't know what else to do?[27]

Tobias goes on to cite Gerald Holton, who has argued that we need a commitment to on-going change as opposed to a series of one-shot cure-alls. *Furthermore, research repeatedly shows the importance of skilled, committed teachers, and of expecting students to excel.*

Let's examine some success stories. The potential for achievement among students of color, even impoverished students of color, when a community and a school work together is illustrated by Ysleta High School in El Paso, Texas. In 1992 five seniors from this school, which serves a poor, almost exclusively Latino community, were admitted to the Massachusetts Institute of Technology. According to Joe Jasso, assistant director of admissions at MIT,

> it is extraordinary for five students from a general attendance high school to be admitted to the same entering class at MIT (although this has happened occasionally with private or specialized public schools). This is all the more impressive because Ysleta High is housed in an old building and has a very limited supply of scientific equipment and computers. According to the principal "We are part of a community that has drugs, violence and gangs. . . . We have our share of students who scorn intellectual achievement. Our dropout rate is as high as any in this area." One of the five students could not speak English two years ago and another works part-time as a janitor. While it's hard to identify the causal factors

with certainty, much of the credit must go to Paul Cain who teaches computer mathematics; each of the five students worked with Cain who "calls himself a catalyst for bright students, [and] credits strong parental support for the students' academic success. . . . Their parents give them direction and care about them. . . . I provide them with an opportunity to display their wares."[28]

Duane Nichols, of California's Alhambra High School, is a math teacher. In addition to chairing the Science Department and teaching regular classes, he teaches a special class about biomedical research three times a week at 7:00 A.M. Thanks largely to his efforts, Alhambra High ranks first among schools west of the Mississippi in the production of finalists in the Westinghouse science talent search. Consider also Richard Plass of Stuyvesant High School in New York City who has taught and developed 181 semifinalists in the Westinghouse competition. Articles about both Nichols and Plass reveal some similar traits. Both make themselves available to their students and work at knowing their students. Both have multiple responsibilities and demands on their time and are constantly busy.

We need to provide more respect and resources for teachers. In hearings before the subcommittee on postsecondary education of the U.S. House of Representatives, I was asked to testify about math and science education. Throughout the day, a number of other scientists, policy analysts, and experts testified. However, the most impressive and memorable statement that day was made by Kent Kavanaugh, a high school teacher from a Kansas City suburb. That spring he had received a national award as an outstanding science teacher from the president of the United States. This is part of what he said to the committee:

> The month before I left for Washington, D.C. to receive the Presidential Award, I averaged 40 hours a week at my job—not my teaching job, my second job as an analytical chemist for the Mobay Corporation of Kansas City. I must work at two or more jobs to make ends meet and to try to pay for college tuition for my son who graduates this spring. Because of this, I often come to school physically and mentally worn out. I am not the exception, I am the rule.[29]

PYGMALION IN THE CLASSROOM

A fascinating study by Professor Robert Rosenthal of Harvard University suggested that the expectations teachers have about a student's potential also exert a strong impact on his or her learning.[30] Rosenthal and his colleagues selected some elementary school students totally at random. The researchers then informed the teachers that these students had tremendous intellectual potential of a kind that had not been revealed on standard intelligence tests. In other words, these particular students were alleged to be potential geniuses in disguise. Once the teachers held these expectations about these otherwise typical children, the students' grades improved dramatically. It turned out that the teachers were spending more time with them, were predisposed in subconscious ways to perceive the students as doing well, and student performance responded to this extra treatment.

This study by Rosenthal has been the subject of some methodological controversy. But the idea is intriguing and powerful. Think of the implications. In fact, the most dramatic recent research about mathematics education emphasized these notions about expectations of excellence.

SUPPORT GROUPS AND CALCULUS INSTRUCTION

Uri Treisman developed calculus workshop study groups in which minority students not only have achieved, but excelled spectacularly. It is very important to understand why the Treisman model has worked and what this means for the development of a talented technocracy in America. As we shall see, there are two crucial components to this success story: students study in groups in addition to their individual study, and students are expected to excel and to do extra, more difficult, homework problems. This is *not* a remedial approach.

Perhaps this model is most noteworthy because of the theories it rejects. The students who succeeded in Treisman's workshops, and in subsequent workshops across the country, were underrepresented minority students, often from poor or disadvantaged backgrounds. Yet their success in the workshop environment sometimes surpassed those Anglos and Asians studying the same subject at the same institution. Thus, these data provide yet another basis for rejecting the notion that some students, because of gender or ethnic background, are less capable of mastering calculus—and, by implication, other mathematical and scientific disciplines.

Treisman's original research has been presented in its most detailed form in his 1985 dissertation, "A Study of the Mathematics Performance of Black Students at the University of California, Berkeley."[31] Treisman observes:

> In the Fall of 1975, while developing a training program for Mathematics Department teaching assistants, I became aware of the high rate at which black students were failing freshman calculus at Berkeley. I had made it my practice to speak with the T.A.s about the weak and strong students in their teaching sections, and the regularity with which black students appeared within the former group and Chinese students within the latter struck me as an issue that should be addressed in the training sessions. With this in mind, I began to seek the reasons for this apparent difference in performance.[32]

Treisman then interviewed 20 black and 20 Chinese students, asking them about their use of instructors' office hours, who they studied with, how much they studied, and so on. Furthermore, he asked the students to prepare a report, from memory, of how they had spent their time during the three days preceding the interviews. So far, these are standard research techniques. But Treisman added another wrinkle that produced startling results. He asked for, and received, permission to accompany the students while they studied. "Many agreed, and over a period of eighteen months I accompanied these students to the library, their dormitory rooms, and their homes in the hope that I might see first-hand how they went about learning and doing mathematics."[33]

What did Treisman find when he compared the study habits of Chinese and black students? First, a black student almost invariably studied alone. In contrast, most of the Chinese students studied with other Chinese students. This allowed them to have support and intellectual exchanges; they tried to work out homework problems and the like; they shared grapevine information about the course and the university. For example, they discovered that the professors' rule of two hours of study for one hour of class was a serious underestimate. The Chinese students averaged fourteen hours per week of study for a four-unit class, while the black students had been devoting the eight hours per week that the professors recommended. The Chinese students critiqued each others' work, correcting errors and suggesting innovative solutions.

Compounding the performance discrepancy was the tendency for black students to avoid remedial tutoring programs; these were students who had excelled in high school, who often were valedictorians, and who identified such programs with low-achieving students. They rarely approached their teaching assistants. "But, even when they did, their inability to define their needs clearly coupled with the low expectations that many T.A.s held for the academic achievement of black students usually precluded a fruitful exchange."[34]

Treisman then designed a calculus workshop experience for the black students that paralleled the structure and processes of the Chinese student groups. What was the impact? "The principal finding is that the average grade earned by black workshop participants has been approximately one full grade higher than that earned by black students not participating in the program."[35]

Additional analysis revealed that the workshop students consistently outperformed nonworkshop black students in the courses following Math 1A—for example, in the second- and third-term calculus courses. Workshop students were considerably less likely than nonworkshop black students to drop out of school in the two years following this calculus course—that is, at the end of 2.5 years of college. Black workshop students were considerably more likely to graduate from college than were black nonworkshop students. Finally, black workshop students were more likely to persist to graduation in a math-based major than were nonworkshop students. In each of these analyses, the graduation rates for black workshop students were roughly comparable to those of nonminority students at Berkeley, while the rates for black nonworkshop participants were substantially lower. When SAT level was controlled—that is, when comparing students who entered with the same SAT level—the black workshop students outperformed all other groups, including the white and Asian students.

Despite these impressive achievements, a reader of this report recently might ask: Would these workshops be effective at other institutions? After all, UC

Berkeley is one of the top universities in the country and students who are accepted there, including minority students, have already demonstrated that they are outstanding. Would these same effects be observed with students from other underrepresented minority groups, such as Latinos?

THE CALCULUS WORKSHOP PROGRAMS AT CALIFORNIA POLYTECHNIC UNIVERSITY-POMONA

Martin Bonsangue has conducted an evaluation of a calculus workshop program, modeled after the Berkeley workshop, at Cal Poly-Pomona.[36] This study focused on a sample of 133 workshop and 187 nonworkshop Hispanic American, African American, and Native American students who were followed for a five-year period. Both the treatment (87 percent) and comparison groups (85 percent) consisted largely of Latino students. Both groups also contained mostly men (74 percent of the workshop group and 80 percent of the nonworkshop group). The workshop program was patterned after the Berkeley experience. Students met in groups to work on calculus problems twice a week for two-hour sessions. Statistical comparisons revealed no significant differences between the workshop and nonworkshop students on background and other *preintervention* variables such as SAT scores, high school grade point average, and a precalculus diagnostic test.

The results: workshop students were significantly less likely to drop out of the institution "with 42 percent (55/131) of the nonworkshop minority students in the 1986–89 sample leaving the institution by spring 1991, compared to fewer than 4 percent (3/78) of the workshop students."[37] "Of those students still enrolled in Mathematics, Science, and Engineering [MSE], more than 90 percent of the workshop students had completed their mathematics requirements for their individual majors, compared to less than 60 percent of the nonworkshop students."[38]

Furthermore, workshop students who persisted in their MSE field achieved higher grade point averages overall than did the nonworkshop students. However, they held only a slight advantage in terms of grades within the major and there were no differences between the two groups with respect to number of units completed overall or within their majors.

The traditional precollege cognitive measures held minimal power in predicting persistence in an MSE major and mathematics completion. Workshop participation was "the only statistically significant predictor of mathematics completion, accounting for 23 percent of the variation in mathematics completion among men, and nearly twice that amount, 44 percent, among women."[39]

An additional aspect of this analysis was to examine the calculus achievement of minority workshop and non-workshop minority and majority students, with workshop students achieving a grade mean nearly one full grade point higher than that achieved for non-workshop minority students. In fact, workshop students earned a calculus grade mean of at least .75 grade points higher than any non-workshop ethnic group, including Asian and white students, even though some precollege cognitive factors for the workshop group were significantly lower than those for white and Asian groups.[40]

The work of Treisman and Bonsangue demonstrates that minority students who traditionally have been underrepresented in science, mathematics, and engineering can excel in these disciplines. The key philosophical components of these workshop programs are an emphasis on academic excellence rather than remediation and the formation of study groups with other students.

STUDENT ACHIEVEMENT AT HARVARD

Now I would like to report a surprising and fascinating research finding from the other end of the academic spectrum: a study of how superachieving students learn best at Harvard College. Richard J. Light conducted extensive explorations with students and other faculty in the Harvard Assessment Seminars. They concluded that "all the specific findings point to, and illustrate, one main idea. It is that students who get the most out of college, who grow the most academically, and who are happiest, organize their time to include interpersonal activities with faculty members, or fellow students, built around substantive academic work."[41]

One of the other principal findings from the Harvard Assessment Seminars related directly to science. Noting that of those who enter college interested in science (more than half the freshmen), one subgroup loves its science experience and plans to study and work more in science. The other subgroup finds its science courses to be dull and loses interest in a technical career. What accounts for the difference? Light concludes that it results directly from how their professors organize their science courses.

> When asked to describe how they approach their work, students from these two groups sound as if they are describing different worlds. Those who stay in science tell of small, student-organized study groups. They meet outside of formal classes. They describe enjoying intense and often personal interaction with a good lab instructor. In contrast, those who switch away from the sciences rarely join a study group. They rarely work together with others. They describe class sections and lab instructors as dry, and above all, impersonal.

Another of the Harvard findings relates to the success of women:

> A note to advisors: while the advantages of study groups are widespread, there is one group of students for whom they seem especially important: young women concentrating in the physical sciences. In her undergraduate honors thesis, Andrea Shlipak (1988) finds that women who concentrate in physics and engineering consider these small working groups a crucial part of their learning activities. Further,

her interviews with women who enter college intending to specialize in the physical sciences reveal a sharp break between those women who join study groups and those who don't. Women who join a small study group are far more likely to persist as science concentrators than those who always or nearly always study alone.[42]

These findings from the late 1980s and early 1990s about Harvard College students parallel the results of an earlier study, completed in the late 1960s.[43] In the earlier research, it was hypothesized that student interaction with reference groups (i.e., faculty, other students, and family) would have an important impact on several key outcomes in the undergraduate experience, including academic achievement. Extensive longitudinal data on a sample of undergraduates in the Harvard classes of 1963–64 were analyzed using multivariate statistical methods (i.e., stepwise multiple regression and canonical correlation analyses). The data had been collected as part of an on-going research project, the Harvard Student Study, and included a variety of psychological and sociological measures. In fact, each student in the sample gave several days to the project every semester he or she was in college. The results revealed the powerful effect of reference groups, especially faculty members. Those students who interacted with their faculty members got substantially more out of the undergraduate experience, in terms of such measures as academic achievement and satisfaction, than did their contemporaries who worked as hard but failed to initiate such contacts.

In summary, educational research has given us the tools to repair our system of mathematics and science instruction. We should implement changes now, before we turn away more talented students.

NOTES

1. Preparation of this chapter was supported, in part, by a grant from the Kluge Foundation. A more extensive treatment of these ideas appears in the forthcoming book by David Eli Draw, *America's Wasted Talent: Why We Must Improve Mathematics and Science Education.*

2. *Building a Quality Workforce* (n.p. 1988), p. 23.

3. J. S. Rigden, "High Schools Don't Prepare Youths for New Workplace," *San Francisco Chronicle*, December 29, 1992.

4. R. B. Reich, *The Work of Nations: Preparing Ourselves for 21st-Century Capitalism* (New York: Knopf, 1991).

5. Ibid., p 228.

6. International Association for the Evaluation of Educational Achievement, *Science Education in Seventeen Countries: A Preliminary Report* (New York: Pergamon, 1988).

7. Ibid., p. 2.

8. B. Cipra, "An Awesome Look at Japan's Math SAT," *Science*, 259 (January 1993): 22.

9. C. Sagan, "Why We Need to Understand Science," *Parade Magazine*, September 10, 1989, p. 10.

10. Paul Jacobs, "Keeping the Poor Poor," in Jerome H. Skolnick and Elliott Cume (Eds.), *Crisis in American Institutions*, 6th ed. (Boston: Little, Brown, 1985), pp. 113–123.

11. D. C. Berliner, "Educational Reform in an Era of Disinformation," paper presented at the meetings of the American Association of Colleges for Teacher Education, San Antonio, Texas, February 1992.

12. C. M. Matthews, *Underrepresented Minorities and Women in Science, Mathematics, and Engineering: Problems and Issues for the 1990s*, a Congressional Research Service Report for Congress, September 5, 1990. The Library of Congress.

13. J. Oakes, *Lost Talent: The Underparticipation of Women, Minorities, and Disabled Persons in Science*, supported by the National Science Foundation (Santa Monica, CA: The Rand Corporation, 1990).

14. Cited in R. Pool, "A Lost Generation," *Science*, 248 (April 1990): 435.

15. H. P. Ginsburg and R. L. Russell, "Social Class and Racial Influence on Early Thinking," monographs of the Society for Research in Child Development (Chicago: Society for Research in Child Development, 1981).

16. Oakes, *Lost Talent*.

17. N. Gray, "Academic Preparation and SAT Scores," Dissertation, The Claremont Graduate School, Claremont, CA.

18. "College Board Issues First Report Card on College Preparation Project for Minorities," The College Board press release dated June 5, 1992.

19. R. Kanigel, *The Man Who Knew Infinity: A Life of the Genius Ramanujan* (New York: Charles Scribners Sons, 1991), p. 4.

20. J. S. Sebrechts, "The Cultivation of Scientists at Women's Colleges," *Journal of NIH Research*, 4(6) (June 1992): 42.

21. S. Tobias, *Overcoming Math Anxiety* (New York: W. W. Norton, 1993).

22. Oakes, *Lost Talent*, p. 39.

23. Sebrechts, "The Cultivation of Scientists at Women's Colleges," p. 24.

24. S. G. Brush, "Women in Science and Engineering," *American Scientist*, 79 (September/October 1991): 413–414.

25. L. Friedman, "Mathematics and the Gender Gap: A Meta-analysis of Recent Studies on Sex Differences in Mathematical Tasks," *Review of Educational Research*, 59(2) (Summer 1989): 185–213.

26. J. S. Eccles, "Bringing Young Women to Math and Science," in M. Crawford and M. Gentry (Eds.), *Gender and Thought: Psychological Perspectives* (New York: Springer-Verlag, 1989).

27. S. Tobias, "Science Education Reform: What's Wrong with the Process?" *Change*, 24 (n. 3) (May-June 1992): 13–19.

28. J. Jasso, quoted in *Los Angeles Times*, April 1, 1992, p. 21.

29. K. Kavanaugh, "Testimony to House Subcommittee on Postsecondary Education," May 1, 1989.

30. R. Rosenthal and L. Jacobson, *Pygmalion in the Classroom* (New York: Holt and Rinehart Publishers, 1968).

31. P. U. Treisman, A Study of the Mathematics Performance of Black Students at the University of California, Berkeley, unpublished doctoral dissertation, University of California, 1985.

32. Ibid., p. 4.

33. Ibid.

34. Ibid.

35. Ibid.

36. M. V. Bonsangue and D. E. Drew, "Long-term Effectiveness of the Calculus Workshop Model," a report prepared for presentation to the National Science Foundation NSF Grant No. MDR-9150212, April 1992.

37. Ibid., p. 9.

38. Ibid., p. 10.

39. Ibid., p. 15.

40. Ibid., pp. 16–17.

41. R. J. Light, *The Harvard Assessment Seminars. Harvard University Graduate School of Education and Kennedy School of Government* (Cambridge, MA: Second Report, 1991), p. 6.

42. Ibid.

43. D. E. Drew, "The Impact of Reference Groups on the Several Dimensions of Competence in the Undergraduate Experience," Ph.D. dissertation, Harvard University, 1969.

Chapter 5

Diversity and the Institutional Transformation of Public Education

Joseph G. Weeres and John Rivera

When John Kennedy was elected president of the United States in 1960, hopes ran high that the nation was embarked on a program that would bring millions of impoverished minority and immigrant Americans into the mainstream of American life.[1] Their poverty, in the midst of plenty, was not only an embarrassment in the Cold War against Communism, but also represented a failure of America's political, judicial, and educational institutions. People lived in poverty, not because they did not have money, but because a segregated social system did not allow them to participate fully in the political process. African Americans, as the most glaring example, did not possess the same rights as most Americans in the judicial system, and were not accorded equal opportunity in the segregated public schools. The 1960s was a decade in which scholars rediscovered the social, political, and economic inequalities that had plagued the nation for more than a century.

In the beginning, the goal of bringing what the Kerner Commission called the "two, separate nations" together seemed well within reach.[2] America had had a long history of successfully integrating immigrants into society, and the task looked feasible, particularly in light the nation's previous successes with European immigrants. The country, moreover, was entering the 1960s from two decades of enormous economic growth, decades in which much of that new wealth went to those at the bottom of the income ladder. For example, from approximately 1940 until 1960, inflation and tax-adjusted incomes of those at the bottom one-fifth of the income ladder rose by over 40 percent, whereas after-tax, inflation-adjusted income for the top one-fifth of wage earners scarcely increased at all.[3] The entire economic tide appeared to be rising, and the dream of an expanding middle class seemed to be being realized—for those who were participating in the system. The task, then, was seen as one of extending these same equal opportunities to the "other Americans."

By the end of the decade, however, most of this optimism had vanished. Although the country had removed many of the formal, legal barriers impeding equal opportunity, and the War on Poverty and entitlement programs had slightly narrowed income inequality temporarily (by the late 1970s most of these gains would be erased), the larger vision of one nation—*E Pluribus Unum*—seemed to be fading. The country appeared either to have forsaken its own expressed destiny, or to have lost its will to realize that destiny.

There are a great many possible explanations for what went wrong in the 1960s. Certainly, assassinations of our most charismatic political leaders, an unpopular and financially expensive war, the social emergence of the "me" generation, and racism all played roles. Another factor was at work that resulted not only in broken promises to the "other Americans," but to an entire generation of white Americans, and their children, who thought they had secured a claim on a position in America's middle class. For while America was seeking to solve the problem of social and economic inequalities, its core industries in textiles, steel, automobiles, and manufacturing were contracting, victims of the emerging transformation from an industrial to a postindustrial economy.

International economic competition and the advent of the knowledge society and information age were putting American workers into wage competition with hundreds of millions of workers from other industrial and developing nations where labor costs were a fraction of what they were in the United States. In the face of these cost pressures, wages of most Americans from the mid-1960s through the early 1990s did not even keep pace with inflation.[4] The results were rising economic inequality (by 1990, the top one-fifth of Americans on the income ladder were earning 52 percent of all wage income, not counting income from stocks, bonds, and savings), and the emergence of political cleavages (notably within the Democratic Party), which sapped the nation's political will to realize *E Pluribus Unum*. The agenda of social and economic inequality was shunted aside in favor of excellence, competitiveness, and developmental politics.

In this chapter we will explore the impact of this economic transformation on American public education. The central argument we advance is that while public education has always served a redistributive function, its primary basis of political and economic support rests on its developmental function: its graduates must be able to contribute to the growth of economic wealth for the nation, for it is this (growing) wealth that provides the (expanding) tax revenue for offering higher levels of public education (elementary, secondary, college) to larger percentages of American youth. To realize this developmental function, the institutional structure of public education must be brought into alignment with the dominant mode of economic production.

This institutional structure consists of four elements: an instructional core (the educational purpose of schools, the pedagogies that are used in public schools, and the organization of teaching itself); an organizational system for controlling and supporting this instructional core; a political system for making decisions; and a funding system for paying for public schools. The instructional core, we argue, is the joining point for institutional alignment between education and the economy; for it is this instructional core that actually produces the necessary human capital. Organizational, political, and funding systems are organized around, and in support of, this instructional core when institutional alignment occurs.

First we will show how these processes of institutional alignment took place during America's transformation from an agrarian to an industrial society at the beginning of this century. The new industrial economy led to a reconceptualization of what would be taught, how it would be taught, and how teaching would be organized. These changes in the instructional core, in turn, required new organizational structures, a redefined political process, and new means for funding public schools. The one-room schoolhouse of agrarian society gave way to large, bureaucratically organized school systems.

Then, we will show how the emergence of the postindustrial economy after World War II began eroding this industrial-based institutional alignment between public education and society. The discontinuities created by this misalignment, however, did not initially manifest themselves in the instructional core. Rather they were perceived as problems of governance, funding, and organization, because it is these systems that provide public schools with most of their immediate feedback about how well society is supporting them. In the 1960s the discontinuities manifested themselves as problems of political power and funding inequality. By the 1980s attention had shifted to problems of organizational design: how to make schools more effective and more efficient. The institutional discontinuity, however, resides deeper than politics, funding, and organizational design. The instructional core needs to be recast to meet the needs of the postindustrial society. That is the challenge public education still needs to confront. Only then can a determination be made as to an appropriate organizational system, a funding mechanism, and a political process for governing public schools.

The chapter concludes by assessing the role people of color might play in shaping this new educational institutional alignment.

FROM AGRARIAN TO INDUSTRIAL SOCIETY

Politically, the last half of the nineteenth century was a long rearguard action by farmers to save farming as a way of life. The Grange, the Alliance, Populism, the free silver movement—all were efforts by farmers to counteract the impact technology was having on their way of life. Technology made agriculture more efficient. A few farmers with machines could produce more crops than hundreds had once been able to grow using manual and animal labor. This efficiency doomed the small subsistence farmer. Farmers with machines grew rich, whereas those who worked with their hands eventually went bankrupt. Many ended up as tenants on the very farms they had once owned. Most joined the great urban migration into the big cities, where industrialization was creating better paying jobs.

The public education system that had been constructed around the rural economy was in visible disarray by the end of the nineteenth century.[5] Throughout the latter half of the nineteenth century, school reformers tried to resolve the "rural school problem."[6] Efforts were made to revamp teacher preparation, to develop new pedagogies, and to broaden the curriculum. These piecemeal approaches to reform, however, failed to stem the decline of the rural school system.

The problem was that its institutional design was structurally inadequate to cope with the impact technology was having on agrarian society. The 200,000 mostly one-room schoolhouse districts that made up the system were organized around small patches of subsistence farmers. Members of rural school boards were comprehensively involved in all aspects of operating their one-room schoolhouses, from hiring the teacher to painting the building. The fiscal viability of this system depended upon the capacity of local farmers to pay for the operation of their schoolhouses. But as technology created severe distribution of income inequalities among farmers, making a few farmers very rich and the majority very poor, most rural schools deteriorated because local, subsistence farmers could not afford to pay for them. Even though machines were making agriculture more efficient, and thereby producing greater wealth, the funding jurisdictions of most of the 200,000 school districts were too small to capture the tax revenue from this new wealth.

District consolidation was the logical answer, but farmers fiercely resisted it. They spoke of democracy and the sanctity of the one-room schoolhouse. But the issue involved more than just a question of power. Farmers wanted political control, because they saw it as a means for transmitting farming as a way of life to their children.[7] In the end, this was the problem. The rural school system was designed to prepare farm children for a way of life that was disappearing. The instructional core of the one-room schoolhouse was incompatible with the needs of the emerging industrial society. School district consolidation eventually was imposed on the rural school system, and today there are fewer than 15,000 school districts nationally, of which there are fewer than 1,500 one-room elementary schools.[8]

INDUSTRIAL-AGE PUBLIC EDUCATION INSTITUTIONAL STRUCTURES

By the early 1900s it was clear, after much political and economic conflict between rural America and big city industry, that a new political climate and industrialized economic base was being established. Schools confronted the challenge of preparing students to do the new work required by America's new economy.

The needs of the industrial labor market required schools to initiate a curriculum that was broader in scope than the 3 Rs of rural schools. Schools needed to prepare students for much more differentiated occupations, and this demanded a more differentiated curriculum than had been provided in the one-room schoolhouse. The curriculum was broadened to include more academic subjects, such as spelling, literature, physiology, natural science, history, geography, as well as vocational training in a wide range of skills including wordworking, machine maintenance, typing, shorthand, and so on. Accompanying this differentiation was curricular tracking with students being shunted into curricular tracks on the basis of their perceived individual capacities for learning and their vocational aspirations. By the 1920s, intelligence tests were beginning to be used to allocate students to these curricular tracks, with the tracks, in turn, containing the educational experiences presumably most appropriate to the kinds of jobs the students eventually would hold—vocational training for those entering the trades, and advanced academic disciplinary work for those destined to move into the professions and management.[9]

The new labor market of the industrial age also required workers to adapt to the regularities of the machine and the assembly line, and the routines of the large corporation. The new instructional core of industrial-age schools consequently placed great emphasis on socializing students in habits of punctuality, listening attentively, obedience, silence, accommodation to routine, regularity in delivering homework assignments, and other social traits they would need to succeed in the new economy.[10] The precise scheduling of students' time, classroom assignments, and seating patterns were among the mechanisms for instilling these habits.[11]

Industrialization gave rise to mass production, mass consumption, mass democracy, and mass media. The economy of the country became increasingly linked. Schools, therefore, sought to transcend the allegiances of particular groups and communities, and assumed the function of instilling national values of citizenship, national loyalty, and allegiance to the rule of law in students. The homogenizing tendencies of industrialization, coupled with liberal immigration policies and a massive population shift from rural to urban America, led to the development of assimilation theories, laws, and practices to reward immigrants with educational opportunity, jobs, and social mobility if they would leave the "old country," with its customs, culture, and language behind. Schools were expected to acculturate these diverse people into a national identity, through the use of a common language, an interpretation of a common history, and the collective enactment of common rituals such as the Pledge of Allegiance and the memorization and recitation of excerpts from the Declaration of Independence and the U.S. Constitution.

Implementation of this new instructional agenda required differentiated pedagogies and more specialized teaching than had been possible in the ungraded one-room schoolhouse of rural America. The efficiency of the transmittal of each subject depended upon a content-specific pedagogy, and the knowledge base demanded by that pedagogy required more formal, specialized teacher training. Normal schools, teacher certification, and the development of elaborate subject-matter-content-specific curricular guides were part of the process for meeting these imperatives. Age-graded classrooms facilitated greater specialization within the teaching force, because a teacher with limited training could become more knowledgeable about the curriculum content for an age-specific group of children than one who was expected to work with children of all ages.

This more differentiated and specialized instructional core necessitated a more formal administrative structure for coordinating and controlling this complexity. And the new nation-building, socialization, and curriculum-tracking functions of public schools required a substantial reduction of direct lay influence on the daily operation of the instructional core. These requirements were met through the establishment of large administrative bureaucracies, staffed by professional education administrators, and by the concentration of political control within the district to a small, single, at-large elected school board. Using the slogan, "let's keep politics out of the schools," a collection of municipal school reformers—composed of business leaders, university presidents, civic leaders, heads of various citywide civic groups, and the owners of most of the mass media—succeeded politically in establishing these structures in most urban cities during the first decades of this century.

Philosophically, municipal reform presumed the presence of a unitary interest for the city as a whole, not just one representing an aggregation of the city's constituent neighborhoods.[12] Government, reformers argued, should serve the city as a whole, not just those of particular neighborhoods or specific groups. Creating a small, at-large elected school board, typically composed of 7–9 members, virtually precluded representation from indigenous neighborhoods and special interest groups, because identification with any particular group worked electorally against candidates who needed to draw support from the city as a whole. Those supported by the media and those who gained the endorsements of citywide civic associations typically had the best chance of winning. It was a structural mechanism for transferring political power from neighborhood communities to economic and social elites.

In spite of this apparent political bias, municipal reform gained broad-based political support from the electorate, including the labor unions, because it offered the hope of economic growth—a future in which most people wanted to participate.[13] Good government would lead to good schools, and good schools would enhance economic growth. An elite presence on the school board reinforced the idea that education was a developmental good—that it was an investment in the future growth of the city and nation. The idea of schools as community-owned property was reinforced in the public's mind by the fact that most of the social and economic elite sent their children to public schools, albeit schools with curricular tracks leading toward the top-tier occupations. Reform embraced a notion of democracy in which elites served as stewards for the community and one in which the legitimacy of competing interests was denied.

A major function of the board and this elite was to secure funding to support the school district. Most of this revenue came from local property taxes. Elites argued that taxes for schools were not only a social good, but also a private one. Good schools would contribute to economic growth, and economic growth, in turn, would increase the property values of taxpayers. Reformers also tied state funding to student attendance. This offered a strong incentive for schools to compel students to attend, and make them participate in the new curriculum.

Municipal reformers also changed the administrative function of the school board. Whereas rural school boards had directly managed and administered the operations of their one-room schoolhouses, reformers sought to separate policy making from administration. This separation, they argued, was essential for making schools economically efficient, and that was important in order to insure that school tax revenue actually purchased more effective schools, rather than getting absorbed in administrative inefficiencies.[14] Professional administrative control over daily operations, they thought, was essential for making school operations more efficient. The task of the board was to set policy; the role of administrators was to implement it as efficiently as possible.

Reformers adopted the organizational principles of unity of administrative command and centralized administrative authority in the hands of a general school superintendent who reported directly to the school board, thereby creating a tight chain of command from school board to superintendent, from superintendent to administrative staff, from staff to school principals, from principals to teachers, and from teachers to students. The structure essentially mirrored the corporate model in industry. Superintendents also borrowed scientific management from industry for guiding their management of the schools—a theory based on breaking complex tasks into their constituent parts, assessing the contributions of each part, and then controlling the interconnections among the parts to achieve maximum, economically efficient production.

In aggregate, these reforms aligned public education to industrialization. The new instruction core was designed to contribute human capital to the industrial economy; the governance, funding, and organizational systems were redesigned by the elites of the new industrial society to support this new instructional core. Schools came to resemble the corporate, industrial model.

Public education greatly benefited from this new institutional realignment. Funding for public education increased substantially, and the provision of public education was extended to include, by the early 1960s, the expectation of universal high school education, with a substantial percentage of high school graduates being able to matriculate to publicly financed colleges and universities. By successfully aligning its educational institutional structures with the needs of industrial society, America had created probably the best mass educational system in the world.

THE EMERGENCE OF THE POSTINDUSTRIAL ECONOMY

The term ''postindustrial'' expresses many different dimensions of the emerging new economy. It has been called the information age, the knowledge society, the new world order. In the beginning, it simply was referred to as the service sector. Beginning shortly after World War II, this sector began growing more rapidly than the industrial sector, and by the early 1960s it produced more jobs than manufacturing. The emergence of this service sector, and the transition into a postindustrial economy, initiated a chain of interrelated institutional adaptations by public education that transformed its outer institutional shell. Each of the components of this outer shell (governance, funding, and organizational structure) reintegrated itself in relation to the others and to perceived changes in the larger, external environment.

However, in trying to reform itself from the outside-in—through reforming governance, funding, and organizational structure—it impaired its capacity to carry out its instructional and socialization functions. Successful institutional alignment, as we saw in the previous section, begins from the inside-out, rather than from the outside-in; for it is the instructional core that develops in the students the cognitive and social skills they will need to contribute to the growth of the new, emerging economy. Once this is configured properly, then organizational, funding, and governance systems need to be designed to support and strengthen this core. But that is not what has been done over the past thirty years. We have been following in the footsteps of the rural school problem reformers of the late nineteenth century.

Changes in Governance

The new service economy that began flourishing after World War II was not as closely tied geographically to the big cities as industrial manufacturing had been. The new economy allowed for a much greater dispersion of the population, and helped feed and support the rapid migration of the population from big cities to the suburbs in the 1950s. The proliferation of these communities rapidly produced a large economic market within each metropolitan area in which businesses, citizens, and governments competed with one another.

In 1956, Charles Tiebout constructed a model to predict the economic distribution of communities that would arise as a result of this competition.[15] His model posited that citizens and businesses would shop among communities to find those that offered the best governmental services for the lowest tax costs, and local governments, in turn, would configure their governmental services to attract residents and businesses with the highest taxpaying capacity. The result, he predicted, would be a metropolitan landscape in which relatively homogeneous communities would be formed that were stratified on the basis of their residents' capacity to pay for governmental services. Communities with affluent taxpayers would have high levels (and quality) of governmental services with corresponding low tax rates, whereas those at the bottom of the hierarchy would have high tax rates but low levels of service. This perverse relationship would develop because communities with affluent taxpayers could have comparatively modest tax rates to generate high levels of tax revenues (because the underlying property values would be large), whereas those with less-affluent taxpayers would need to impose high tax rates to achieve an acceptable level of tax revenue to operate their governments.

This market, economists argued, offered a partial substitute for politics, because citizens eventually would distribute themselves on the basis of their preferences for governmental services and on their capacity to pay for those services. An exit option would substitute for political voice because governments would need to provide services tailored to hold desirable taxpayers in their communities. If those services were not forthcoming, residents could exercise the exit option and move to a more desirable community.[16]

Tiebout's model, however, ignored the transaction costs of moving in and out of the market (e.g., the costs of buying and selling a home: realtor fees, closing costs, new mortgage financing, etc.). The inefficiencies imposed by these transaction costs significantly constrained the exit option for many Americans and made communities much more heterogeneous in their composition than the economic model had predicted. This breakdown in market controls, coupled with the absence of a clearly identifiable economic elite in most suburban communities, raised the level of political voice to the discordant, particularly as communities became more socially and economically heterogeneous in their composition.[17]

The governance system of public education became increasingly politicized with unstable school board majorities and the predominating influence of narrow-issue special interest groups. In the big cities, most of the social and business elites departed to a few insular suburban enclaves, and school politics within these cities increasingly came to reflect the ethnic and neighborhood divisions within the city. Today, many big cities have abandoned altogether the municipal reform device of at-large elected school boards in favor of regional representation.

The primary consequence of this political fragmentation has been the withering away of the capacity of school boards to articulate a unitary interest for the district as a whole, and to formulate a coherent and stable set of educational policies. The absence of a relatively cohesive voice at the apex of the institutional structure has significantly diminished the capacity of the system to coordinate and control its administrative and instructional components.

Changes in Funding

The proliferation of suburban communities on the basis of market principles generated substantial inequalities in the capacity of local school boards to fund their local school systems and to provide quality educational services. America, as Theodore Lowi observed, had never really been a melting pot; it always had been a boiling pot, with one group trying to get away from another, and the affluent trying to escape contact with the poor.[18] By the early 1960s it was painfully evident that big cities no longer had the fiscal capacity to remedy their deteriorating educational systems. Fiscal problems, however, were not the special province of just the big cities. By the early 1970s the inner ring of suburban communities was in economic decline, and this process has continued to spread outward over the past two decades. But at the beginning of the 1960s much of this economic deterioration still was confined to the big cities. As mentioned at the outset of this chapter, it was the overlay of these economic conditions with racial and ethnic segregation that prompted the nation to take action in attempting to resolve the problems of inequity and unequal opportunity. America also perhaps was moved by a better understanding of its own history.

During much of America's history, people of color were considered natural resources. They were fungible elements in the formula for extracting wealth, and were legislated out of the political culture. They were not considered part of the configuration designed to achieve congruence between the institution of public education and the political and economic systems of wealth creation.

The battle to win equal educational opportunity was a long and difficult one led by large segments of America's diverse racial and cultural populace. Legislation had rendered equal educational opportunity almost nonexistent for nonwhites. In 1850, after a successful pre-Civil War movement to prevent African Americans from obtaining an education, only 6 percent of the "free Negro children" attended school nationwide, while nearly 60 percent of white children went to school. By the end of the nineteenth century the African American school-age population had grown by 25 percent, yet the percentage of children attending school was less than twenty years before.[19]

In those rare instances where people of color did participate in the educational system, public education's resources were directed toward the white students. The federal government established inferior schools for Native Americans with acculturation as the primary purpose. Mexican American children were subjected to the "separate but equal" doctrine that had been applied to African American children in the South.[20]

Much of the national educational agenda of the 1960s was concerned with finding (at least partial) remedies for these inequalities. Federal and state governments increasingly were called upon to redress fiscal inequality, and when legislative bodies refused to act, advocates for fiscal redistribution turned to the courts to force redistributive assistance. As federal and state sources of revenue increased, property taxes diminished as a means of funding public schools. By 1980, property taxes comprised less than 50 percent of school revenues for most school districts nationally.

These actions helped make per pupil expenditures among school districts more equal, but they also created more divergent points of accountability in the funding environment of public schools. For each source of money there inevitably were strings attached, not all of which could be woven into a single fabric. Each often pushed the instructional core in different directions, thereby making the mission of public schools less clearly defined and less compelling a target for action.

Change in Organizational Structure

Multiple-sourced funding, coupled with political fragmentation, altered the organizational structure of public education. In the industrial model, public education's administrative bureaucracy had been designed to have a unitary structure, where all components were tightly interconnected and controlled by the general superintendent. In the new fiscal and political realities of the 1960s and 1970s, however, many school districts, especially the big city ones, began proliferating horizontal and vertical differentiation, overlapping jurisdictions, and multiple lines of authority in order to allow constituent organizational subunits to respond separately to conflicting external demands.

This new institutionalized form of organization allowed public school administrators to more readily secure political support and fiscal resources from a more differentiated funding environment and more politically fragmented governance system. But it also weakened the structure's capacity to maintain constancy of purpose.[21] By sacrificing unity of command and functional integration, and by trying to be all things to all those with money and power, public schools no longer had an organizational structure capable of delivering consistent, cohesive educational services, much less doing so with economic efficiency.

The Need to Work from the Inside-Out

By the early 1980s, school reformers began to recognize the significance of the emergence of postindustrial economy for the future of public education. A global economy would require the graduates of America's public education system to compete for jobs with workers from around the world. Wage rates for non- and even semiskilled labor would fall until equilibrium was established in the international labor market. To secure the higher paying jobs, workers would need better skills and training.

This realization that America had entered a postindustrial economy shifted the debate over public schools from equity to excellence. But throughout much of the 1980s, school reformers turned to making schools better—to issues of quality, efficiency, and organizational effectiveness. These issues, however, do not fully come to grips with institutional misalignment. Trying to improve organizational designs is not likely to succeed when the political and funding systems surrounding these structures impose contradictory and continually changing demands on school administrators. Piecemeal reforms will not work in a system in which the components of the institutional structures are tightly interconnected. The devolution of the industrial public educational institutional framework in the face of an emerging postindustrial economy produced discontinuities with that new economy. Politicized governance, multiple-sourced funding, and institutionalized organizational structures are all tightly coupled, and reflect interrelated responses by public education to the discontinuities being created by the transition to a postindustrial society.

The problem, however, is not one of interconnectedness, but starting points. Because public education gains most of its immediate feedback about its performance through the governance system, the institutional discontinuities with the emerging postindustrial economy initially manifested themselves in this domain. Trying to resolve discontinuities in governance led to other problems in funding and organizational structure. School reform in the latter half of this century is strikingly similar to what took place during the latter half of the nineteenth century when America's rural school system sought to cope with the emergence of industrialization. Efforts to resolve the rural school problem did not work until public education recognized that its institutional core needed to be brought into alignment with the needs of an industrialized society, and then its governance, funding, and organizational systems were redesigned to serve that new instructional core.

Today, public education faces a similar challenge. It needs to redesign its instructional core so that its graduates can participate as wealth producers in the postindustrial economy. This process must start from the inside-out, rather than, as has been the practice over the past thirty years, from the outside-in. Once the instructional core is aligned to the new postindustrial economy, then an appropriate outer shell of the institution can be designed to support this new core. This form of institutional realignment will be necessary for public education to improve its capacity to contribute toward, and benefit by, the new wealth that can be created in postindustrial society.

CONCLUSION

Economics has been called the dismal science, because it takes as its starting point a lower boundary estimate of the human condition. It begins with a selfish, cunning set of individuals and seeks to identify the conditions wherein their rational self-interests might intersect to produce moments of cooperation. Applying this framework to our analysis of the institutional transformations that have taken place in public education over this past century, the most depressing aspect with respect to people of color is that the country could shunt aside such a large number of people and still prosper as it did. We believe that the country would have been even more prosperous if it had made its institutional structures more inclusive. But the fact that so many human resources could be squandered and the country still succeed is a sobering reflection as to where a lower boundary estimate of a postindustrial society might fall.

Our historical analysis of the institutional transformation of public education from an agrarian to an industrial society also suggests that elites will play a major role in shaping the new institution of education in postindustrial society. People of color may be able to exert sufficient power to play a role in this process. There is nothing deterministic about the relationship between economy and education. The patterns of reinstitutionalization of education in the wake of industrialization have varied among industrialized nations, depending upon the distribution of political power in those countries.

There is some evidence that the new postindustrial economy is fragmenting and decentralizing political power. Technology is making information and the means of communication available to a much broader array of citizens. Just as a videocamera altered the power relationship between Rodney King and the police in the City of Los Angeles, the new technologies of postindustrial society may not have the centralizing impact that manufacturing exerted on industrial society. More fluid and shifting coalitions may arise as a consequence of greater information and communication, potentially giving people of color greater political power.

In order to participate in the process of shaping the new institution of public education, people of color will need to restructure their political agendas. The developmental, rather than the distributive, function of education will need to be emphasized, and a connection established between that function and the role people of color can play in producing the new wealth of the postindustrial society. However, even this may not be sufficient in a society where racial and ethnic biases remain so deeply ingrained.

Apart from the level of impact people of color will have in shaping the institution of public education in postindustrial society, there is another equally important dynamic at work, one this chapter has not addressed, and the existence of which has never depended upon the choices made by the mainstream, dominant society. American history reveals countless stories from Chicano/Latino American, Native American, African American, and Asian American cultures that recount the ability of people, regardless of the intensity of oppressive treatment, to struggle against that oppression and, through that struggle, not only to survive, but to achieve. In stories such as these, achievement is secondary because human attributes such as compassion, courage, hope, struggle against oppression, the will to survive, and the desire for justice must be central before achievement itself will be recognized as meaningful. The desire for this kind of meaning is as much a part of human rationality as is the calculation of self-interest.

NOTES

1. Michael Harrington, *The Other America: Poverty in the United States* (New York: Macmillan, 1962).

2. United States Kerner Commission, *Report on Civil Disorder* (Washington, DC: National Advisory Commission on Civil Disorders, 1968).

3. Newton Edwards and Harman Richey, *The School in the American Social Order* (Boston: Houghton Mifflin, 1963), p. 466.

4. Barry Bluestone and Irving Bluestone, *Negotiating the Future: A Labor Perspective on American Business* (New York: Basic Books, 1992).

5. David Tyack, *The One Best System: A History of American Urban Education* (Cambridge, MA: Harvard University Press, 1974).

6. Ellwood Cubberley, *Rural Life and Education: A Study of the Rural-School Problem as a Phase of the Rural-Life Problem* (Boston: Houghton Mifflin, 1922).

7. Arthur Vidich and Joseph Bensman, *Small Town in Mass Society: Class, Power and Religion in a Rural Community* (Princeton, NJ: Princeton University Press, 1968).

8. Emil J. Haller and David H. Monk, "New Reforms, Old Reforms, and the Consolidation of Small Rural Schools," *Educational Administration Quarterly*, 24(4) (1988): 470–483.

9. Ellwood Cubberley, *Public School Administration* (Boston: Houghton Mifflin, 1928).

10. Joel Spring, *The American School 1642–1990* (White Plains, NY: Longmans, 1990).

11. Willard Waller, *The Sociology of Teaching* (New York: Russell and Russell, 1961).

12. Edward Banfield and James Q. Wilson, *City Politics* (Cambridge, MA: Harvard University Press, 1963).

13. Paul Peterson, *The Politics of School Reform 1870–1940* (Chicago: University of Chicago Press, 1985).

14. Raymond Callahan, *Education and the Cult of Efficiency* (Chicago: University of Chicago Press, 1963).

15. Charles Tiebout, "A Pure Theory of Local Expenditure," *Journal of Political Economy*, 64(4) (1956): 416–424.

16. Paul Peterson, *City Limits* (Chicago: University of Chicago Press, 1981).

17. Joseph G. Weeres and Bruce Cooper, "Public Choice Perspectives on Urban Schools," in James G. Cibulka, Rodney J. Reed, and Kenneth K. Wong (Eds.), *The Politics of Urban Education in the United States* (London: The Falmer Press, 1992), pp. 57–70.

18. Theodore Lowi, *The End of Liberalism* (New York: W. W. Norton, 1969).

19. Robert Blauner, *Racial Oppression in America* (New York: Harper and Row, 1972).

20. John Fernandez, *The Diversity Advantage* (Lexington, MA: Lexington Books, 1993).

21. Joseph G. Weeres, "The Organizational Structure of Urban Educational Systems: Bureaucratic Practice in Mass Societies," in Stanley W. Rothstein (Ed.), *Handbook of Schooling in Urban America* (Westport, CT: Greenwood Press, 1993), pp. 113–130.

PART II

CULTURE

Chapter 6

The Concept of Culture

Walter F. Beckman

Language is the way we think and feel about the world we live in.[1] It allows us to remember and to pass on to our children the values and beliefs of the group. This is the cultural system of human beings and it helps us to make sense of what is happening in our daily lives. It is something that is found in all human communities and helps in the establishment of marriage rules, economic relationships, art, science, and so on. Culture is transmitted through speech and language, organizing the universe in ways that give human life meaning and direction. Rules for marrying and family life, as one example, have changed a great deal over time, yet such rules continue to persist even when they are broken by increasing numbers of people in modern society.[2] Such rules are formed in language and become part of the symbolic order, revealing themselves as ideas that fix and rationalize the physical and social order. The symbolic order of words describes the world in terms of beginnings and endings, good things and bad things, and synonyms and antonyms, producing the cultural habits of society. These are relayed through the language of parents, the church, and educational systems, forming a web of social, economic, and political structures that become the givens in the world of infants and young children.

Nevertheless, it is always within the language (and ideas) of a people that its culture is generated and sustained. Language alone is the transmitter of traditions and order, providing newborns and their families with their place in social status system of the modern world.[3] In words, beliefs, and life traditions, the family transmits to children a knowledge of their family's culture and class, assuring them of their physical and mental support during the most vulnerable, early years of life.

In language, infants are enveloped in a social system long before they can take their place as subjects in the world of adults. This happens before they can acquire the speech and language skills they will need to communicate with others effectively, before they are a functioning individual. Moreover, it is in the formalization of the marriage rules that language makes its unique contribution to family life, providing a powerful social mechanism that transmits to new generations information about the social and economic relationships of the system. These themes of cultural heritages are partly determined by class positions: these provide family members with a basis to determine their attitudes towards art, science, religion, diet, and strangers. It is true that later learnings can alter some of these earliest teachings, but it seems foolish to ignore the power of these earliest understandings of individuals.

To repeat, then, the relations of family members are controlled by speech and language and the ideas they generate: these provide the basis upon which all thoughts are formulated and revealed. Why is this important? Because people need to make their intentions known to one another, they need rational forms of communication based on the language they learned from their parents. They have no other way of sending or receiving complex messages. Only those who learn the language of the culture will benefit from it; punishment and disgrace often await those unfortunates who, for one reason or another, are unable to make the transition from the natural to the cultural order during their first years of life.

Chapter 7, "Italian and Mexican Responses to Schooling: Assimilation or Resistance?" by Richard J. Altenbaugh, shows how the language and culture of two immigrant groups in the United States influenced their efforts to assimilate into the wider American culture at different moments in the nation's history. This is followed by Chapter 8, "Emerging Educational Structures: The Impact on Leadership 'Culture' " by Andrew E. Dubin. Dubin shows how the speech and language of students has influenced the educational structures that are emerging in our inner cities.

NOTES

1. Stanley W. Rothstein, *The Voice of the Other: Language as Illusion in the Formation of the Self* (Westport, CT: Praeger Publishers, 1993), Chapter 1.

2. Ruth Benedict, "Continuities and Discontinuities in Cultural Conditioning" in Patrick Mullahy (Ed.), *A Study of Interpersonal Relations* (New York: Hermitage Press, 1949), pp. 304–307; Claude Levi-Strauss, *The Elementary Structures of Kinship* (New York: Beacon Press, 1969).

3. Claude Levi-Strauss, *The Savage Mind* (Chicago: University of Chicago Press, 1966), Chapter 2.

Chapter 7

Italian and Mexican Responses to Schooling: Assimilation or Resistance?

Richard J. Altenbaugh

Our task is to break up these groups or settlements, to assimilate or amalgamate these people as part of an American race.
Ellwood P. Cubberley (1919)

In Texas the teacher beats you for using Spanish in school to remind you that you are an American. Your friends beat you after school to remind you that you are a Mexican.
Quoted in Joan W. Moore (1976)[1]

INTRODUCTION

The cover of a 1993 special issue of *Time* magazine proclaimed the "new face of America," illustrated by a computerized composite of a woman "from a mix of several races." The lead article, entitled "America's Immigrant Challenge," and written by the editors, warned its readers that the concept of "minority" will be redefined because of the rapid and large influx of immigrants: "sometime during the second half of the twenty-first century the descendants of white Europeans, the arbiters of the core national culture for most of its existence, are likely to slip into minority status." This prospect, the article continued, "hardly pleases everyone." It warned that a majority of "normally tolerant Americans," frightened by the "newcomers' contributions to crime and disease," want to "limit immigration more strictly." This article concluded with a contradiction: it praised "diversity" yet upheld "assimilation" as the ultimate solution.

The article that followed, "Not Quite So Welcome Anymore," proved to be alarming. Based on a *Time*/CNN poll, 73 percent of Americans want to "strictly limit immigration," and 49 percent favored a constitutional amendment preventing children born here from becoming United States citizens unless their parents were also citizens. Revealing how distorted this society's perceptions are concerning immigrants, Americans believe that 64 percent of immigrants enter the country illegally while the actual figure is only 24 percent.[2] The authors of these articles maintained a disturbed, if not shocked, tone.

This controversy, often manifested in outright hostility, is not surprising when analyzed against the backdrop of history. Prejudice and intolerance have greeted newly arrived immigrants as early as the colonial period, establishing a "standard for the future."

> The English colonists and later Americans of the majority group appreciated the labor that the newcomers could provide, but expected the immigrants to absorb the dominant customs while shedding their own as quickly as possible. Minority group members were sought for their labor yet were despised for their ignorance of English, their attachment to culture and faiths prevalent in the Old World, and the lack of understanding of the American Way.[3]

Fearful Americans used education to facilitate the acculturation process. According to Stephen Brumberg, "the dominant American culture, working through its public schools went about imposing the hegemony of Anglo-Saxon culture upon an alien culture."[4]

This perception has led one historian to blatantly label schools as "culture factories." Public schools ably fulfilled this role during the Irish immigration of the early nineteenth century.[5] With the massive migration of southern and eastern Europeans between 1880 and 1920, frightened Americans again looked to their schools to assimilate the newcomers. This represented a conscious, blatant, and methodical process, hoping to attain Anglo-conformity. Ellwood P. Cubberley, a leading educator, self-righteously proclaimed in 1909:

> These southern and eastern Europeans are of a very different type from the north Europeans who preceded them. Illiterate, docile, lacking in self-reliance and initiative, and not possessing the Anglo-Teutonic conceptions of law, order, and government, their coming has served to dilute tremendously our national stock, and to corrupt our civic life. The great bulk of these people have settled in the cities of North Atlantic and North Central states, and the problems of proper housing and living, moral and sanitary conditions, honest and decent government, and proper education have everywhere been made more difficult by their presence. Everywhere these people tend to settle in groups or settlements, and to set up here their national manners, customs, and observances. Our task is to break up these groups or settlements, to assimilate or amalgamate these people as part of an American race, and to implant in their children, so far as can be done, the Anglo-Saxon conception of righteousness, law and order, and popular government, and to awaken in them a reverence for our democratic institutions and for those things in our national life which we as a people hold to be of abiding worth.[6]

While many immigrant groups acquiesced to this transformation, others resisted it.[7]

Given the historical experience of immigrants in this country, what will be the fate of Mexicans and their children? It has been estimated that almost 10 million Mexicans, the largest and most prominent of the Hispanic cohorts, reside in this country. "By the year 2000, in key areas of this nation, the majority population will be Hispanic."[8] How will (do) they perceive schooling? How will (do) they respond to this assimilation process?

These questions remain largely unanswered by academics. We have witnessed a renaissance of studies in social history that focus on the relationship between ethnic minorities and education, but a paucity of literature exists that concentrates on the educational past of Chicanos. And what little there is may be categorized into two basic "approaches": institutional-based and minority-group activities themselves. The former covers public school policies, including long-term discrimination, chronic underachievement, and assimilationist curricula; while the latter stresses the Mexican American quest for educational equality— namely, efforts to curb school discrimination and campaigns for the linguistic and academic needs of their children. Yet one overriding question remains: How unique is their experience? Similarities exist in the educational experiences of Chicanos and other language minority groups of European descent. But, as Guadalupe San Miguel concludes, "new studies comparing and contrasting the educational experiences of Mexican Americans with other minority and immigrant groups are needed."[9]

One manner of addressing these questions is to analyze the historical experience of a comparable immigrant group—Italians. Why study Italian immigrants in order to gain insights into the Mexican experience? From 1881 to 1920, 4.5 million Italians sailed for the United States, representing the largest of the southern and eastern European groups. These two immigrant groups not only dominated their respective time periods in sheer numbers, but their premigration and postmigration experiences appeared to be similar. Italians and Mexicans emigrated from environments of poverty, often saw themselves as temporary residents, largely settled in urban areas (this, of course, does not ignore the rural settlements of Italians as well as Mexicans), "recognized the Roman Catholic religion, cultivated a strong sense of community, and viewed American institutions, especially public schooling, with suspicion."[10]

More significantly, both groups presented the existing North American culture with a profound challenge: how to school, and ultimately assimilate, this massive body of non-Americans.[11] Leonard Dinnerstein and David Reimers have pointed out that immigrants who had low economic and educational aspirations lacked mobility and were least likely to accept the American way of life. Italians and Mexicans certainly would be included in such categories.[12] Because of their resistance to these assimilation processes, the Italian family represented the most formidable social institution that the school system ever encountered; its cultural resistance persisted over three generations. Finally, no comprehensive educational history of Italians and Mexicans exists. This chapter attempts to reconstruct and synthesize their public school experiences from existing secondary sources, and will rely heavily upon works by Leonard Covello and Gilbert Gonzalez.[13]

American perceptions of culture have guided this society's responses to immigrant groups. School personnel have viewed immigrant children either as the product of an inferior culture, as in the case of Italians, or as victims of cultural deprivation, as in recent years with Mexicans. Whatever the perspective, immigrant cultures have been regarded as unacceptable; Anglo values have been seen as superior. Thus, the public schools, reflecting American values, have consistently attempted to reshape immigrant experiences and perceptions of culture.

ITALIAN SCHOOL EXPERIENCES

American public schools, between 1880 and 1920, mobilized to assimilate the children of the massive influx of southern and eastern Europeans. Marion Brown, principal of New Orleans' City Normal School, a teacher training center, self-righteously proclaimed to the 1902 meeting of the National Education Association that American educators served as missionaries, saving these unfortunate and misguided children. She argued that we must

> bring them to the Anglo-Saxon standard, train them to self-control that means freedom, the love of country that foreshadows the brotherhood of men, the developing personality that can take only justice and right as its standard, a consummation possible only thru [*sic*] knowledge of the mazes of inherited tendencies, by sympathy with the soul struggling in shackles of ancestral bondage.

She categorized each European ethnic group for the audience in this run-on sort of way. Regarding Italians, she began by generalizing about the "Latin race,"— Spanish, French, and Italian—then moved to specific descriptions about Italian immigrant children. Classrooms where such Latin children learned were always noisier and less-well-disciplined than others. They were more subject to outbursts of emotion. The effects of their cultural history, or their heredity, caused them to show less self-restraint and antidemocratic sentiments and ways of doing things. With such children, a directive and authoritarian influence was most successful. Brown recited other insights into the character of Italian children— "ardent lovers of beauty, excellent in form, quick to learn a new tongue, keen at the bargain, loving music and rhythm, passionate, revengeful, proud to shine, easily antagonized"—warning listeners that such un-American behavior needed "to feel a strong hand at the helm."[14]

By 1930, 4,456,875 Italian immigrants and their "American-born children" lived in the United States, and 60 percent of them resided in cities. Leonard Covello, who intensely studied the East Harlem Italian community, argued in his classic 1942 study that they effectively resisted assimilation, setting the stage for cultural conflict that often assumed "open hostility to American patterns in every way." The family served as the key social institution in the Italian community, as it had in Italy. All social control emanated from the values and moral imperatives of this group.[15] Italian family priorities superceded, and often confronted, American school requirements. The root of this conflict grew out of the economic and cultural needs, values, and traditions of the past.

Southern Italians respected "work" in its broadest terms; they saw it as dignified while idleness was viewed as shameful. Their traditions dictated that "all children" serve as "useful and effective members of their families from an early age." Parents perceived adolescents as young adults who were supposed to assume domestic responsibilities as well as work outside of the home; they failed to understand why Americans insisted on extending childhood into their teen years. Such parents felt uneasy about the idleness of youngsters expected to work once they reached the age of twelve. These children were expected to contribute to the household economy, as well. As one parent summarized this "shameful" situation for Covello: "In America it's all play, and I see young men who should be contributing to their families, still going to school and playing ball in the streets."[16]

A second economic reason stemmed from the fact that Italian immigrants often required that their children find jobs to ensure the very survival of the family. Parents made a rational and conscious choice here. They sacrificed their children's individual success for the family's well-being. Schooling held long-term, intangible promises while working guaranteed immediate survival. In 1905, 79 percent of Italian sons and 82 percent of daughters, 15 to 19 years old, abandoned the Buffalo schools. As Virginia Yans-McLaughlin explained it, Italian children had to pay this price of lesser job mobility. Even upwardly mobile second-generation Italians failed to join the ranks of doctors and lawyers in sufficient numbers. This did not preclude mobility, however; property acquisition simply replaced occupational advancement. "The desire to own a home can be seen as the wish of former peasants to possess—even at great sacrifice—something which had been desired for so many generations."[17]

Italians thus became notorious for saving money to invest in property. Some wives and mothers generated income by collecting boarders' fees or finding occasional part-time work. Families too delayed material gratification, purposefully sacrificing a higher standard of living in order to conserve money. Finally, children played a key role in purchasing a house. It remained a simple fact that most families could not afford a home until the children grew up and found jobs, and "Italian children took their obligations seriously." Sons contributed to house payments more out of a sense of family loyalty than over a concern for economic survival. Italian parents must not be condemned for selfishly neglecting their children's interest or future: property—a tangible asset—could be proudly bequeathed to children, serving as a mode of upward mobility.[18]

The Italian family saw the school's cultural role as its most dangerous threat.

Covello captured the significance of this conflict. Because of its official character, and its insistence upon American values and mores, it remained a constant enemy to family cohesion. Only when children were forced to attend schools did the family begin to feel the power and force of the alien, Anglo culture. Parents instantly realized the peril to their fundamental social values and traditions. They saw the school's authority—namely, compulsory attendance—as a threat to their economic survival.[19]

Schools contaminated their children with ideas and moral understandings that were at variance with what they had taught their children from childbirth. Covello pointed to this conflict as the source of the problems between Italian families and the schools. In the schools, their children were made to feel that they were incompetent and ignorant and that their family heritage and culture was somehow deficient. The Italian family was unpatriotic because it resisted the Americanization process. The preferred ideas and behaviors of the school were taught to children, and they were seen as being preferable to what they had learned at home. The school sought to teach the immigrant children an allegiance to the flag, the nation, and the American way of doing things. However, in doing this, it attacked the children's loyalty toward their parents and families. Italian students told Covello that teachers made them feel inferior and that these ideas were reinforced by American children. The entire school experience contained moralizing teachers, intolerant classmates, ethnocentric subject matter, and American values that challenged the Italian heritages of children. At the same time Italian children were reprimanded at home and in their communities for adopting American manners, tastes, and conduct. They were called Americanos, and this was a term of reproach that even the youngest of children understood.[20]

Although Italian parents pragmatically, yet reluctantly, accepted elementary schooling, their attitudes toward secondary schooling ranged from latent resistance, at best, to overt hostility, at worst. Covello summarized this experience by noting the conflict that occurred between this legal-rational authority and the traditional authority of the Italian immigrant. They found compulsory attendance laws an intrusion upon their family life, especially in high school. They found the curriculum and moral content of classrooms as contrary to their norms, values, and beliefs.[21] Many Italian parents openly defied compulsory attendance laws, cleverly circumvented them, or made a mockery of them as Irish immigrants had done in the 1840s.

As a result, Italian children were seen as problem cases by many American teachers. Covello reported one teacher's perceptions. The children were often truant and the boys a constant irritation that created difficulties for the school.[22] Truancy, cutting classes, tardiness, and disciplinary infractions were problems of greater frequency among Italian elementary students than non-Italians. While Italian parents sabotaged the elementary school's influence, they often demonstrated outright belligerency toward the high school experience. Attendance, academic achievement, and school completion remained extremely low, as Michael Olneck and Marvin Lazerson demonstrate.[23] School education for girls particularly irked parents. Adolescent girls simply did not need schooling in Southern Italy, but American schools required their attendance. One mother expressed doubts about the benefits of emigration by lamenting the fact that girls of thirteen and fourteen wasted good time in schools when they could have earned money for their families.[24] Her doubts about emigrating to America were widespread, and Italians, more than any other group, often returned to their homeland. The Italian government estimated that 1.5 million immigrants repatriated between 1900 and 1915. In 1903, one Italian observer wrote: "The language, the religion, the traditions and the hope to return are all strong ties for the emigrant. A favorite phrase among the Italian immigrants is 'Italy is always Italy.' " Consequently, Italians remained resistant to assimilation, as Luigi Villari, Italian Consul in Philadelphia, observed: "The Italians of the first generation conserve their national characteristics . . . they are so difficult to assimilate and so many of them repatriate." Finally, an Italian embassy official reported to his government in 1902 that these " 'birds of passage' . . . hate everything which is American except the gold which takes them away."[25]

For those immigrants who remained, they preserved their culture through their children. School absenteeism appeared to be prevalent among Italian youths. A frustrated truant officer assigned to an East Harlem high school described the resistance process he encountered. Italian children did not respect the attendance laws, and truant officers were seen as hostile government agents whose arrival at home caused great discomfort. Neighbors refused to help officers locate the homes of truants and saw their visits as intrusions into their private lives.[26] The entire Italian community participated in these subterfuges, aiding and abetting the poor fugitive, because school attendance was seen as a family affair. While many non-Italian hookey-players feared retribution from their parents, this was not so with Italian youths. By absenting themselves from school and working to help support the family, Italian youths were praised by parents and community leaders alike.[27]

Covello further contended that family tradition asserted itself during adolescence. Children became more hostile to public schooling and more supportive of the mores of their families and communities. Throughout the 1930s, a complex process of assimilation and then reassimilation occurred, as older children were quick to recall. As children many of them were ashamed of everything Italian. They often denied their own parents while hating to come to school each day. Later, many of these children learned that the family was something to be valued over the schools. It was a source of *gemeinschaft*—warm family relations that could not be duplicated elsewhere. Older children saw that the opportunities of America were proscribed for many of them and they counted the days when school would be over. While schools and teachers attempted to seduce younger immigrant children into the American way, older children rejected them because of their unpleasant experiences. When Covello surveyed Italian youths, they retained three basic Italian values: family solidarity, male superiority, and the economic oneness of the family.[28]

Within this context, Covello presented fascinating insight into the complex assimilation process from the immigrant's perspective. Many Italian high-school-aged children had learned to play the game of Americanization. However, their acculturation was only skin deep.[29] Italian students spoke American slang, adopted many American symbols, and in numerous ways appeared to be American in order to survive the school's unwelcome environment, but in reality they still retained their family values.

Human agency expressed itself in many ways. Collaboration existed between Italian parents and their children that largely sabotaged "the process of formal education." Parents knew of, and in some cases approved, violations of school attendance regulations by their adolescent children. Covello found such resistance manifested through the third generation—that is, those born of native parentage.[30] The 1970 Census indicated that over 4 million people claimed the Italian language as their mother tongue, with 1.4 million speaking it in their homes.[31]

MEXICAN SCHOOL EXPERIENCES

Mexican migration appeared to be more complex than the Italian experience. Only a small number of Mexicans emigrated to the United States prior to 1900. Nevertheless, the Mexicans did not represent a stranger to the Southwest. "The area had been populated by people of Mexican descent since the late 1500s. All citizens of the United States who came to the area after 1848 had been confronted with the presence of the Mexican and his language, architecture, religion, and food."[32] Mexican emigration began in earnest during the late nineteenth and early twentieth centuries as a southwestern regional experience, focusing on agricultural and railroad work. With the Quota Acts of 1921 and 1924, which severely restricted southern and eastern Europeans, especially Italians, Mexican emigration assumed a different character; midwestern industrial employers now began to use Mexican workers to fill the void left by their European counterparts. Their "homing pigeon" instinct made them particularly appealing to American employers: "The general presumption was that members of this group worked in local fields or mines for a season or two and returned to Mexico to spend the money they had earned for improvements on their family property somewhere south of the border."[33]

Thus the Mexican migration spread regionally, unlike the Italian movement, but overlapped chronologically with the Italian influx. Fording the Rio Grande ultimately replaced crossing the Atlantic Ocean.[34] Thomas Carter and Roberto Segura point out that with increasing Mexican migration to the Southwest, Anglo society turned to the public schools to assimilate them, to inculcate the "richness of American civilization and culture and ultimately overcome the inadequacies attributed to the Mexican race or culture."[35]

Gilbert Gonzalez, focusing too on the Southwest, maintains four distinct periods in the history of twentieth-century Chicano education. The first, known as the "era of de jure segregation," began in 1900 and continued for fifty years. Americanization marked this period, representing the "prime objective of the education of Mexican children." The popular press and academic literature blatantly stereotyped them as "dirty, selfish, promiscuous, and prone to drinking, violence, and criminal behavior."[36] A contemporary paternalistic, yet no less biased, view summarized Mexican culture as "gay, light-hearted," devoted to "color, music, and dancing."[37] A Los Angeles school superintendent expressed his desire for Americanization in 1923, when he addressed district principals: "We have these [Mexican] immigrants to live with, and if we Americanize them, we can live with them."[38] Assimilationists therefore not only saw Mexicans as foreigners but perceived Mexican culture, like many other cultures, as inferior. "Popular as well as academic opinion held that Mexicans posed an 'educational problem,' a consequence of alleged intellectual, social, economic, cultural, moral and physical inferiority."[39]

Classroom practice assumed a set routine; intolerance and humiliation permeated the classroom environment. As Gonzalez explicates it, "teachers urged Mexican children 'to make fun of the lazy ones' in the classroom; to overcome uncleanliness by making a dirty child feel uncomfortable; to compare Mexican and American homes for the sake of imitation; and to overcome the "racial" desire to show off by ridicule."[40]

Language instruction, however, served as the primary approach to the Americanization of Mexican children. "The superintendent of the Eagle Pass, Texas, schools followed conventional wisdom when he wrote that a Mexican child 'is foreign in his thinking and attitude' until he learns to 'think and talk in English.' "[41]

The Great Depression stimulated rural Mexican migration to American cities, and this created a "problem" for urban school systems. Educational literature uniformly described Mexicans in derogatory terms, labeling them as "disease-ridden, inclined towards violence and crime, innately inferior, yet simple and artistic."[42] English represented the instructional language regardless of the number of Mexican children. During the 1930s, "in San Antonio half of the school population was non-English-speaking, the vast majority Spanish-speaking." Gonzalez concludes:

> Americanization, as a curricular activity, endured well into the late thirties, and even then educators did not abandon the objective of assimilating Mexicans into the dominant culture; they merely changed the appearance of the program. Proponents of "Americanization" ceased referring to it as such, but the essential features of the program endured.[43]

This meant that the culture and language of Mexican students remained under attack.

American schools also confronted Mexican families. "Educators perceived the Mexican home as the source of Mexican culture and consequently as a reinforcer of the 'Mexican problem.' " The schools tried to drive a cultural wedge between parents and their children, "separating children in such a way that they would come to desire a home and family of a different [and better] kind."[44]

The schools seldom succeeded because Mexicans resisted. During the early decades of this century, many Mexican immigrants, like their Italian counterparts, planned to return to their homeland, a short train ride away—even for those residing as far away as Chicago. Mexicans maintained a low naturalization rate, the lowest of all immigrant groups. In 1920, only 22,732, or 4.8 percent, of the 478,383 Mexican-born residents had chosen to become American citizens. Ten years later this rate had risen by only one percentage point. As one laborer, who toiled on the Southern Pacific tracks and in the Colorado beet fields, expressed it, "for my part, all the time that I have been in this country I have always thought of going back to my country."[45] Much of this attitude reflected cultural preference, as Elias Garza, field hand and railroad worker, expressed it: "I don't like the customs of this country. . . . Although my children are already grown up I don't want their children to be *pochos*. That is why we are all going so that their children will be born over there and they will be brought up good Mexicans."[46]

This choice stemmed not only from cultural preference but also from nativist hostility. "The Mexican never believed that he could become an integral part of American society." Discriminated against in the workplace, in housing, and in the judicial system, many Mexicans felt little allegiance to this country. And American citizenship failed to ameliorate their subordinate economic and social position, as one Mexican commented: "They talk to us about becoming citizens, but if we become citizens we are still Mexicans. They look at our hair, and listen to our speech and call us Mexican. Even my boy who was born in the United States is a Mexican it seems. He has to go to the Mexican school. There is always a difference in the way he is treated."[47] Assimilation produced yet another twist; it failed to confer equality. Americanization appeared, therefore, to be hollow.

Nevertheless, through segregated schools, American educators hoped to " 'Americanize' the child in a controlled linguistic and cultural environment." Since Mexican students were poor, Gonzalez asserts that social class played a part in this process as well, serving social reproduction. Segregation assumed many manifestations in this context. Mexican children either attended separate schools, often firetraps or condemned buildings, or were in isolated classrooms in mixed schools. In most mixed schools, Mexican students found themselves tracked into "slow learner classes."[48] Beginning in the 1930s, tracking programs emphasized vocational and manual arts training, English, health and hygiene, as well as values like cleanliness, thrift, and punctuality. Carter and Segura assert that "fear of social or racial contamination . . . assumed . . . the implicit, but real, argument for racial segregation."[49]

Americanization rarely occurred in such segregated settings, however. In spite of the efforts of Anglo teachers to ridicule or ignore Mexican culture, obliterate the Spanish language, and track Mexican children in the early grades, Mexican cultural heritage endured. Poor Mexican families, like their Italian counterparts, needed their children's income to survive. Because of family economic needs, these children were simply absent from this cultural cleansing. As one migrant mother explained it: "I can't keep both of my children in school every day . . . if their father works alone he can only make $4 a week, while if one of the boys works with him, they can earn $6 or $7." No more than 25 percent of migrant children attended school in agricultural Texas during the 1930s. "By their sixteenth birthdays, many children had barely reached junior high, and the dropout problem, which subsequently became notorious, began to manifest itself."[50] This decision did not depend solely on the economic condition of Mexican families, because, according to Gonzalez, boards of education and educators often barred migrant children from schools because they were not residents.

The public schools, the principal American cultural institution, confronted other, even more resilient and immutable, social institutions: the immigrant family and community. Mexican parents and communities organized and protested against segregation, beginning in 1943 in southern California, in a case that became known as *Mendez et al. v. Westminister School District of Orange County.*[51]

Although de jure segregation legally ended in the Southwest in the late 1940s, the "pattern of segregation remained between 1950 and 1965," Gonzalez's second period of Chicano educational history. The concept of cultural deprivation drove educational policy—"that is, Chicano culture was recognized as an ingredient to Mexican-American adaptation to Anglo-American culture."[52] The 1960s War on Poverty translated into school programs to break the generational cycle, as it was perceived. "Educators accepted attempts to improve the school as long as the changes were based on assumptions to improve the school as long as the changes were based on assumptions inherent in the idea of cultural deprivation and did not involve structural modification of their institutions." Schools neither implemented fundamental curricular changes nor introduced intercultural heritage materials.[53] They accepted funds for more and better equipment, smaller classrooms, remedial or compensatory programs, and teacher development and aides, but resisted desegregation and community involvement.

The third period, the "militant and reformist era," in Gonzalez's periodization scheme occurred between 1965 and 1975. The Chicano, or La Raza, movement confronted American society and its schools, forcing many changes. The community—*el barrio*—demanded an equal, if not dominant, voice in educational decision making. The movement also attacked the inherent assumption of Mexican cultural deprivation within compensatory and remedial education programs.[54] "Programs such as bilingual and bicultural education, affirmative action, integration, curriculum reform, special admission to higher education, and financial aid, provided a substantially modified educational atmosphere."[55]

In spite of these many demands, the schooling process appeared to experience little change. The Chicano movement advocated bilingual education, but, according to Carter and Segura, "most bilingual programs, unfortunately, still incorporate cultural deprivation assumptions."[56] The classroom, generally speaking, continued to serve as the stage for cultural conflict. Citing the 1973 *Mexican-American Education Study*, Richard Valencia summarized that "based on systematic observation and evaluation of behavior in over 400 classes in New Mexico, California, and Texas, . . . Chicano students, compared to Whites, received significantly less praise and encouragement from teachers. Furthermore, teachers were found to spend less time in asking questions of Chicanos."[57] One-third of Chicano students reported teacher prejudice—that is, "stereotypic comments voiced in front of class; cultural clashes; being punished or embarrassed for using their native language."[58]

Gonzalez appears to be ambivalent about any progress since 1975, which marked the beginning of his fourth period in twentieth-century Chicano educational history. On the one hand, by the late 1970s Chicanos maintained their insistence on better and culturally sensitive teachers, integration, demand for more Chicano subject matter, and, most importantly, an ascendancy of bilingual/cross-cultural schooling. The new rationales of cultural differences and cultural-linguistic pluralism gained advocates. On the other hand, opponents persisted; this era has been dominated by "political conservatism." Decreased federal spending has further undermined Chicano goals for schooling. At best, for Gonzalez, this period, which is still unfolding, has witnessed a "rollback of the reforms enacted during the previous one."[59] At worst, as Carter and Segura maintain, "some of the older discriminatory patterns, policies, and practices of the schools have been modified, but few have been eliminated or radically changed."[60]

This situation does not bode well for Chicano students. The more recent influx of Mexican immigrants into the United States has sparked sharp debate, spurred reactionary legislation, and generated ill-conceived policy implementation, especially in the area of education.[61] The result is, as the findings of the National Commission on Secondary Education for Hispanics (NCSEH) indicate, "that a shocking proportion of this generation of Hispanic young people is being wasted. Wasted because their educational needs are neither understood nor met."[62] Consequently, the dropout rate for Hispanic students has steadily increased, during the past decade, to a current rate of 40 percent, far in excess of the national average of 25 percent.[63] This situation exists because school personnel tend to interact more negatively with Spanish-speaking students than with other language minority students.[64]

CONCLUSIONS

The responses to American schools by Italian parents and their children are strikingly similar to the Mexican experience. From a historical perspective, the school performances of immigrant children rested solely on the cultural fit between their ethnic culture and American school values. Schools, as we have seen, seldom adapted to them; for success, immigrants had to adapt to American culture and their children had to adjust to the schools—that is, embrace the assimilation process.

Some immigrant groups resisted, however. Truancy served as one means of protest. If immigrants resisted the predominant culture propagated by the schools, then their children paid the price, experiencing outright hostility and academic failure; none of this rested on their innate ability. Confrontation represented another form of resistance. Mild cases included Italian parents' efforts to sabotage truant officers while serious clashes occurred in the courts, with suits filed by angry Mexican parents. Finally, these "birds of passage" and "homing pigeons" also exercised the ultimate form of cultural preservation, returning to their homelands.

The tragedy here is that American society, in spite of these historical lessons, continues to insist on assimilation while paying lip service to diversity. That special issue of *Time* included an article, "Teach Your Children Well," which noted the "Eurocentric bias of U.S. education." Multicultural education, which has had an impact on college and university campuses, "does not seem to have leached into the primary and secondary schools."[65] This shortsighted and insensitive approach sets the stage for continued cultural conflict in American classrooms, in particular, and society, in general.

NOTES

I want to thank Bruce Nelson, Northwestern University, for reading an early draft of this chapter. As always, his comments proved insightful. The chapter does not necessarily reflect his interpretational framework, and he is in no way responsible for any errors in it.

I presented an early version of this chapter at the annual meeting of the American Educational Research Association, New Orleans, April 5–9, 1988.

1. Ellwood P. Cubberley, *Public Education in the United States: A Study and Interpretation of American Educational History* (Boston: Houghton Mifflin, 1919), pp. 15–16; Joan W. Moore, *Mexican Americans* (Englewood Cliffs, NJ: Prentice-Hall, 1976), p. 125.

2. See the entire issue of *Time*, September 23, 1993.

3. Leonard Dinnerstein and David M. Reimers, *Ethnic Americans: A History of Immigration* (New York: Harper and Row, 1988), p. 11.

4. Stephen H. Brumberg, "Tales Out of School: Reports of East European Jewish Immigrants in New York City Schools, 1893–1917," *Issues in Education*, 2 (1984): 94–96. Also, refer to John Higham, "Integrating America: The Problems of Assimilation in the Nineteenth Century," *Journal of American Ethnic History*, 1 (Fall 1981): 7–25.

5. Stanley K. Schultz, *The Culture Factory: Boston Public Schools, 1789–1860* (New York: Oxford University Press, 1973).

6. Cubberley, *Public Education*, pp. 15–16.

7. For immigrant responses to assimilation, see Brumberg, "Tales Out of School,"

pp. 91–109; John Bodnar, Roger Simon, and Michael P. Weber, *Lives of Their Own: Blacks, Italians, and Poles in Pittsburgh, 1900–1960* (Urbana: University of Illinois Press, 1982); and Michael R. Olneck and Marvin Lazerson, "The School Achievement of Immigrant Children: 1900–1930," *History of Education Quarterly*, 26 (Winter 1974): 453–482.

8. National Commission on Secondary Education for Hispanics (NCSEH), *"Making Something Happen": Hispanics and Urban High School Reform* (Washington, DC: Hispanic Policy Development Project, 1984), p. 3. Also see Dinnerstein and Reimers, *Ethnic Americans*, p. 108.

9. Guadalupe San Miguel, Jr., "Status of the Historiography of Chicano Education: A Preliminary Analysis," *History of Education Quarterly*, 26 (Winter 1986): 523, 536.

10. For evidence to substantiate these generalizations, refer to scattered sections on Italian and Mexican immigrants in Dinnerstein and Reimers, *Ethnic Americans*. Specific references to Italians can be found in Richard D. Alba, *Italian Americans: Into the Twilight of Ethnicity* (Englewood Cliffs, NJ: Prentice-Hall, 1985); Betty Boyd Caroli, *Italian Repatriation from the United States, 1900–1914* (New York: Center for Migration Studies, 1973); Humbert S. Nelli, *From Immigrants to Ethnics: The Italian Americans* (New York: Oxford University Press, 1983); Virginia Yans-McLaughlin, *Family and Community: Italian Immigrants in Buffalo, 1880–1930* (Ithaca, NY: Cornell University Press, 1977). For Mexicans, see Lawrence A. Cardoso, *Mexican Emigration to the United States: 1897–1931* (Tucson: University of Arizona Press, 1980).

11. Rodolfo Acuna, *Occupied America: A History of Chicanos* (New York: Harper and Row, 1981), p. 311.

12. Dinnerstein and Reimers, *Ethnic Americans*, pp. 187–188.

13. Leonard Covello, *The Social Background of the Italo-American School Child: A Study of the Southern Italian Family Mores and Their Effect on the School Situation in Italy and America* (Leiden: E. J. Brill, 1967); and Gilbert G. Gonzalez, *Chicano Education in the Era of Segregation* (Philadelphia: Balch Institute Press, 1990). Also refer to San Miguel, "Status of the Historiography," pp. 523–534. This chapter avoids treating the immigrant parochial school experience because few secondary sources exist. Italians ignored them for a long time, and did not open many.

14. Brown's speech is quoted in Clarence J. Karier, *Shaping the American Educational State: 1900 to the Present* (New York: The Free Press, 1975), pp. 255, 271, 272.

15. Covello, *The Social Background*, pp. 276, 279, 280.

16. Ibid., pp. 288, 289; the parent's quote is on p. 292.

17. Yans-McLaughlin, *Family and Community*, pp. 172, 177. This was not unique to Italians because other immigrants and workers employed similar strategies. See Stephen Thernstrom's treatment of "property mobility" in *Poverty and Progress: Social Mobility in a Nineteenth-Century City* (Cambridge, MA: Harvard University Press, 1964). Also refer to David J. Hogan, "Education and the Making of the Chicago Working Class, 1880–1930," *History of Education Quarterly*, 18 (Fall 1978): 227–270.

18. Yans-McLaughlin, *Family and Community*, pp. 176–177. Parts of this section appear in Richard J. Altenbaugh, "Urban Immigrant Families: A Comparative Study of Italians and Mexicans," in Jean E. Hunter and Paul T. Mason (Eds.), *The American Family: Historical Perspectives* (Pittsburgh: Duquesne University Press, 1991), pp. 125–141.

19. Covello, *The Social Background*, p. 314.

20. Ibid., pp. 335, 336, 337–338.

21. Ibid., p. 316.

22. Ibid., p. 283.

23. See Olneck and Lazerson, "The School Achievement."

24. Quoted in Covello, *The Social Background*, p. 292.

25. All of the quotes in the latter half of this paragraph are from Caroli, *Italian Repatriation*, pp. 54, 76, 77.

26. Quoted in Covello, *The Social Background*, pp. 382–383.

27. Ibid., p. 386.

28. Ibid., pp. 347–348, 360–381; the quote is from p. 347.

29. Ibid., p. 350.

30. Ibid.

31. Alba, *Italian Americans*, p. 90.

32. Cardoso, *Mexican Emigration*, p. 21.

33. Ibid., p. 22. See also Mark Reisler, *By the Sweat of Their Brow: Mexican Immigrant Labor in the United States, 1900–1940* (Westport, CT: Greenwood Press, 1976), pp. 3, 14–15, 16–17.

34. Reisler, *By the Sweat*, p. ix.

35. Thomas P. Carter and Roberto D. Segura, *Mexican Americans in School: A Decade of Change* (New York: College Entrance Examination Board, 1979), p. 17.

36. Gonzalez, *Chicano Education*, pp. 30, 36.

37. Quoted in ibid., p. 40.

38. Quoted in ibid., p. 36.

39. Ibid., p. 22.

40. Ibid., p. 39.

41. Ibid., p. 41.

42. Carter and Segura, *Mexican Americans in School*, p. 17.

43. Gonzalez, *Chicano Education*, pp. 41, 45.

44. Ibid., p. 47.

45. Quoted in Reisler, *By the Sweat*, p. 111. The statistics in this paragraph are from the same page in Reisler.

46. Quoted in Manuel Gamio, *The Mexican Immigrant: His Life-Story* (originally published in 1931; New York: Arno Press, 1969), p. 148.

47. Reisler, *By the Sweat*, p. 113. The quote in this paragraph is on this same page.

48. Gonzalez, *Chicano Education*, p. 22.

49. Carter and Segura, *Mexican Americans in School*, p. 17, agree with Gonzalez on this latter point—that is, Americanization occurred best through the isolation of Mexicans from Americans.

50. Gonzalez, *Chicano Education*, pp. 23, 25, 99. This mother's quote is in Gonzalez, p. 122. Carter and Segura, *Mexican Americans in School*, p. 17.

51. Gonzalez, *Chicano Education*, pp. 147–148. He cautions, on pp. 35–36, against simplistic comparisons between Mexican and European educational experiences.

52. Ibid., p. 14.

53. Carter and Segura, *Mexican Americans in School*, pp. 20, 21.

54. Ibid., pp. 25–26.

55. Gonzalez, *Chicano Education*, p. 14.

56. Carter and Segura, *Mexican Americans in School*, p. 26.

57. Richard R. Valencia, "The Plight of Chicano Students: An Overview of Schooling Conditions and Outcomes," in Richard R. Valencia, *Chicano School Failure and Suc-*

cess: Research and Policy Agendas for the 1990s (London: The Falmer Press, 1991), p. 11.

58. Ibid., p. 13.

59. Gonzalez, *Chicano Education*, p. 16.

60. Carter and Segura, *Mexican Americans in School*, p. 28.

61. Guadalupe San Miguel, Jr., "Mexican American Organizations and the Changing Politics of School Desegregation in Texas, 1945–1980," *Social Science Quarterly* 63 (1982): 701–715.

62. NCSEH, *"Making Something Happen,"* p. 3.

63. L. Steinberg, P. L. Blinde, and K. S. Chan, "Dropping Out Among Language Minority Youth," *Review of Educational Research*, 54 (1984): 113–32.

64. Moore, *Mexican Americans*, p. 85.

65. See *Time*, p. 69.

Chapter 8

Emerging Educational Structures:
The Impact on Leadership "Culture"

Andrew E. Dubin

What is the process by which change occurs in schools that considers both the organizational need and the societal mandate? The literature is rich with organizational processes that address change components. The most important change element deals with the human component. People allow change to occur. That element is most critical in making change operational. Of course, without considering and allowing for the varied and complex aspects of the organizational enterprise to evolve, the ability to change will be significantly constrained. Clearly, the need for organizational features of centralization, bureaucratization, and politicalization, which predict and control the behavior of all those involved in the organization, are central to the stability and management of a system and must be factored into this complex equation. This has been the traditional, inherent, and mechanical force behind our schools. Stanley Rothstein points out that in the historical model, the military organization, it was also confronted by the problem of controlling, training, and moving large numbers of people in confined spatial areas. Such institutions felt a strong affinity for geometric and uniform formations and constructions. Buildings and tents were assigned specific locations, entrances, and exits.[1]

As well, H. Warren Button also offers a backdrop to the mechanical orientation that overlies the schooling structure:

> The aim of the "greatest good for the greatest number" was to be implemented by knowledgeable reformers; utilitarians were often not only reformers but also authoritarian. Potemkin was also a staunch advocate of prisons built on panopticon (all-seeing) principles. . . . These principles were taken originally from Prince Grigory Alcksandrovich Potemkin (1739–91) an advisor of Catherine the Great, Empress of Russia, as a strategy to control and manage the behavior and movement of workers.[2]

We can draw historical references to the schools' primary and traditional functions as being the socializing and sorting agent for society's labor function. As such, the organizational features are so ordered to accommodate those primary functions. But the alarming and all-encompassing current and systematic breakdown of our family system is generating a reaction in our schools that is causing a different type of change and expectation to occur. This is producing a function that is creating a form change. Of course, the role or function of the school still must be to respond to the labor demand, which has even greater global implications today, but now must do so with the admixture of demographic and consequently political changes in our society. There is a different human element operating today that is a departure from the past. This is affecting the leadership authority, school organization, and "culture" in a different way. While order and systematic process must be maintained, it must be done in a different arena, one that is more subject to outside intervention than has been the pattern in the past. In doing so, the characteristics of authority and leadership that have been manipulated in the past by the organizational structure, grounded by inherent legal and traditional roles, have been altered by a new force.

Rothstein and others point to changing and emerging societal forces that have begun to depart from the more docile, controlled, and innocent traditional populations of the past. These "historic" populations were generally victimized by the systematic sorting mechanisms of our schools as a means to accommodate our labor force.[3] This new order, I believe, is trumpeting in the open arena for cultural leadership and organizational change. Deeper understandings and sophistication of the populace, more powerful political forces, and more legitimate revelations regarding class biases and systematic subjugations of populations of people by our governments have given rise to a lessened personalization posture that in the past typified our society. We are seeing ourselves as less responsible, inferior, and guilty for the failure we have realized in school. We are identifying less with the school projection of our responsibility for this failure. We are now reflecting a more angry and distrusting perspective that is far more challenging and demanding of the system. We have only to look at the litigious school environments, the impact and power of the press, the continual altering of extreme political positions influencing the power structure of the schools, to appreciate the fluid, challenging, and unpredictable condition in which we find ourselves. Indeed, the closed system that was the cornerstone and bedrock of our system is no longer closed.

Considering the inclusion of these outside forces and in the context of the new open system, it is important to consider and understand the ways in which the traditional power structures will attempt to adapt to these changes. This open system, or "integrative model," which must include various interests and groups, still must be within the control and management of the school organization and subtly and adeptly be balanced within the purview of the school organization.

REALITIES OF SOCIAL AND ORGANIZATIONAL CHANGE

To what extent this current of change truly impacts the system is under considerable debate. And in what ways will the leadership "culture" be required to effectively adapt to these changes? Joseph Weeres' commentary on political systems points out that

> to transform the political economy of urban school systems would require an institutional redesign of public education perhaps greater in scope than what took place at the beginning of this century—one involving federalism (the respective roles of federal, state, and local governments), funding, governance, and, finally, organizational structure. Achieving that kind of transformation must come from outside urban public school systems, because today, unlike nearly 200 years ago, big cities occupy the periphery rather than the center of our economic and political institutions.[4]

Can an argument be made that addresses these areas of change? Is there evidence upon which we can draw that identifies the various agencies interacting with and being responsive to these changes? Are federal mandates, funding sources, legislative and political forces attempting to redesign public education?

Before we look at the question of changing leadership "culture," let us establish the existence of significant efforts and forces producing change. These are the issues central to organizational change and will reconstitute the leadership "culture" of our schools.

A 1993 Association of Teacher Education *Newsletter* recently commented on this very topic:

> State and national policy makers are beginning to recognize the need for new organizational relationships at the family and community levels among schools, health agencies, and other human service organizations. Collaborative reform is central in the new directions proposed by President Bill Clinton's education, health, and human services team: Secretary of Education Richard Riley and Secretary of Health and Human Services Donna Shalala. The integrated services concept is included in the Kildee Education Bill, H.R. 4323. The concept is also reflected in several newly established entities such as those created and supported by Ernest Boyer and former Surgeon General C. Everett Koop—the National Ready to Learn Council, the Carnegie Task Force on Meeting the Needs of Young Children, and more.
>
> Fifteen states (at last count) have passed legislation fostering the coordination of health, social services, and education—for example, the far-reaching bill in Kentucky creating family resource centers and youth services agencies, and the Communities in Schools programs in California, New Jersey, and Texas. Many other states are considering variations of the Kentucky plan, and in some states the education, health, and human service agencies are writing coordinated strategic plans and creating sites where multiple agencies are located for easy access.
>
> Foundations have funded numerous programs fostering collaboration, such as

the Annie Casey New Futures Program and the Danforth Community Leadership Project.[5]

These data and project initiatives would certainly suggest large-scale efforts being entertained in substantive ways and by politically powerful interests that undergird the change movement.

Other efforts can be identified as well. Jeanne Jehl and Michael Kirst's article, "Getting Ready to Provide School-linked Services: What Schools Must Do," highlights a relatively new project in San Diego.[6] The program, known as "New Beginnings," focuses on the linkages between the family and the school. The program

> is a collaborative effort involving the City of San Diego, County of San Diego, San Diego City Schools, San Diego Community College District, and San Diego Housing Commission. These agencies have planned a new system of services for children and families. The system is grounded in four basic principles: (1) services will focus not only on individual school-age children, but also their families; (2) services will emphasize prevention, rather than costly crisis intervention; (3) to avoid reliance on outside funding sources, each participating agency will redirect existing resources to this effort to the greatest extent possible; and (4) plans will be made to adapt the model to other communities and school sites in San Diego County.

Jane L. David's work, *Restructuring Schools: The Next Generation of Educational Reform*, identifies a host of reform efforts throughout the country that speak to the internal changes that schools and leadership are undergoing. To state just a few of these efforts:

> To learn more about the extent to which school districts can transform themselves and what it takes to do so, we studied three districts that have undertaken restructuring efforts. We began with a telephone survey of over a hundred districts to locate those that best represented districts whose actions have led to new roles and relationships and organizational arrangements. We selected three districts for more intensive study: the Dade County Public Schools (Miami, Florida), the Jefferson County Public Schools (Louisville, Kentucky), and the Poway Unified School District (Poway, California).
>
> These districts are by no means the only ones undergoing significant change.[7]

NEW AGE RESEARCH/EFFECTIVE SCHOOLING MOVEMENT

A belief system upon which the effective schooling movement is predicated involves the strongly held point of view of New Age reformers. They hold the belief that schools are capable of and have demonstrated significant and meaningful impact on children of all socioeconomic groups and strongly counter the arguments attributed to the likes of Christopher Jencks, James Coleman, et al. who take the position that schools make little difference and the family background, social class, location (northern or southern), urban or suburban school settings, and peer influence and traditions were the significant variables in successful student outcomes.[8] In their pursuit of models of practice that would support this contention, Coleman et al. identified schools of student composition of equal socioeconomic levels in order to determine success outcome differentials. They determined that there were definite school and teaching characteristics they could identify that transcended the student variables identified earlier in Coleman's and Jencks' work and separated the effectiveness of one school from another.

They listed leadership, school climate, teaching practices, and school structure as characteristics that made a substantive and lasting impact on learning for students. This is not to say that the research and position of Coleman and others did not have a significant impact on the learning process—indeed it did—but there was a growing body of research that refuted the absolute claims attributed to that research. In addition, the effective schooling movement advocates also take aim at those more "progressive" theorists who take the position that the schooling system is designed to perpetuate the ruling middle and upper classes and is quite successful at its inherent and subversive mission. The research from which I draw reflects the Coleman et al. position, which sees the schools as altering these class relationships and offering opportunities for all students regardless of background.

As a starting-off point, the effective schools research points out highly significant findings regarding the learning atmosphere. In addition to the socioeconomic factors ascribed to earlier, there are many other conditions that alter learning outcomes. For one, attitudinal distinctions often contribute to learning outcomes. This is relatively simple and argues that predispositions of teachers or students effect the ways in which students are perceived and perceive themselves. These, essentially, are self-fulfilling prophesies. These research findings have "led to improvements in student achievement, self-concepts, and school attitudes; improvements in teachers' instructional skills and sense of professional efficacy; principals' expertise in managing reforms; improved teaching of at-risk and special-needs children; and a clearer vision of school goals for administrators, staff, and students."[9] When administrators, teachers, students, and parents are provided opportunities to identify preconceived notions about others, in a supportive and constructive environment, change occurs. This is a complex, sensitive, and time-consuming process, but it is reflected in the literature.

In what is considered the direct challenge to the research findings identified by Coleman's work, R. R. Edmonds reviewed the research findings in the hope that he would uncover effective schools' characteristics.[10] From this voluminous research material, 55 schools were identified as having instructionally relevant approaches and effects on students when the family background and home environment were controlled (e.g., parents' education, parents' occupation, percentage of white students, family size, and percentage of intact families).[11]

Based upon that reexamination of Coleman's EEOS data (Equal Educational Opportunity Survey), Edmonds proposed that effective schools:

1. Have strong instructional leadership, without which the elements of good schools cannot be created nor held together.

2. Have a climate of academic expectations in which all personnel seek to be instructionally effective for all students and no children are permitted to fall below minimum levels of achievement.

3. Have an atmosphere that is "orderly without being rigid, quiet without being oppressive, and generally conducive to the instructional business at hand."

4. Make it clear that the acquisition of basic skills takes precedence over all other school activities.

5. If necessary, divert energy and resources from other business to further the fundamental objectives.

6. Frequently monitor student progress by either classroom tests or system-wide standardized tests in order to relate pupil progress to instructional objectives.

From this research Edmonds concluded that "in and of itself, pupil family background neither causes nor precludes elementary school instructional effectiveness."[12] Within this analysis, the element of attitudes becomes a centerpiece for the effective schools' practices.

FAMILY SYSTEMS PARADIGM

This writer believes that the changes we are experiencing in public schools, organizationally, have considerable commonalities with a "family systems model," which views the individual, within the context of the family, in a multidimensional way. Although there are variations of this model, there are many characteristics they all have in common.

Families are seen as systems—rule-governed systems with a tendency toward stability or homeostasis. If a family member deviates from the family's rules, this constitutes feedback, and if the family reacts to it as negative feedback, they try to force that person to change back. Families, like other living systems, maintain their interactions within a relatively fixed range in order to remain stable in the face of normal environmental stresses. In structural family theory the same point is made by saying that families have a relatively stable structure, which enables them to function effectively as a system, with various subsystems each fulfilling part of the family's overall task.

Families must also change to adapt to changing circumstances. To do so they must be capable of revising their rules and modifying their structure. Dysfunctional families are distinguished by their rigidity and inflexibility; when circumstances change, they do not.

How can a family systems model be effectively integrated into the organizational structure of the school? Although we will be reviewing a model grounded in psychotherapeutic theory and in some instances it is not transferable, there are many elements of the model that are present in all organizations that are rooted in individual and group behavior. Because more human and social services are being introduced to schooling environments, there is considerable overlay between the family systems model and the organizational one.

A family systems model is highly integrative and attempts to address individual needs within the context of the environment, both historic and present.[13] Within the context of the school organization, its application would be to replace or augment the societal and family elements that have been decomposing through our capitalist system over the past decades and direct those interactions and activities to the school. This model reflects sensitivity, compassion, and trust, underscoring the family structure, and views children (individuals) as something beyond the prospective "labor worker" entities of the past. This is a more organic model and dynamic process, not the controlled and static organizational one to which we have become accustomed.

I believe that we are already experiencing characteristics of the family systems model within the restructuring efforts of these projects identified earlier in this chapter. When viewing a system or individual from a family systems perspective, the initial changes that members within the organization undergo involve behavioral or interactional change, which we have been experiencing in these initiatives over the past decade. This can be viewed as a "first-order change as opposed to a second-order change, which occurs when the rules of the system that govern those interactions change."[14] If this period of our schooling can be viewed as the first-order change, and I believe it can, it is represented in a somewhat amorphous shape since it is essentially finding itself.

Various new reform efforts, projects, programs, and the like reflect the attempts being made for a workable and viable model. Behaviors are being adjusted but the rules that underlie these behaviors are undefined and are waiting for a more clearly defined foundation for systematizing themselves.

Michael Nichols and Richard Schwartz's family systems paradigm identifies specific characteristics that can easily be transferred over to the organizational setting. Again, we are already seeing this type of model in various reform movements throughout the country. These characteristics would have application in what is defined as an effective school, in the following ways:

1. able to adapt to change;
2. able to view problems as organizational with specific concerns assigned to individuals;
3. cognizant of traditional and historic backgrounds that affect the current culture of the school;

4. characterized as resilient and flexible to accommodate individuals personally—that is, on an individual basis and also institutionally (from an organizational vantage point);

5. decentralized and capable of managing its own decision-making processes;

6. responsible to and reinforcing of difference;

7. capable of seeing people as emotional and rational;

8. aware of the personal and organizational interests of its students;

9. maintaining and perpetuating the health of the organization and the self-esteem needs of its membership;

10. perpetuating and reinforcing strong interactional elements within its membership so that no one is dealing in isolation.[15]

This model extends the school in ways that reflect the changes and considerable needs in the family structure, which is requiring more and more outside support. This of course has always been the dilemma of the school, to reflect society while attempting to shape and direct it. But we are experiencing greater and different expectations from our families from that of the past. While the organization traditionally has offered a fixed structure that has accommodated a select, predictable, subservient, and somewhat functional population, it can no longer choose to do so because of this changing environment and family structure. It must be accommodating in different ways. Before, the considerable slant was for organizational conformity. Now, the balance has shifted toward the individual. Of course, the extent that an equilibrium between the organization and the individual can be developed will ultimately determine the overall health of the organization.

Talcott Parsons addresses this salient aspect when defining social systems:

A social system consists in a plurality of individual actors interacting with each other in a situation which has at least a physical or environmental aspect, actors who are motivated in terms of a tendency to the "optimization of gratification" and whose relation to their situations, including each other, is defined and mediated in terms of a system of culturally structured and shared symbols.[16]

Reflecting his definition of the social system within the parameters of the family systems model, it is clear to see why the system is undergoing such intense adjustment. The "culturally structured and shared symbols" to which Parsons alludes are not shared and are literally undergoing restructuring, and so the social system (the school) will be altered to accommodate these dynamic and volatile external forces.

Parsons continues:

A social system is only one of three aspects of the structuring of a completely concrete system of social action. The other two are the personality systems of the individual actors and the cultural system which is built into their action . . . each is indispensable to the other two in the sense that without personalities and culture there would be no social system.

It seems quite clear that when we compare the characteristics of effective school reform and change to the family systems model, we can see significant similarities. Let's look at a distillation of many variables of effective schools represented in the work of Gary Davis and Margaret Thomas,[17] and compare those to the characteristics stated earlier regarding the family systems paradigm:

1. School site management. Principals, teachers, and other staff need considerable building-level autonomy to determine how to increase student achievement. A unique combination of these factors logically demands flexibility, creativity, and building-level independence.

2. Strong instructional leadership by the principal, which is essential to initiate and maintain the school improvement process. The pivotal, causative feature of virtually every effective school is a principal with vision, energy, and a dedication to leading the staff and students toward better school attitudes.

3. Staff stability. Once a school experiences success, keeping its staff together is important for maintaining its effectiveness and promoting further success. Good interpersonal relationships lead to shared goals.

4. In secondary schools, a planned and purposeful program.

5. An effective schoolwide staff development program aimed at altering attitudes, expectations, and behavior while teaching teachers new skills and techniques. There should be peer supervision—teachers observing and coaching each other.

6. Parent involvement and support and parent awareness of school goals and student responsibilities, especially in regard to homework. If parents thoroughly understand school expectations regarding homework, whether at the elementary or secondary level, they can help arrange the home environment to accommodate that homework.

7. Schoolwide recognition of academic success; publicly honoring academic achievements.

8. Maximizing learning time, which means devoting a greater proportion of the school day to academic subjects. This is active learning.

9. District support for fundamental changes and improvements, building-level management, staff stability and so forth. Guiding and helping is probably the best role for the district office.

10. Collaborative planning and good collegial relationships, both of which are essential for change.

11. A schoolwide sense of community and the individual's sense of being a recognizable member of that community. This may be created by the appropriate use of ceremony, symbols, rules, and such.

12. School social structure, which includes allowing students to talk and work together, time allocations, differentiation in students' programs, parent involvement, and teachers' satisfaction with the school structure.

13. Students need to have control over their academic work and to know that the school system is not stacked against them. (Students in low-achieving schools feel the system functioned so that they could not achieve and that teachers were not committed to high student achievement.) Teachers and the school need to show concern for individual students' welfare; there should be feeling among students that they can talk to staff members about personal problems.

14. Providing a clean, comfortable, and pleasant working environment.

15. Assigning responsibilities for school and personal duties to a large proportion of students.

When we examine the variables represented in this list, the overlap of the family systems paradigm focuses on issues of validation, both to the various players of the system and the system itself. Expectations within the organization of well-defined and challenging academic expectations emerge quite significantly in the literature. As well, characteristics of individual validation are prominently reflected in the effective schools.

One extremely important element in this complex overlay of characteristics that makes operational practices functional or dysfunctional resides in the communication procedures and underlying structures. When we consider communication, we are identifying both unspoken and spoken behaviors present in a social context. It is often said that the most important means of communication are those things that are not said. As well, communication also involves those symbols and clues utilized by members of an organization in providing and interpreting meaning.

In this sense, it is clear to see how important the leadership component is since the decision makers must create an atmosphere of trust where communication can operate as functionally as possible. In addition, the skill involved in interpreting this behavior, which often operates on an intensely subtle level, must be particularly sophisticated.

Some critical areas of understanding and skill application are addressed in the following questions:

1. What are the socially acceptable ways to act, ways approved by others?

2. What behavior will please or displease others?

3. Why do others respond as they do?

4. What are they after?

5. What are their intentions toward us?

6. What are they reporting about themselves?

7. How do we appear to others?

8. How do others see us, evaluate us, respond to us?

9. What are our own intentions?

10. What do symbols, both cultural and organizational, mean to its members?[18]

CULTURAL IMPACT ON LEADERSHIP

How does this alteration in the school organizational process affect the leadership of a school from macro-micro management perspectives? What more specific changes are we experiencing that are impacting the characteristics of our leaders in our schools today?

Central to any effective organization is the vision and skill of its leadership. Understanding the underlying motives behind action and the methods by which the goals, driven by motive, can be successfully realized, is the formula for effective and responsible leadership. In this context there are two central aspects to leadership that need to be addressed. One focuses on centralized leadership and policy development. Here, on the federal, state, or district level resides the centralized leadership component that often drives the processes of the local schools. We see this actualized in federal mandates, state initiatives, or more local board-generated procedures. The other leadership focus lies in the decentralized model where the power resides with the local school level, where the decision-making apparatus rests with the people most affected by those decisions—the principal, teachers, parents, students, and community. Although there is much to consider regarding the overarching and "common good" orientation and contribution of the centralized approach, the decentralized model provides the healthiest structure for our schools by the nature of our pluralistic society and need to be responsive to our extremely fast-paced environment.

The leadership of the "decentralized model" departs from the traditional one and offers a new leadership culture. Its orientation becomes one that defines the organization as far more malleable. As a result, it must be flexible and far-ranging in order to accommodate this more fluid and complex organizational state. As identified within the family systems paradigm, the leadership of a school must work to balance the various agendas of this integrative organization by utilizing appropriate leadership skills. While it is crucial to be able to develop planning procedures that address the short- and long-term projections, it is more the role of the administrator that must undergo change.

Leadership can no longer attempt to assume responsibility for every aspect of school operations. It is an impossible task, particularly in light of the complexities of the modern-day school. Also, incorporating the talents and psychological support of the school membership is the cornerstone upon which effective schools are defined. This new cultural role definition demands that administrators be aware of that which drives them. They need to be more reflective and communicative. They must be able to understand the dynamics of their schools and communicate this understanding to their communities. This will require transitioning their teachers and parents to assume roles they traditionally did not assume. They must also understand those outside agencies that have become a part of the school fabric. These agencies will include social services, security, and funding sources—organizations generally on the periphery of the schools' jurisdiction and interest, indeed, a new culture in an open system arena. Another important aspect to this new culture resides in a belief system grounded in the effective schools research. This, too, will be a departure from values associated with a fixed and static organizational class system to one predicated on significantly affecting the learning process.

A framework of perspectives and administrative areas that would be reflected in this new cultural leadership would be as follows:

1. Establish as the primary role of the leadership to be facilitator and organizer—that is, directing the talent, energy, and funding to appropriate members of the school community in order to increase the learning outcomes. This would involve stimulating research and student and adult growth opportunities.

2. Develop a sense of involvement and commitment to those within the organization—that is, a devotion to quality work and service. Inspirational leadership is an important administrative skill in this area.

3. Improve the organizational process features that identify areas of concern while they are occurring, rather than a product-oriented organizational system that identifies flaws after they have happened.

4. Begin to interact with the organizational membership more substantively, so that histories can be developed. In this way greater commitment will develop and the monetary element will be less important in the decision-making process.

5. Develop reflective practices and environments so that self-growth can be initiated and continued.

6. Develop matrix organizational structures so that boundaries between and among groups become eliminated. This promotes greater linkages, support, and general offerings in emotional involvement and professional expertise.

7. While maintaining a flexible and adaptable organizational environment, conducive to change, begin an institutionalization of the process for long-term planning and stability.

A CASE STUDY

The following school situation analysis is drawn from a recent consultancy I conducted in which the need for new and dynamic leadership was clearly evidenced. This leadership approach was predicated on the type of skills reflected in the material outlined in this chapter, which incorporated a family systems orientation. As well, it also involved a strong understanding of the political dynamics of the school organization. On the one hand, being cognizant of, and sensitive to, the organizational need for control and equilibrium was essential in this analysis in order to be effective. In addition, it was vital to create a climate or culture that would be responsive and adapt to the needs of the open environment of the school. After outlining the school organization, I've presented some of the areas that would need to be evaluated and analyzed when assessing the needs of the school. I've offered questions to consider in these areas.

The school reflected many of the characteristics of a traditional school organizational model, with a top-down leadership/administrative configuration. This was an inner-city high school of approximately 800 students of multicultural backgrounds. The administration consisted of a principal, two assistant principals, two guidance counselors, a resource specialist, and approximately 130 faculty members. The student body was changing rapidly, reflecting a community in flux. As well, there was a significant dropout rate due to the chasm that existed between the school and the community. The curriculum no longer reflected the traditional linkages with the student population. I was asked to review their school program and make recommendations regarding the improvement of their test scores and communication between and among the faculty and administration, community, and students.

The administration had been there for 20 years, and the faculty was seen as somewhat entrenched. There appeared to be a less-than-congenial relationship between them as evidenced in a recent accreditation review questionnaire. In addition, the students were particularly somber and apathetic regarding their attitudes toward the school. In the past, the school had had a strong and credible reputation in the community for high academic standards, but it now realized a less-than-favorable feeling among the parent groups. In fact, parents were becoming resentful of the decline of the school's educational program and were placing more pressure on the teachers and the administration to raise their expectations regarding school work and to become more committed to the school program. Other parents were writing letters to the school board complaining of the situation and requesting transfers for their children to other schools in the district. Prospects of the school being absorbed into other neighborhood schools were being entertained.

There were a number of areas or focal points that had to be identified before any specific action could take place. And of paramount consideration for all proactive planning was the allowance for process—that is, in order for any plan to be successful, there had to be a legitimate time frame for this to occur with appropriate contingency arrangements. Each area or focal point would generate what I call, "outcome objectives," which would be the mechanisms for future planning. They would represent finite possibilities of action although there would be enough flexibility to consider unanticipated aspects of the situation.

These are the areas of focal points I considered:

1. *Historical context.* What background characteristics of the school were important? Who were the important teachers, parents, and others that played central roles in the operation of the school? Had other consultants been invited to conduct such a review? Were there reports, surveys, questionnaires, or interviews, from which I could draw to give me a better background of the school and its needs?

2. *Documentation.* Were school reports available? For example, had an accreditation review been conducted recently or a Program Quality Review? What were the findings? Were there problems identified in the educational program, personnel, support staff, counseling, finances, and so on?

3. *Personalities.* Who were the "power" people in the organization? What were the factions within the school and the community? How did they interact? What was the informal organizational power structure?

4. *Politics.* What groups existed in the community and how influential were they? Were these groups undergoing change? What were the relationships among those directly involved in the school?

5. *Funding.* What were the funding sources? Who controlled them? Were there opportunities that could be explored for external funding?

6. *Leadership Styles.* What type of leadership was present? How long had the administration been at this school? What type of leadership would be most effective coming in the wake of the present administration?

7. *Faculty.* What were the characteristics of the faculty? This analysis would be based on a number of characteristics such as gender, years of experience, advanced degrees, years at the school, size of the departments or programs, and relationships among faculty members.

8. *Students.* What was the demographic breakdown of the students? Was this student population involved in the school program? What were the test scores, attendance records?

9. *Short- and Long-Term Plans.* What types of plans would be most appropriate to meet the needs of the school within the context of educational planning, faculty ability, financial appropriations, and general vision or philosophy of the school? Were the needs of the school recognized, understood, and supported by all school community?

10. *Time Involvement.* In light of the present needs of the school, was there adequate time to allow the plans to come to fruition? Which plans should be pursued immediately and what reaction would this generate? Which plans should be pursued in the future and what reaction would this generate? What is the relationship between the short-term and long-term plans?

11. *Governance.* What were the governance issues? Did the school require structural or process governance adjustments? How would this be received? How much time would this require?

Underscoring all these areas of investigation would be to develop an organization that provides opportunities to examine itself objectively and substantively. Initially, when an organization undergoes such a review and process for change, there is significant resistance. Reducing this resistance requires leadership to incorporate strong involvement from those affected by these changes. Although a leadership vision and direction will be desired and expected, it must be offered tactfully and within the context of the situation. A process for mutual approval needs to be established.

As indicated, the historic school models were structured to adapt the environment to meet the needs of the organization.[19] The leadership requirement now needs a more responsive level of understanding and far greater responsibility to adapt itself to the emerging characteristics of the constituent groups within the school organization.

CONCLUSION

Schools are undergoing enormous change—from a closed system and highly predictive structure to an open system model. This departs from the static and controlled organizational structure that has typified our schooling enterprise. This has occurred as a matter of necessity, owing to significant global changes and societal problems, and has demanded that our leaders be far more reflective and adaptive. It has also pressured our schools to accommodate those populations of students and parents that have historically escaped our system by organizational choice and circumstance.

The organizational mandate to accommodate these new constituent groups has taken the form of a family systems model that focuses on individual need. This new school role traditionally resided in the family but now is being assumed by an integrative school process and structure. At this time, it is incumbent for our leadership to be sensitive to this need and skilled in order to effectively deal with this new organizational challenge. Self-reflection, understanding of one's motives and those of the constituent groups, and strong interpersonal skills underscore the leadership requirements.

Finally, schools can and must be significant factors in determining and advancing students to attain academic skills and social understandings to make them successful and contributing members of our society. Orchestrating that process and creating the organizational "culture" is what is demanded of our leadership today.

NOTES

1. Stanley William Rothstein, "A Short History of Urban Education," in Stanley William Rothstein (Ed.), *Handbook of Schooling in Urban America* (Westport, CT: Greenwood Press, 1993), p. 7.

2. H. Warren Button, "City Schools and School Systems," in ibid., p. 47.

3. Rothstein, "A Short History."

4. Joseph G. Weeres, "The Organizational Structure of Urban Educational Systems," in ibid., p. 127.

5. Dean Corrigan, "An Idea Whose Time Has Come—Again," ATE *Newsletter*, 27 (1) (1993).

6. Jeanne Jehl and Michael Kirst, "Getting Ready to Provide School-linked Services: What Schools Must Do," *Educational Leadership* (Burlingame, CA: ACSA, 1992).

7. Jane L. David, *Restructuring Schools: The Next Generation of Educational Reform* (San Francisco: Jossey-Bass, 1990), p. 211.

8. J. S. Coleman, E. Campbell, C. Hobson, J. McPartland, A. Mood, F. Weinfield, and R. York, *Equality of Educational Opportunity* (Washington, DC: U.S. Government Printing Office, 1966).

9. R. Peterson, "Educational Reform Implementation and Impact in South Carolina," paper presented at the annual meeting of the American Educational Research Association, New Orleans, April 1988.

10. R. R. Edmonds, "A Discussion of the Literature and Issues Related to Effective Schooling" (St. Louis: CEMREL-ERIC Document Reproduction Service No. ED 142 610, 1978), reprinted in Gary A. Davis and Margaret A. Thomas, *Effective Schools and Effective Teachers* (Boston: Allyn and Bacon, 1989).

11. Davis and Thomas, ibid.

12. Edmonds, "A Discussion."

13. Raymond J. Corsini and Danny Wedding, *Current Psychotherapies* (Itasca, Ill.: F. E. Peacock Publishers, 1989).

14. P. Watzlawick, J. Weakland, and R. Fisch, *Change: Principles of Problem Formation and Problem Resolution* (New York: W. W. Norton, 1974).

15. Michael P. Nichols and Richard C. Schwartz, *Family Therapy—Concepts and Methods* (Needham Heights, MA: Allyn and Bacon, 1991).

16. Talcott Parsons, *The Social System* (New York: The Free Press, 1951), p. 5.

17. Davis and Thomas. *Effective Schools.*

18. Virginia Satir, *Conjoint Family Therapy* (Palo Alto, CA: Science and Behavior, Inc., 1983).

19. Charles Perrow, *Complex Organizations* (Palo Alto, CA: Scott, Foresman, 1972).

PART III

RACE

Chapter 9

Race Relations and Segregation in the United States

Walter F. Beckman

Not too many years ago, slave auctions were a regular part of the American scene. It was not until 1865 that this evil practice, and the system of slavery it supported, ended.[1] From the beginning of the slave trade, many slaveholders sought justification for their actions in the writings and traditions of the Holy Bible. They enslaved men, women, and children in the name of natural law, often separating families in order to create more docile and obedient slaves. And through these pernicious practices they provided many of the understandings and attitudes that exist in our own times.

Moreover, in cities and towns of the North, where slavery was unknown, similar attitudes developed as African Americans moved there in search of freedom. Schools, families, governments, and religious bodies taught racist attitudes and beliefs to their children, and they, in turn, passed them on to their children. Between these teachings and those of southerners there was only a difference in intensity. Judging from the newspapers of the times, the same stereotypes of people from other races were used to influence the public throughout the nation. We leave it to others to determine whether such attitudes were, and are, pathological in the clinical sense, but they were used to keep African Americans separate and apart from the mainstream of American life.

Furthermore, it should not be forgotten that the slaves had an important part in building and maintaining the economic system of the new nation. Their segregation was not merely to keep them confined and exploitable. Even after the Emancipation and into the modern age, unemployment and underemployment for African Americans was always twice as high as it was in corresponding white and immigrant groups, and these figures cannot be taken at face value.[2] During bad times African Americans were the first to be laid off, while in good times they were always the last to be rehired. Race prejudice, then, was a socioattitudinal way of justifying the exploitation of their labor by referring to inferiorities and deficiencies that were first articulated during the slavery era. The goals of race prejudice sought to limit the opportunities of African Americans while preventing them from assimilating into the American culture. They insisted that the former slaves remain as they had always been—a group that was outside the mainstream of the America economy.

How do these ideas affect children in American schools today? Children are likely to experience race prejudice at an early age, long before they enter schools. Nevertheless, the schools do their part, as they have done in the past. Schools have been and are bastions of exclusion in the inner cities of the United States today, and have been essentially segregated since their earliest days. There was the period after 1954 when the Supreme Court mandated integration in the nation schools.[3] But these judicial demands were resisted throughout the country, and today the inner-city school districts of the United States are more segregated than ever before. So children are forced to attend segregated schools, where their culture and language are subjected to discriminatory attitudes and practices. These experiences are part of the socialization wherein persons from different races and cultures learn how different they really are when compared to the dominant white culture.

The mistreatment that African American children experience in schools can sometimes be akin to what working class white children experience.[4] But the experiences are not identical by any means. Maintaining social distance is quite different from maintaining racial difference, although some of the effects are similar. Discrimination against youngsters because of their race causes confusion and anguish in children who experience it.

The textbooks used in our schools seldom show African Americans in favorable ways, and children soon learn that their racial backgrounds are not valued by their teachers and schools. They learn that teachers judge them by their work in class *and* by the color of their skin. The suffering that this causes is severe, since it conflicts with the personal identities that children possessed before they entered such schools. Children may become self-conscious of their color in such situations, reproaching their families and themselves for the experiences they have in classrooms. When these incidents are added to those that develop in families that are struggling to survive on the fringes of an exploitative labor market, loneliness and self-rejection often result.[5]

The outcome of these social-psychological pressures to conform to a culture and society that will not allow it to successfully do so produces a self-deflating effect. Schooling seeks to teach African American children their lack of importance in the educational and social worlds. It demands that they accept schooling's definitions and points to the incredibly high rates of academic failure as proof of African American inadequacies. By shaming, excluding, devaluing, and alienating African American children, teachers give youngsters a truer sense of where they stand in the social system of the United States. In these acts of inculcation and socialization, African American children learn that they probably will not be president of the United States—that is, they learn their place in the economic and social pyramid.

Some learn the messages of racism and lose much of their self-esteem, becoming ashamed of their families and heritage. Other African American children respond to the racist messages of state schools by shutting them out, seeking to reaffirm their identities as competent and worthwhile persons by going back to familial, neighborhood, or nationalist groups. They accentuate the values and worldviews of their race and try to understand the exact nature of the racism that is arrayed against them. While schooling is teaching such children they are unworthy and incompetent, African American organizations are trying to counteract these teachings and their effects on the social and personality structures of children. Now and then these ideas find their way into parts of the curriculum of an individual school. But these learnings are soon overwhelmed by the other pedagogic demands of state schools, demands that focus on test scores that are racially and culturally biased against African Americans.[6]

To summarize, then, the slave system gave bondage a religious and economic sanction. Beginning in the seventeenth century, slavery was customarily explained by quotations from the Bible and observations of the wretched condition of the slaves themselves. These allusions to the Bible, in the North as well as the South, provided the religious sanction for the rationalization of an evil and inhuman system of forced labor. In the post–Civil War era, segregation was quickly adopted as a way of maintaining the economic and social inequalities of the past. Whereas according to Constitution and northern practice, the country was committed to a democratic and egalitarian ideology, slavery and then segregation led much of the nation to embrace antidemocratic and stereotypical ideas. The Bill of Rights was ignored and black Americans were seen as inferior beings and chattel property. But the contradictions produced dissenters who argued against these immoral and illegal practices: against slavery, which made white Americans overseers; against avarice, which allowed men to treat their fellows in inhuman ways; against bigotry and discrimination, which permitted white Americans to exploit the labor of their fellow countrymen. The abolitionists merely followed the teachings of the Bible and their own political institutions when they implored the nation to destroy first slavery and then the segregation system.

However, this tiny band of abolitionists had little in common with the general populace. Most Americans continued to receive and accept uncritically the stereotypes and justifications for slavery and segregation. Nevertheless, the idea of racial integration persisted, even though it did not attract large numbers. Its appeal was rational, moral, and intellectual. But segregation met the economic and social needs of American industrialism, and black unemployment and underemployment cushioned the shocks of many of the nation's severe economic downturns. All this was concealed from the national consciousness by segregation and the media: few nations carried such severe, contradictory ideas about equality and special privilege, about democracy and plutocracy, into the twentieth century.

There is little doubt that the maintenance of the segregation system for more than 100 years has much to do with the economic needs of an unrepentent system. The first years of the segregation era were characterized by severe repression of blacks; and in the sharecropping system that replaced the old plantation system we see one tyranny and oppression replacing another with little change in the living standards of the newly freed slaves. Booker T. Washington, in his founding of vocational education at Tuskegee Institute, typified the compromises that many black leaders were forced to adopt in order to survive in a dangerous and repressive America: during the latter part of this period, the Niagra Movement and especially W.E.B. Du Bois began to articulate new goals and demands that focused upon a free and unfettered training of the mind. But if knowledge was so important to the emerging black leadership, ignorance was equally important to those who wished to retain the segregation system. If education could provide black Americans with the training and insights they needed to succeed in American society, it was dangerous to those who had always lived off the subordination and labor of the former slaves.

Today, the same issues of racial segregation are being played out everywhere in the United States, and especially in our inner cities and schools. The prejudices of countless generations have been used to deny Afro-Americans what they need and want: knowledge so they can know and compete; opportunity so their families will not have to bear the shocks and burdens of poverty and alienation; equality and access so that the privileges of a small group will give way to greater equality of opportunity and access for all Americans.

NOTES

1. Peter I. Rose, *They and We: Racial and Ethnic Relations in the United States* (New York: McGraw-Hill, 1990), pp. 20–29.

2. Kurt B. Mayer and Walter Bickley, *Class and Society* (New York: Random House, 1970), Chapter 20.

3. August Meier and Elliot Rudwick, "Radicals and Conservatives: Black Protest in Twentieth Century America," in Peter I. Rose (Ed.), *Old Memories, New Moods* (New York: Atherton, 1970), pp. 124–125.

4. Stanley W. Rothstein, "The Ethics of Coercion: Social Control Practices in an Urban Junior High School," *Urban Education*, 22 (1) (April 1987): 53–72.

5. Arnold M. Rose, *The Negro's Morale* (Minneapolis: University of Minnesota Press, 1949), pp. 85–95.

6. John U. Ogbu, *Minority Education and Caste* (New York: Academic Press, 1978), pp. 221–227.

Chapter 10

Race, Class, and the Educational Marginalization of African Americans: A Historical Perspective

Mougo Nyaggah and Wacira Gethaiga

In the American community, education has always been a critical issue in the struggle to achieve full human rights. This struggle began in the colonial era early in the seventeenth century, when stereotypes of Africans as animals, perceptions of their inability to comprehend the written word, and denial of literacy for fear of awakening a desire and a demand for rights led to substandard, rural-based training after emancipation, segregation (*Plessy v. Ferguson*), and resegregation (after *Brown v. Board of Education*). Thus it is clear that the history of education for African Americans has been informed by structural institutional racism designed to keep them at the bottom of the social system.

BACKGROUND AND INTRODUCTION ABOUT AFRICA

Contrary to myths and "traditional wisdom," African American education predates the American experience. Slaves in the New World left records that attest to their prior education in Africa before enslavement. One freed slave, Omar ibn Obeid, who gained his liberty after over twenty years, recounted how he had studied Arabic from his father and uncle in West Africa.[1] Before their arrival in the New World, many such slaves knew how to read, write, recite, and pray in Arabic—the language of Islam—which had been introduced in Western Africa from across the Sahara Desert starting in the tenth century.[2] Islam thus played a major role in the development of West African civilization in medieval and postmedieval times. It was adopted by the African political elite, notable among whom were Mansa Musa and Askia Muhammand, the rulers of the great empires of Mali and Songhay, respectively. These rulers went on to recruit Muslim scholars and start centers of learning at Timbuktu and Gao.[3] Literate people at the courts of the African rulers were employed as scribes, government commercial representatives in north Africa, or as merchants or teachers.

Around AD 1200 the Mali empire emerged with its rulers embracing Islam and using it as a unifying ideology and as the basis of solidarity with the Muslim merchants who participated in the salt and gold trade in this region. While the Mali and Songhay rulers' pilgrimages to Mecca fulfilled one of the five tenets of Islam—a visit to Mecca at least once in one's lifetime—such journeys were also advertisements for trade and served to attract intellectuals to these states as it became clear that West African political acumen and economic growth gave foreign scholars confidence to locate there.[4]

The Berber merchants also brought Islam across the Sahara to the Kingdom of Ghana, where some were employed in the capital, Kumbi, as record keepers or trade facilitators. The purist Almohads and Almoravids also contributed to the spread of Islam in Ghana and eventually to the downfall of this kingdom. This contact between Islam and the African kingdoms accounted for the literacy of some Africans who were captured into slavery.

Once the Portuguese and other Europeans reached West Africa in the fifteenth century, the decline of the western Sudanic states accelerated in proportion to the increase of the European activities on the Gulf of Guinea—a coastal region extending from Senegambia to the Congo. The western Sudanic savanna political states, which were maintained by the revenues derived from trans-Saharan trade, declined as those funds plummeted following the diversion of that trade to the coastal regions. West African exports and imports passed through the coastal trading depots set up by various European powers.[5] This shift led in turn to the rise of new forest region states—Asante and Dahomey. The older forest states—Benin, Yoruba, and Igbo city states[6]—also became stronger.

The decline of the Sudanic states in the seventeenth century coincided with the European exploration of and expansion into the Americas, the subsequent decimation of the Native Americans and Bishop Las Casas' theological justification for the importation of African slave labor to continue the production of raw materials—sugarcane, cotton, tobacco, and minerals—for European markets. The slaves sold in the coastal slave marts came from the coastal as well as from the Sudanic states, where many had acquired literacy and were already followers of Islam.[7] These slaves would constitute the black gold exported to the Americas legally until 1807 and as part of illegitimate trade for most of the nineteenth century to the end of the Civil War.

The number of Africans seized on that continent and brought to the Americas and Caribbean islands during the four and half centuries since Columbus' landing in Santo Domingo is still a topic of disagreement among scholars. Although earlier estimates ranged as high as 45 million Africans, recent figures are around 10 million.[8] This figure does not include those who died either in the internecine wars to supply slaves or on the high seas in the Middle Passage. While disagreements about the numbers exist, there is general consensus on how they were captured and who was sold to the European merchants: wars and conflicts between one state or community and another resulted in captives and prisoners who were assimilated in the society of the captors or sold to reduce the adversaries' potential military recruits in the future or for economic gain.[9] European slave adventurers working with paid African collaborators pursued and captured Africans along the coast; African long-distance traders brought the slaves as far as 200 miles from the Sudanic savanna to the coastal trading depots.[10] Many of those slaves were Muslim and had studied the Quran.

When the Asante King Osei Bonsu was asked why he sold his fellow Africans into slavery, his response was that he believed that the African slaves under the Europeans lived under the same conditions as slaves lived in Africa.[11] This was a major misunderstanding: slaves in Asante, the king's reference point, enjoyed numerous rights:[12] they could marry free men or women; their children could move up the political and social ladder (two of the Asante kings in the nineteenth century were sons of a beautiful war captive who married into the royal family); slaves and their descendants could own and dispose of property as well as engage in trade;[13] and slaves were eventually assimilated into the society of their captors through marriage to free men and women. This gave slaves firm roots in their new homeland. In the Songhay empire, eunuch slaves were an important higher administrative cadre.[14] What the Asante king did not know was that the slaves in the Americas were chattel, property without the rights accorded many slaves in Africa.

SLAVERY CULTURE AND EDUCATION BEFORE THE CIVIL WAR

The slavery culture era, from the founding of the Virginia colony through the War of Independence to the Civil War, was dominated by conflicts centered on African American roles in the political economy that disempowered and marginalized them. The white landowners—planters or yeoman—constituted part of the larger dominant class, which originally came from England to exploit the resources of the new colonial economy established under the philosophy of mercantilism.[15] In order for them to maintain their dominance over the colonial political economy, still tied to the metropolitan motherland, the colonial state sanctioned the importation of slaves and devised elaborate systems to control them and minimize competition. Financial interests that sanctioned the fifteenth-century exploration were also influential in lobbying for legislation to set up joint stock ventures or chartered companies, like the Virginia Company, which founded colonial settlements in America.[16] This same financial class dominated and exploited the well-known "triangle trade" between Europe, Africa, and America. Slaves were the most important "commodity" in this trade, and the wealth derived from them was critical in England's capital accumulation through the Industrial Revolution.[17]

Under mercantilism the colonial economy was closely tied to the economic policies of the English capitalist state.[18] When the slaves arrived in Virginia early in the sixteenth century, they were regarded as labor resources for producing wealth from the land just as were the indentured servants or the Native Americans. The Africans who came to Virginia early were accorded the same rights as the white indentured servants: they were given land and freedom after their indenture service. Blacks who gained freedom and property proved their ability to achieve success if there were no racial or class-based barriers. This early success was a manifestation of their work ethic from Africa rather than from their white neighbors, who adhered to the Calvinistic work ethic and the spirit of capitalism.[19] However, demands for plantation production and labor scarcity in the middle of the sixteenth century ushered in enslavement laws against the Africans.[20] The beginning of the slave laws in Virginia and their spread to other colonies as similar capitalist demands dictated them was also the start of the marginalization of African Americans, which continues to the present.

The African slaves in the American colonies found their lives dependent on and controlled by these capitalist social relationships and the legal norms of the political economy that existed in the colonies. Considering the concepts of seventeenth-century mercantilism and the function for which the colonies were founded, the slaves were part of the emerging pre-Industrial Revolution capitalist economy.[21] Columbus' accidental landing in America while looking for much-desired East Indian spices led to the discovery of fertile land and mineral resources that required an abundant source of labor.[22] The new colonies, the native inhabitants, and the slaves from Africa were to be put into a production relationship by the owners of investment capital from the nations that supported the establishment of such colonies. In the ensuing production arrangements the welfare of African Americans was immaterial: they were often forbidden to have families, children could be separated and sold, and family stability was rarely encouraged because it hindered effective market exchange of slave production units.

As with family life, education was considered unnecessary for the slaves in their designated tasks in the mines or in the sugarcane or cotton plantations. During the colonial era and the early nineteenth century, education for the Africans in the Americas was considered dangerous: it raised their consciousness and encouraged revolts. While the American colonies did not support education for African Americans—this was to wait until after the Civil War—the prevailing myths and stereotypes helped perpetuate the denial of education even to those Africans who had encountered it in Africa.[23] These were the same myths used to justify enslavement and to relieve Europeans of their guilt: the slaves brought here were saved from cannibalism, they would be baptized and readied for salvation, and they would benefit from contact with the white man's civilization under slavery.[24] Ironically, there was a prevailing fear in colonial America and in the early nineteenth century that teaching slaves about Christianity would be harmful because slaves might equate their situation with that of the Jews in Egypt and expect a "messiah" to liberate them as Moses did according to

Biblical accounts. Indeed, African Americans cited the Bible to question the master-slave relationship based on exploitation, the greed and cruelty of masters, and other contradictions found in analyzing the slave owners' Judeo-Christian morality contrasted with their commitment to laissez-faire capitalist practices.

In spite of a systematic policy of denying slaves education, there were African Americans who were able to educate themselves during the colonial era and from Independence to the Civil War.[25] As Henry Bullock points out, most opportunities were inadvertent, when the slave master's relatives taught slaves to read and do arithmetic, or when the children of the liaisons between the master and slave were manumitted with provisions for an inheritance that could be used to pay for education.[26] Sometimes a little education was provided by the slave master in order to improve the slaves' skills in crafts; some slaves were given basic literacy skills to function as bookkeepers on the plantation or to read measurements in carpentry. Some notable slaves who were availed such opportunities manifested their ability to learn and left their biographies.[27]

The marginalization of African Americans in the colonial state could therefore be mitigated by manumission or the purchase of freedom, followed by the acquisition of education to assure mobility into the ranks of professionals, skilled craftsmen, or the yeoman class.[28] Most whites in the South did not own slaves, and free African Americans made a living like most of these whites: they were hired as laborers or as craftspeople—carpenters, masons, shoemakers, boatmakers, spinners, seamstresses—if they had apprenticed to a trade and gained the necessary skill.[29] Others owned property they had bought or inherited from their former masters after manumission, while a smaller group owned their own businesses.

Although education was not readily available for most people in the colonies, its accessibility to African Americans was limited even more by the common myths and stereotypes about the Africans. The views held by the Euro-American investors justified the notion that African Americans were suitable only for manual labor and were not endowed with high intellect.[30] However, there were many who believed that African Americans had the capacity to acquire knowledge and ideas and use them to their own advantage. As Bullock has pointed out, the established policy was to keep the African Americans illiterate, since no education was essential to do the bulk of plantation or domestic work. But various economic and social factors intervened and resulted in blacks acquiring education, which they subsequently used for their advancement.[31]

However, the decision to provide or withhold education was a critical variable in the overall economic, social, and political order. In the southern states education was less important to all classes than in the northern states, where literacy was valued and its provision to the public was part of the Puritan value system with its emphasis on reading the Bible for salvation. Education was accessible to blacks in the private homes of their masters, in the church-sponsored Sunday or sabbath schools, and in the public schools in the northern states.[32] Many blacks, either brought directly from Africa as slaves or born in slavery and manumitted, aggressively utilized educational opportunities and later became famous: Phyllis Wheatley—who studied the classics in Latin, as well as history, geography and, astronomy; Benjamin Banneker—who studied mathematics and surveying; and many nineteenth-century slave leaders, abolitionists, and ordinary slaves.[33]

Such demonstrable intellectual abilities by African Americans affected the slave-culture capital class paradoxically. On the one hand, they promulgated the myth that slaves were incapable of learning; on the other, they feared that education of the slaves contributed to production "depressions" due to slave dissatisfaction with their lot. In their view, these problems could be prevented only through a variety of strategic political and religious manipulations to deny education to the blacks. Indeed after the revolts led by Denmark Vesey, Gabriel Prosser, and Nat Turner, and the issuance of David Walker's fiery Appeal calling for black rebellion,[34] many states enacted tighter laws restricting African American movement, gatherings, and access to education.[35] Conflicting arguments were articulated: some opposed these restrictions and contended that religious education could be used to control blacks if they could read the Scriptures and learn the catechism and hymns; others argued that such literary knowledge could be used for intra- or interplantation communication, circulation of ideas of discontent, reading of abolition tracts, and writing to encourage flight to the northern states or Canada.

On the proeducation side, several religious or philanthropic groups had merged in the colonial side that were dedicated or financially committed to promoting African American access to education. The Quakers worked primarily in Pennsylvania and neighboring states; the Manumission Society began funding the African Free School in New York shortly after Independence; and the Society for the Propagation of the Gospel started schools in several states. Most of these groups advocated the educational ideas formulated in 1685 in Europe by a Swiss Quaker named Thomas Budd.[36] He believed that schools should be started in every town for the instruction of boys in both academic and trade subjects like mathematical instrument making, jewelry, or shoemaking, and of girls in subjects like spinning, sewing, and knitting. This is the kind of education that was set up in the private or church-supported schools. In one African American school in New Jersey in 1819 the emphasis was solely on academic subjects: reading, writing, spelling, English grammar, geography, arithmetic, and, for advanced students, natural philosophy, astronomy, theology, and ecclesiastical history.

Unfortunately, in many towns and counties where local decisions were made for funding education or determining teachers' salaries, African Americans did not have any political power through the vote to elect the leadership entrusted with making decisions, some of which affected their welfare adversely: underfunding education or paying African American teachers lower salaries than whites. In other areas, there was no political will by school officials and administrators to enforce the state laws promulgating compulsory education for all children. For example, in New Jersey African American children were refused admission to schools and the funds allocated for their education were returned to the county at the end of the year.[37]

Although the slave trade "ended" in 1808, economic development on the frontier, in the western territories, and in the Southwest with the Louisiana purchase five years earlier led to an increased demand for slaves to use in agricultural production in the new territories.[38] This demand for more labor coupled with the prohibition of the external slave trade led to the rise of slave breeding and the internal slave trade between the upper southern states, such as Maryland, Virginia, and North Carolina, and the deep southern states, such as Louisiana, Mississippi, Georgia, and Alabama. The economic investments and returns were so attractive that English financiers extended credit in that region, resulting in increased cotton production and stricter control of the African Americans.[39] These restrictions, new capital investments, and production relationships led to northern and southern conflict, which was accelerated by price fluctuations and interminable debates on slavery.

NEO-SLAVERY CULTURE AND EDUCATION AFTER THE CIVIL WAR

The North and South conflicts over slave-based political economy and culture culminated in the Civil War—the worst bloodbath in the nation's history—and, ultimately, in the emancipation of the slaves. While the end of the war witnessed the physical liberation of African Americans, their handicaps and marginalization continued in the postwar years.[40] After a hiatus of two decades of relative progress during Reconstruction, the old production and class relations were restored under the Jim Crow laws and the implementation of the late-nineteenth-century new state constitutions in the south. The economic security of the famous "forty acres and a mule" that the slaves had hoped for were dashed by white sympathies for the south.[41] Neither Abraham Lincoln nor his successors supported the proposed land acquisition and distribution to the freedmen. Such a program would have provided economic stability and fostered development of African American competitiveness and viability. In contrast, the denial of land led to the continuation of the culture of poverty and dependence created during slavery, and it was now buttressed with violence and new antiblack laws. The political empowerment gained during and after the war was lost and this meant the reestablishment of the old slavery culture of black marginalization, including limited access to education.[42]

These events did not cause African Americans to falter, however; following the Civil War, their faith in education intensified and was translated into the advocacy of free compulsory education for all children. Northern teachers who came to the South commented on the determination of the southern black children and their enthusiasm and eagerness to learn. The debate over the value of academic versus industrial/vocational education raged for the next forty years.[43]

It eventually split African Americans into two camps, one led by Booker T. Washington, the founder of Tuskegee University, and the other by W.E.B. Du Bois, the founder of the National Association for the Advancement of Colored People (NAACP). The substance of the Washington-Du Bois debate, taken together with the institutionalization of black education due to increased funding by private sources or public funds, is central to our argument in this chapter that the slave and neoslavery cultures have contributed to African American marginalization.

At that time, there were public discussions and policy statements asserting the role of the state in the provision of education and economic support to the emancipated African Americans. The ideas that emerged and were implemented under the aegis of a new agency—the Freedmen's Bureau—were interconnected with the existing political economy and continuing production relationships modified only briefly by the short-term loss of the ownership rights of the planter class.[44] Some aspects of the relationship between the former slaves and their masters might have changed but not so the economic production relationships, which came to resemble those between free laborers and the plantation class in the South or between the laborers and the industrial capitalists in the North, in the sense that subordination and exploitation continued based on race and class variables.

Education, as one of the key variables, could not be provided and paid for without economic benefits to the providers. Issues included the kinds of schools, curricula, pedagogy, funding, compulsion, and control, as well as the contribution of education to the political economy.[45] Whether formal education was going to be academic or industrial/vocational, the important consideration was that it should provide the students with the skills useful to the existing agricultural political economy or the emerging industrial capitalist state.

African American marginalization was also intensified by the violence and intimidation of the post-Reconstruction era, the Great Compromise of 1878, and the Jim Crow laws that lasted until the 1950s and 1960s.[46] By the end of the nineteenth century the blacks had lost the minimal political power and related rights they had gained after the Civil War: the provisions of the Fourteenth and Fifteenth constitutional Amendments were diluted in 1883 by the nullification of the slaughterhouse cases dealing with the 1875 civil rights law; various states enacted discriminatory constitutions; segregation in transportation, hotels, education, and other facilities was accomplished by the United States Supreme Court's sanction of the separate but equal doctrine based on *Plessy v. Ferguson*;[47] and the agricultural production relationships entrenched a neofeudal exploitation system between the planter class and sharecropping serfs.[48]

In spite of Booker T. Washington's success in gaining funding support to establish vocational schools, the emerging black vanguard, who articulated their ideas in the Niagara Movement,[49] challenged Washington and added another dimension to the proletarianization of the African American. Du Bois argued that black acquisition of industrial education would be meaningless if blacks were not accorded the other rights guaranteed under the law and Constitution, the most important of these being political power gained through suffrage.[50] Essentially, Du Bois believed that a special type of education for blacks limited their opportunities for advancement; therefore, the black child should be accorded the same rights as the white students, either to academic or to industrial education.

In reality, the blacks lacked land, the main source of revenue to support an educational system. They became "wards" of the new economic order, and thus the survival of their educational institutions depended on the good will of their enemies. Whatever they received was given grudgingly and they paid for it through hard work in sharecropping or low-paying manual jobs in the budding industries.

The split in the black intelligentsia extended into the black communities and was reflected in local debates, both in the South and the North, just as it is today. There were those in the community who advocated segregated industrial schools, partly to provide employment opportunities to African American teachers who were not hired in mixed or white schools, and partly for the psychological support provided by black teachers to black students.[51] The other side in the community saw the racially separate schools as limiting their children's access to the professions and social mobility. It was the rejection of these limitations and the search for improved production relationships that led many African Americans to flee to the North in the first two decades of the twentieth century.

But the northern states were not the promised land they were expected to be.[52] While in the South the political economy and the production relationships were based on demands of the slave-holding class, in the North they were based on the demands of industrial capitalists. The industrial moguls who had contributed funds to establish schools or support the special curricula for former slaves expected skilled graduates to increase productivity in new manufacturing ventures, transportation infrastructures, and export and import commercial activities.[53] The blacks found themselves in economic and job competition with the poor or lower class whites, many of them recent immigrants from eastern and southern Europe or descendants of the earlier Irish immigrants.[54] Often there were clashes of these exploited proletariats. In most cases the blacks lost because of the preference of industrial capitalists for white workers.

The most formidable obstacle to the African Americans in the North was, as in the South, the legal system. Numerous local and state laws were enacted and implemented to institutionalize the nineteenth-century Jim Crow doctrine. The NAACP and, to a lesser degree, the Urban League challenged these laws in court and had some successes.[55] However, many capricious laws were upheld by biased local, state, or federal courts. Among this legislation the worst, in terms of limitations on education, were concerned with residential segregation; restrictive covenants excluding African Americans from certain neighborhoods encouraged school officials and administrators to set up separate districts or to gerrymander the boundaries for racially segregated schools. For African American children residing in the "wrong" school districts, the separation was accomplished by forced transfers or in some cases by setting up separate classrooms for different races.[56]

As education was the avenue to job opportunities and class mobility, African American frustrations intensified when organized labor mounted opposition against blacks.[57] The 1920s witnessed massive industrial expansion and productivity. At the same time, the pens of Harlem Renaissance writers celebrated black pride but also attacked the methods used to keep the blacks down, and equated the northern political, social, and economic control of neoslavery to that of slavery.[58] This was not lost on the students in the segregated schools and resulted in the student riots of the 1920s. These riots could be seen as the continuation of the slave revolts due to their limited potential for success, but also as the forerunners of the sit-ins and protest marches of the 1960s, which were decidedly successful after the Supreme Court struck down the Jim Crow legal yoke, *Plessy v. Ferguson*, by overturning the school discrimination laws in *Brown v. Board of Education*.[59]

MARGINALIZATION SINCE THE 1954 *BROWN* RULING

The Supreme Court ruling on the *Brown v. Board of Education* case in 1954 did not end the lack or denial of education of African Americans. Segregated education had meant inferior education, which in turn led to low-income jobs and marginalization of the majority of the blacks' lower class status. The curriculum, even in the states that pretended to provide "separate but equal" facilities, was substandard. Most educators believed, with Mississippi's Governor James K. Vardaman, the "White Chief," that too much education would render blacks "unfit for work which the white man has prescribed and which he will be forced to perform." The long period of separation had also taught white children that they were better than African Americans. The national socialization process on the inferiority of the blacks permeated down to children as young as age four. It was obvious to them that blacks were not fit for anything beyond being servants and garbage collectors.[60]

It can be argued that the rejection of school integration nationally may have had something to do with racism against the African American, but may also have reflected the fear by people in the educational hierarchy about the kind of education the blacks have had in those substandard schools. Integration was certainly not a panacea. In areas where integration of the schools has taken place, black students still fail. Some African American scholars have explored a return to separate schools, while some maintain that integration still offers more opportunities to children of all ethnic groups and is more appropriate in a pluralistic society. The fact is that conditions in most residentially segregated ghettoes have not changed. School boundaries and districts have remained technically the same and still promote segregated facilities, including school systems.[61] Flight to the suburbs by black middle-class professionals, while benefiting the individuals, has arguably deprived the ghettoes of important leadership and role models.

With these factors in mind, we can see why the problems are still with us. Joel Perlman has recently argued that it is difficult to determine exactly what has contributed to African American marginalization.[62] It could be because of their own slave culture and tradition—here he is in company with Thomas Sowell—or it could be because of racism and discrimination—here Du Bois would be a supporter. Our discussion leads us to conclude that the slave culture, buttressed by denial of economic resources and free political choices and institutionalized through intimidation and violence, resulted in a national policy of segregation and substandard education, which has militated against the movement of the African American community away from marginalization toward the mainstream.

NOTES

1. See Omar ibn Obeid, *American Historical Review*, 30 (July 1925).

2. J. F. Hopkins and Nehemia Levtzion (Eds. and Trans.), *Corpus of Early Arabic Sources for West African History* (Cambridge: Cambridge University Press, 1982), 285–297; E. W. Bovill, *The Golden Trade of the Moors* (London: Oxford University Press, 1958).

3. Nehemia Levtzion, *Ancient Ghana and Mali* (London: Methuen, 1973), and *Muslim and Chiefs in West Africa* (Oxford: Clarendon Press, 1968). See also his article in *Journal of African History*, 4 (3) (1963); H.A.R. Gibb, *The Travels of Ibn Batuta, A.D. 1325–1354* (Millwood, NY: Kraus Reprint, 1986), and *Mohammedanism: An Historical Survey* (London: Oxford University Press, 1969); J. Spencer Trimingham, *Islam in West Africa* (Oxford: Clarendon Press, 1959), and *The Influence of Islam upon Africa* (New York: Praeger, 1959).

4. John Hunwick, "Songhay, Bornu and Hausaland in the Sixteenth Century," in J. F. Ade Ajayi and Michael Crowder (Eds.), *History of West Africa*, Vol. I. (New York: Longman, 1971), pp. 202–239.

5. Daniel P. Mannix and Malcolm Crowley, *Black Cargoes: A History of the Atlantic Slave Trade, 1518–1865* (New York: Viking Press, 1962), pp. 1–49, 69–103; Edward Reynolds, *Stand the Storm: A History of the Atlantic Slave Trade* (New York: Allison & Busby, 1985), Ch. 1, 2.

6. I. A. Akinjogbin, *Dahomey and Its Neighbours, 1708–1818* (Cambridge: Cambridge University Press, 1967); G. I. Jones, *The Trading States of the Oil Rivers: A Study of Political Development in Eastern Nigeria* (London: Oxford University Press, 1963); Karl Polanyi, *Dahomey and the Slave Trade* (Seattle: University of Washington Press, 1966).

7. Hopkins and Levtzion, *Corpus of Early Arabic Sources*, pp. 294–296.

8. Philip D. Curtin, *The Atlantic Slave Trade: A Census* (Madison: University of Wisconsin Press, 1969). His questioning of earlier figures of slaves brought to the Americas and conclusion that slightly less than 10 million arrived in the new world sparked a heated debate among scholars. The consensus is that this figure ranges between 10 and 12 million (p. 253); J. E. Inikori, "Measuring the Atlantic Slave Trade: An Assessment of Curtin and Anstey," *Journal of African History*, 17 (1976): 197–223.

9. The fall of the Congo kingdom of Nzinga Mbemba—a.k.a. Afonso I—in the sixteenth century is a classic example of an African state's political disintegration under heavy intervention by Portuguese traders to generate slaves for Brazil.

10. Elizabeth Donnan, *Documents Illustrative of the History of the Slave Trade to America*, 4 vols. (Washington, DC: Carnegie Institute, 1930–1935). This is the best collection of material dealing with this subject until the abolition of the trade by the British in 1807.

11. Nana Owusu Ansah, oral interview, April 3, 1971.

12. Robert S. Rattray, *Ashanti Law and Constitution* (London: Oxford University Press, 1929); Mougo Nyaggah, "Social Origins of the Asante Traditional Administrators: 1700–1900," unpublished Ph.D. dissertation, University of California, Berkeley, 1974.

13. In Igboland, Nigeria, one of the leading businessmen, Jaja, was a former slave who rose to be the leader of trading "canoe house" group. Ajayi and Crowder, *History of West Africa*, p. 88.

14. Levtzion in ibid., pp. 146–147.

15. Susan P. Lee and Peter Passell, *A New Economic View of American History* (New York: Norton, 1979), pp. 15, 28.

16. Ibid., Ch. 1.

17. Ibid., p. 19.

18. Ibid., Ch. 2.

19. John Hope Franklin and Alfred A. Moss, Jr. *From Slavery to Freedom: A History of Negro Americans* (New York: Knopf, 1980), pp. 55–59.

20. Max Weber, "Protestant Ethic and Spirit of Capitalism," in Poggi Giafranco (Ed.), *Calvinism and the Capitalist Spirit* (Amherst: University of Massachusetts Press, 1983).

21. Lee and Passell, *New Economic View*, Ch. 2.

22. Walter Rodney, *How Europe Underdeveloped Africa* (Washington, D.C.: Howard University Press, 1982), Ch. 2; Eric Williams, *Capitalism and Slavery* (New York: Oxford University Press, 1966).

23. Philip D. Curtin and Paul Bohannan, *Africa and the Africans*, 3rd ed. (Prospect Heights, IL: Waveland Press, 1988), pp. 3–18, 50–61. Many blacks opposed this strenuously. For the views of two free blacks in 1813, see Herbert Aptheker (Ed.), *Documentary History of the Negro People in the United States* (New York: Citadel Press, 1963), pp. 57–65.

24. Curtin and Bohannan, *Africa and the Africans*, 6–8.

25. See Henry L. Gates, Jr. (Ed.), *The Classic Slave Narratives* (New York: New American Library, 1987) for the life stories of Olaudah Equiano, Mary Prince, Frederick Douglass, and the controversial Harriet Jacob. For black college education before the Civil War, see Frank Bowles et al., *Between Two Worlds: A Profile of Negro Higher Education* (New York: McGraw-Hill, 1971), Ch. 2.

26. Henry A. Bullock, *A History of Negro Education in the South from 1619 to the Present* (Cambridge, MA: Harvard University Press, 1967).

27. Gates, *Slave Narratives*.

28. The existence of thirteen colonies has no bearing on the "state" in the political sense, as the slave laws and conditions varied only in degree from one colony to the other, and, in fact, the political economy of the new republic continued the same production relationships. Our concept of marginalization refers to consequences of articu-

lated or implied assumptions and actions that hinder most African Americans from mainstream American society, deny them equal opportunities and rights, and relegate them to the societal periphery on the basis of historical mythologies and stereotypes about the African race. And our class concept relates to the group consciousness existent in any society-based political economic ideology and production relationships that are manifest in the social stratification. African American marginalization and lower class strata converge, albeit since colonial Virginia days the African Americans who owned land (yeoman), skilled craftspeople or business owners and managers, professionals (engineers like Benjamin Banneker, doctors like James Darman, or academics like Du Bois) clearly do not belong to that class. But they too suffered from the consequences of marginalization based on dominant class assumptions, racist ideology, mythologies, and stereotypes.

29. Marion M. T. Wright, *The Education of Negroes in New Jersey* (New York: Columbia University Press, 1941), 40.

30. Lee and Passell (*New Economic View*) point out that U. B. Philips "believed that the African Negroes were inferior in intelligence to whites; thus they were fit only for work on southern plantation," p. 162; this was contrary to what a free black, George Lawrence, had argued in 1813: "There could be many reasons given, to prove that the mind of an African is not inferior to that of an European; yet to do so would be superfluous. It would be like adding hardness to the diamond, or lustre to the sun." Their talented minds were stifled by "the merciless power of their masters." Aptheker, *Documentary History*, p. 58.

31. Bullock, *History of Negro Education*, p. 15.

32. Carleton Mabee, *Black Education in New York State: From Colonial Times to Modern Times* (Syracuse, NY: Syracuse University Press, 1979), pp. 1–45, 69–84.

33. Robert Sherer, *Subordination or Liberation: The Development and Conflicting Theories of Black Education in Nineteenth Century Alabama* (Tuscaloosa: University of Alabama Press, 1977), p. 33.

34. Thomas R. Frazier, *Afro-American History: Primary Sources*, 2nd ed. (Chicago: Dorsey Press, 1988), pp. 49, 91. This is a good source for primary material in one volume. For other useful edited books on blacks, see Howard Broz (Ed.), *African-American Social and Political Thought, 1850–1920* (London: Transaction Publishers, 1992); Darlene C. Hine, *The State of Afro-American History* (Baton Rouge: Louisiana State University Press, 1986); a comprehensive one volume by African American specialists is John P. Davis (Ed.), *The American Negro Reference Book* (Englewood Cliffs, NJ: Prentice-Hall, 1966).

35. Joel Williamson, *The Crucible of Race* (New York: Oxford University Press, 1984), pp. 16–18; Thomas Sowell, *Ethnic America: A History* (New York: Basic Books, 1981).

36. Wright, *The Education*, p. 32.

37. Ibid., p. 45.

38. Douglass C. North, *The Economic Growth of the United States, 1790–1860* (New York: Norton, 1966), p. 201, Ch. 9. The increased investment in slaves from 1802 when a prime slave cost $600 to 1860 at $1,800 reflected the crop value increase per slave during the same period from $14.68 to $101.09, p. 128.

39. Ibid., p. 187; Richard Kluger, *Simple Justice* (New York: Knopf, 1976), pp. 40–42.

40. Bowles, *Between Two Worlds*, Ch. 3.

41. Kluger, *Simple Justice*, p. 44. According to Kluger, Andrew Jackson "hated slavery more for what it had done to the poor-whites of the south than to those in actual bondage"; Donald Spivey, *Schooling for the New Slavery* (Westport, CT: Greenwood Press, 1978), pp. 3–37; Robert A. Margo, *Race and Schooling in the South, 1880–1950* (Chicago: University of Chicago Press, 1990), Chs. 1–2.

42. Kluger, *Simple Justice*, p. 257.

43. Bowles, *Between Two Worlds*, p. 36.

44. Eugene D. Genovese, *Political Economy of Slavery*, 2nd ed. (Middletown, CT: Wesleyan University Press, 1989).

45. Kluger, *Simple Justice*, pp. 632–634; Sherer, *Subordination*, pp. 7–10, 147–148.

46. W.E.B. Du Bois, in *The Negro American Family* (New York: Negro University Press, 1969) has shown that social differentiation or class distinctions among African Americans existed based on education, occupation, income, property, and the residential areas, pp. 64–96, 134–148.

47. Kluger, *Simple Justice*, pp. 73–76.

48. Marc Bloch, *Feudal Society: Social Classes and Political Organization*, Vol. 2 (Trans. L. A. Manyon) (Chicago: University of Chicago Press, 1961), pp. 443–446.

49. Elliot M. Rudwick, *W.E.B. Du Bois: Propagandist of the Negro Protest* (New York: Atheneum, 1978), Ch. 5. See pp. 96–98 for the demands of the Niagara Movement.

50. Page Smith, *The Rise of Industrial America*, vol. 6 (New York: McGraw-Hill, 1984). Smith quotes William Sinclair to illustrate the lost power: "with the ballot the negro is a man; an American among Americans. Without the ballot he is a serf, less than a slave, a thing," p. 619.

51. Judy J. Mohraz, *The Separate Problem: Case Studies of Black Education in the North, 1900–1930* (Westport, CT: Greenwood Press, 1979).

52. Joel Perlman, *Ethnic Structures: Schooling and Social Structure among the Irish, Italians, Jews, and Blacks in an American City, 1880–1935* (New York: Cambridge University Press, 1989). He writes that "the social-class of the black groups worked against their school progress," p. 180. They were also discriminated against in employment, and tracking and segregation in schools led to low grade attainment, Ch. 5.

53. Bowles, *Between Two Worlds*, pp. 44–47; John E. Fisher, *The John F. Slater Fund: A Nineteenth Century Affirmative Action for Negro Education* (New York: University Press of America, 1986), pp. 111–117.

54. Stanley Lieberson, *A Piece of the Pie: Blacks and White Immigrants since 1880* (Berkeley: University of California Press, 1980). Oscar Handlin, *The Newcomers: Negroes and Puerto Ricans in a Changing Metropolis* (Cambridge, MA: Harvard University Press, 1959).

55. For the initial objectives set by the founders of this organization, see Bullock, *History of Negro Education*, p. 212.

56. Mohraz, *The Separate Problem*, p. 31, has shown how this system worked in three northern cities.

57. Du Bois, *The Negro American Family*, pp. 69–79.

58. Aptheker, *Documentary History*, pp. 68–70.

59. Bullock, *History of Negro Education*, pp. 216–249; J. Harvie Wilkinson III, *From Brown to Bakke: The Supreme Court and School Integration, 1954–1978* (New York: Oxford University Press, 1979), pp. 11–26.

60. Video: "Black History: Lost, Stolen or Strayed," 1968, narr. by Bill Cosby.

61. Rosemary Salomone, *Equal Education Under Law: Legal Rights and Federal Policy in the Post-Brown Era* (New York: St. Martin's Press, 1986), Ch. 2.

62. Perlman, *Ethnic Structures*, pp. 215–219; Thomas Sowell, *Ethnic America: A History* (New York: Basic Books, 1981).

Chapter 11

Serving Asian American Children in School: An Ecological Perspective

Mikyong Kim-Goh

Despite rapid growth of the Asian American population in recent decades, there is a paucity of research on this group in general, and on children in particular. According to the 1990 Census, Asian Americans are the fastest growing ethnic group in the United States, showing 108 percent growth since 1980.[1] Immigration accounted for three-fourths of the population increase among Asian Americans during the 1980s.[2] This population is expected to continue to grow rapidly with a rate of over 150 percent growth between 1990 and 2020.[3] Currently, the Chinese are the largest group, following by Filipinos and Japanese; however, the numbers of Asian Indian, Korean, and Vietnamese are growing rapidly and may soon surpass the larger groups.[4]

Asian Americans have typically been perceived as the "model minority," and their educational achievement and economic success have been well documented.[5] However, the stereotype of model minority with few social or psychological problems obscures the serious needs that exist in many Asian American communities. It ignores the heterogeneity and diversity among these groups and vast problems encountered by recent Southeast Asian refugees and new immigrants in accessing the services available. In fact, even though the average family income of Asian Americans is slightly higher than that of whites, their personal incomes are lower than whites; the poverty rate of Asian Americans is nearly twice that of whites, and poverty is especially prevalent among the Southeast Asian refugees.[6] The geographical distribution of Asian Americans reflects a strong concentration in the West (55.7%) as opposed to the Northeast (18.3%), Midwest (10.6%), or South (15.4%).[7] In comparison, only 21.2 percent of all Americans live in the West.[8]

Although Asian American children comprise only 3.4 percent of the total enrollment in public elementary and secondary schools in the United States, they represent a substantially larger proportion in some regions, such as Hawaii and California, 67.9 and 10.8 percent, respectively.[9] The objective of this chapter is to examine problem areas pertinent to Asian immigrant children in American school systems, and to provide practical suggestions that offer viable field-based solutions. To accomplish this task, an ecological perspective is useful in that it enables one to examine various levels of an environmental system and the interaction between individuals and the environment.[10] The ecological perspective views the growing child as an active agent in a series of interlocking systems, ranging from the microsystems of the family and the school to the macrosystem of governmental, social, and economic policies.

Each of these systems poses risks and opportunities for the child interacting with the environment at successive developmental stages. Because of its broader orientation to view an individual within one's larger contextual environment, this ecological perspective is especially relevant in analyzing the impact of poverty, immigration, and discrimination on the psychosocial development and adjustment of minority children. For instance, one cannot understand the current experiences and needs of Asian American children without the background knowledge of Asian immigration history and the societal and political context of their immigration. Similarly, Confucian traditions, although the level of impact may vary according to different Asian American groups and their degree of acculturation into the Western society, still exert a significant influence on Asian American families. Hence, this chapter will begin with a brief presentation of the history of Asian immigration to the United States and Asian cultural traditions, followed by discussion about special needs of Asian immigrant children and practical suggestions for intervention.

HISTORY OF ASIAN IMMIGRATION

The first Asian group to immigrate to the United States was the Chinese. Although Chinese were present in the United States in the 1700s, they did not begin to arrive in significant numbers until the middle of the nineteenth century, when they were drawn by the discovery of gold in California in conjunction with increasingly harsh economic and political conditions in China.[11] Most of these immigrants were Cantonese-speaking males from southern parts of China such as Hong Kong and Canton. Facing an economic downturn and agitated by increased anti-Chinese sentiment among white workers, Congress passed the Chinese Exclusion Act of 1882. This was the first legislation that specifically targeted a particular ethnic or racial group for exclusion.[12] Subsequently, many Chinese returned to China. Those who remained in the United States suffered innumerable humiliations, racial violence, and loss of property and, at times, life. It was not until 1943 that Chinese Exclusion Act was repealed, in part because China was a wartime ally of the United States.[13]

The Japanese were the second major Asian group to immigrate to the United States as a source of cheap labor for West Coast businesses. Like the Chinese before them, the Japanese faced the hostility of white workers who felt that their wage levels were being undercut by these new immigrants.[14] This antagonism finally culminated in the Gentlemen's Agreement of 1907, whereby the Japanese government agreed to limit migration to the United States to nonlaborers. The agreement did, however, permit the wives of local Japanese residents to enter the United States, and many Japanese brought in "picture brides"—brides from Japan selected by emigrant men through the exchange of pictures.[15]

In 1882, the United States became the first Western nation to sign a trade and friendship treaty with Korea. In the succeeding years, spurred by famine and political instability, over 7,000 predominantly male Korean workers immigrated to Hawaii and filled the labor vacuum left by the Chinese on the sugarcane and pineapple plantations. In 1905 Korea became a colony of Japan, and the Japanese government enacted a law that prohibited Koreans from emigrating to the United States.[16] Between 1907 and 1924, most of the Korean immigrants were women—picture brides for the older male Korean population. After the Korean War in the 1950s, a large number of immigrants and refugees, many of whom were wives of U.S. servicemen, arrived in the United States.

Filipinos originally immigrated to Hawaii to work on the plantations. During the 1920s, Filipino migration to the U.S. mainland gained momentum, coming either directly from the Philippines or indirectly through Hawaii. Because Filipinos were nationals of the United States, they were not subject to legal or quota restrictions. The Tydings-McDuffie Act of 1935 changed this situation, however. While granting future independence to the Philippines, it also placed Filipinos under an alien status, thereby restricting their immigration to 50 persons per year.[17]

The racist and exclusionist immigration policies of the United States toward immigrants of Asian ancestry were further reinforced through the passage of the Oriental Exclusion Act in 1924, which banned all immigration from Asia. The McCarran-Walter Act of 1952 rationalized the existing immigration policy, maintaining quotas for Asians: 105 immigrants from China, 185 from Japan, and 100 each from the Philippines and Korea.[18]

In 1965, in the midst of the civil rights movement, the Immigration and Nationality Acts Amendments provided the first real reform of immigration policy in the twentieth century. The law abolished the national-origins quotas, which favored immigrants from northwestern Europe. The principal of family reunification and the emphasis on scarce occupational skills became the major criteria for the admission of immigrants. Unlike the earlier immigrants, many of these post-1965 immigrants were from middle-class or affluent families, possessing higher level skills and education.

The Southeast Asians, most of whom have arrived since 1965 and especially since the fall of Saigon in 1975, represent the newest group of Asian immigrants in this country. Although often treated as a monolithic and homogeneous group, they are in fact very diverse culturally and linguistically, coming from Vietnam, Laos, and Cambodia. The first wave of Southeast Asian refugees primarily came from Vietnam. This group tends to be highly educated, with marketable skills, American contacts, and economic resources. The second wave consists of Vietnamese "boat people" and refugees from Cambodia and Laos, who lack human and economic capital. They are in general poorly educated and unprepared for an advanced industrial society such as the United States.

CULTURAL AND FAMILY TRADITIONS

Although Asian Americans show much diversity in the areas of linguistic, historic, economic, and social development, this chapter will focus on the commonly shared features of cultural and family traditions that exist among Asian American groups. The traditional family structure of Asian Americans primarily derives from Confucianism and Buddhism. These systems do not stress independence and autonomy of the individual but rather that the individual is superseded by the family. Moreover, the family adheres to the Confucian tradition of specific hierarchical roles established for all members. An individual's response and adherence to this code of conduct becomes not a reflection of the individual but of the extended family to which he or she belongs.[19] Key factors to be considered when applying the concepts presented here to any particular Asian American family are its social class, geographic origin, birthplace, and generation in the United States.

Family Roles

According to the Confucian ethics, roles and expectations in the family were clearly defined. Based on a hierarchical role structure, the father assumed the role of an ultimate decision maker, while the mother's role was primarily seen as the nurturant caretaker of her husband and children. The father was responsible for the family's social status and economic well-being. Until recently, women were discouraged from working outside the family.[20] As an emotionally devoted parental figure, the mother would intercede with the father, who was often emotionally distanced, on behalf of their children. Certain duties and privileges were associated with gender and birth order. Following the tradition of male domination, sons were more highly valued than daughters. The family name and lineage were passed through the male side, while married women were absorbed into the families of their husbands. The oldest son in particular received a preferential treatment as well as more responsibilities for the family.[21]

As Asian countries have modernized, however, traditional attitudes towards distinct gender roles are loosening. An increasing number of women, including mothers, are entering the job market. Women in the family are no longer relegated to subordinate roles only. Such a trend is even more pronounced in Asian immigrant families in the United States. In acculturated Asian American families, mothers may play a much more active role in decision making regarding family or business matters, while fathers are often the figurative heads of families. Similarly, differential treatment for sons and daughters is not so pronounced as in the past.

In the process of migration, Asian families experienced severe disruption in their extended kinship network that was traditionally the primary unit of society in their native countries. Many Asians in America, however, find a substitute for a kinship network through a membership in "clan" associations or ethnic churches. These extended kinship networks often provide social and financial support for the Asian immigrant families.

Obligation and Shame

Contrary to the Western tendency toward contractual obligation based on reciprocity, within Asian cultures the unspoken obligatory reciprocity that arises out of a relationship has a significant influence on the person's behavior. Obligation can be derived from personal relationships—that is, parent to child, teacher to student, and employer to employee—or incurred through kind or helpful actions. Behavior is often dictated by a sense of obligation or a desire to avoid being in a position of obligation.[22] Shame and loss of face are similarly powerful mechanisms of guiding behavior and motivating forces for conforming to societal or familial expectations. The concepts of shame and loss of face involve not only the exposure of the actions for all to see, but also the withdrawal of the family's, community's, or society's confidence and support.[23] In societal structures where interdependence is so important, everything an individual does is viewed as a reflection of the family as a whole, and bringing shame on one's family is avoided at all costs.

Communication Patterns

In Western society, the ability to openly express ideas and feelings is highly valued. We are encouraged to "speak our mind." However, within most Asian cultures there is a different attitude toward open communication of thought and feelings. Similar to rigid rules of role structure, rules of communication are governed by specific characteristics of the persons involved. For example, personal attributes such as age, gender, education, occupation, social status, and marital status determine the initiator of conversation, the structure of the language used, the topics to be addressed, and the degree of open expression allowed.[24] Because harmonious interpersonal relationships are so highly valued, outright confrontation is avoided whenever possible. Even today in many Asian families in the United States, open expression of emotion is generally frowned upon; suppression of undesirable thoughts or emotions is highly valued.[25]

SPECIAL NEEDS OF ASIAN IMMIGRANT CHILDREN IN SCHOOL

Linguistic Adjustment

Many researchers and practitioners have agreed that language difference is the biggest problem for immigrant children.[26] For the majority of Asian immigrant children, there is often limited or no use of English at home, and home-school interface is minimal, thus limiting language skills further.

Handicapped by their language barrier and culture shock, the children tend to resort to passivity and conformity, taking an invisible role in a school that rewards the assertive and highly verbal behavior. As a form of solution, bilingual education was originally intended to help develop the intellectual abilities of each child by using the child's native language to enable him or her to acquire proficiency in English. Children are usually able to overcome the language barrier after residing in the United States for six or more years.[27]

With regard to language differences, several studies have examined the relationship between second language proficiency and social and emotional adjustment among immigrant children. Some found a correspondence between problems of an emotional nature and linguistic inadequacy, the most common ones being extreme shyness, silence, and submissiveness.[28] However, in a study of immigrant pupils in Sweden, there was no direct relationship between "pure" language skills and the social and emotional adjustment.[29] Based on this finding, the author concluded that the acquisition of the new language is a necessary, but not sufficient, condition for the promotion of a good overall adjustment.[30] A study of Korean American families showed that 94 percent of the 400 families interviewed spoke Korean language at home.[31] Interestingly, the authors noted that language was a source of cultural conflict between parents and children. The authors concluded that parents who insisted on continued use of Korean at home may be working against their own high expectations for the children's academic success and ultimately success in the American job market.[32]

Educational Adjustment

When immigrant children arrive in an American school, it is often difficult to distinguish children with low intelligence and ability from those suffering from culture shock and from the need to withdraw into themselves in the process of adjustment. Similarly, linguistic and cultural complications, economic and health factors, attitudinal factors, sociocultural peer group expectations, cross-cultural stress, and intergenerational conflict frequently deflect the efforts of educators to recognize giftedness in these children and provide for them.[33] This is a time when children may give quite a false impression of themselves and it is easy to make wrong assessments of them. In particular, children who have already received part of their education abroad have special difficulties. It is likely that their previous educational experiences will be dissimilar from what they find in the United States. The level of some children's previous education may not be adequate for them to join a class of students of their own age, thus creating a socialization problem.

The difference in educational system may be one of the factors that make the adaptation of immigrant school children difficult. Most children who come from non-English-speaking countries will have to learn the language of instruction. Some will have to adjust to different teaching styles and different modes of learning. Some children may also be hurt by discriminatory comments or acts by their classmates and teachers. A child who is the only one in the school who speaks a particular language, or who belongs to a particular culture, can experience a desperate state of isolation. On the other hand, children enrolled in schools containing a high percentage of students speaking the same language may have difficulty integrating with native-born peers because of potential divisions along ethnic lines, and thus there is little opportunity for them to begin the process of stepping into the new society and making friends, and the period of alienation from those with whom they must eventually work is extended.

Emphasizing family ecology as a context for human development, Urie Bronfenbrenner reported that closer ties between families and their children's classroom teachers may positively benefit the children's academic achievement in school.[34] However, a study of Asian children in Chicago and Los Angeles revealed that the home-school communication tends to move in one direction only—usually from school to home.[35] Rates of contact between teachers and parents were relatively low, and such contacts were valued by teachers only when the teachers initiated the contact.

In general, Asian American students are the most successful group in school and are most likely to believe that doing poorly in school has negative repercussions.[36] The Asian children devote relatively more time to their studies than other groups, are more likely to attribute their success to hard work, and are more likely to report that their parents have high standards for school performance.[37] An examination of the family characteristics of Asian-American and white high-achieving students showed that the family life of white students tended to be less structured and provide less formal educational experience for children after school and on weekends.[38] However, both groups shared high parental expectations, concerning parents, stable family environment, and close-knit family relationships.[39]

Under the influence of Confucianism, which stresses the virtue of scholarly pursuit, most Asian immigrant parents value education highly and are very anxious that their children should do well at school. Indeed, their main reason for immigration is often to provide their children with good educational opportunities. Some immigrant families may also have unrealistic ambitions for their children as part of the apparently hopeless and desperate effort to improve their position substantially in this society. From the beginning, therefore, children are loaded with a great sense of obligation toward the family for uprooting itself for their sakes. Children also realize a tremendous sense of responsibility for fulfilling the parents' dreams and wishes through their educational achievements. This sense of obligation can overwhelm children with feelings of guilt in case of failure.

In spite of the high expectation of their children, many immigrant parents are unimpressed and bewildered by some aspects of the American educational system. They think the discipline is far too lax or nonexistent, and they see schools as providing opportunities for their children to become ill-disciplined and disrespectful to them like "American" children. The school in this respect can be a source of disruption and strain as well as achievement. Since most parents anticipate and fear that schools will produce cultural conflict between them and their children, the parents may be prone to overreact to the more or less inevitable behavioral changes their children will undergo as a result of development and socialization to the environment. Moreover, the school personnel may feel far more sympathetic to immigrant children than to their parents, whom they sometimes see as harsh disciplinarians making quite unrealistic demands on their children.

Cultural Adjustment

In families who have recently immigrated, children are often in conflict between two competing sets of values and norms, which require them to develop one set of behaviors in the family setting and another set in school and community settings. When these behaviors are diametrically opposed, emotional stress inevitably results.[40] Many Asian immigrant children are socialized by their parents to appreciate the continuity of their family, to respect elders, and to forego individual gratifications that are at the expense of the family or group.[41] Children are often discouraged from expressing their thoughts and emotions overtly in public. Overemphasis on obedience and conformity in child rearing practices among some Asian immigrant families is thought to hinder the development of self-reliance, and to create a child who functions better in structured settings than in unstructured settings.[42] Subsequently, Asian immigrant children are often viewed by educators as shy with their teachers and friends in the classroom and reluctant to assert their own views. Such a phenomenon often leads to race stereotyping of Asian American children. In fact, teachers tend to perceive passive Asian American children as being better adjusted to the classroom as compared to passive Caucasian children.[43] Cultural differences in listening behavior are sometimes perceived negatively by the teacher. Response behavior patterns such as lowering of the eyes when being addressed, or passive, seemingly unresponsive staring are frequently misinterpreted as inattentiveness.[44]

The children are often torn between a wish to identify with their friends and share their privileges and way of life, and their loyalty to their parents, who may wish them to retain the culture of their native countries. Parents tend to lose a great deal of the respect and authority that they had in their home country when they immigrate. Instead of children looking to their parents for guidance, support, and leadership, the roles are now reversed. In addition, both parents in the immigrant family often have to work long hours away from home. As a result the children are greatly influenced by peers or by the American public school system.[45] Many refugee children in particular often face temporary or permanent separation from their parents during the escape from their native lands and resettlement in the United States. Considering the finding that prolonged and traumatic separations experienced by children in the course of migration were principal antecedents of the immigrant children's disorders such as depression and anxiety, the Southeast Asian refugee children, especially unaccompanied minors without adult family members or relatives, are extremely vulnerable to mental problems.[46]

Some of the most complex problems facing Asian immigrant families with older children cluster around the degree of independence these children want and are allowed. This demand to be free of some of the bonds of the family can be a source of anger and concern for their parents because it may be seen as a threat to the structure of the family and a desertion of traditions, which not only are important in themselves but also provide immigrants with security in an unfamiliar country and a link with their native lands. Possibly immigrant parents' greatest cause for concern revolves around the discipline of their children and the standards of behavior they wish them to adopt. Many parents are unimpressed by the independence of older American children and the apparently laissez-faire attitudes of their parents. And yet they realize that their traditional methods of upbringing are not entirely appropriate for children whose friends and school companions enjoy a much greater degree of independence. Some parents see that adaptation must be made, but are uncertain how to do this, and, for many of them, there is an absence of acceptable models. Such conflicting features within different cultures can create a sense of confusion and psychological moratorium for the immigrant children who are susceptible and sensitive to societal influences, and may lead them to question their own values and to doubt the worthiness of their original cultural background.

Behavioral Adjustment

Although our knowledge of Asian American children with emotional or behavior problems is extremely limited, existing research on the mental health of immigrant children in general offers some insight into the problem. Earlier studies tended to highlight more behavioral problems such as antisocial disorder or conduct disorder among immigrant children than nonimmigrant groups.[47] Interestingly, in an extensive survey of West Indian children in London, M. Rutter and colleagues discovered that conduct disorder among the immigrant children was manifest almost entirely at school and not at home, indicating the immigrant children's particular difficulties in adapting to the school system.[48]

Another major area of disorder, among adolescent immigrants specifically, is in the domain of self-concept, identity conflicts, and conflicts with parents. None of these are, of course, the exclusive prerogative of immigrants, but the literature suggests that the experience of migration and culture change may exacerbate these normal developmental crises for immigrant adolescents. Self-deprecation and low self-concepts are thought to be common among immigrant adolescents who come from ethnic minority groups that are devalued by the majority culture.[49] In a deep desire to be accepted as natives, some children refuse to speak their home language and are ashamed of their parents when they speak their own tongue in public. This rejection by the child of the first language and culture can spell the beginning of a serious identity crisis. Acute identity crises may also develop among immigrant adolescents who feel impelled to make a forced choice between the values and identities of their old and new cultures.[50] The stress thus engendered may lead to grossly deviant behavior and even graver psychopathology. For example, suicide has accounted for a much larger proportion of deaths among Asian American youths than among white Americans, and the suicide death rate for foreign-born Asian youth has been consistently higher than that found for the U.S.-born.[51]

Children, however, often accept the differences in their lives in and outside the family and make good adjustments to the dual demands on them, even though this may be achieved only after some pain and conflict. Parental attitudes to social change and new experiences were found to be significant predictors of the adjustment in school of immigrant and native children.[52] A recent study in Canada claimed that immigrant children were not at increased risk for psychiatric disorder or poor school performance and that they used mental health and social services significantly less often than do their nonimmigrant peers.[53] Similarly, analyzing the data from the Los Angeles County Department of Mental Health, Khanh-Van Bui and David Takeuchi found that both Asian American and African American adolescent clients had lower rates of conduct disorder than White counterparts.[54]

STRATEGIES FOR SERVING ASIAN IMMIGRANT CHILDREN IN SCHOOL

As a human service institution with the broadest and most immediate contacts, school systems are in a unique position to assist immigrant families with children. If problems are encountered by members of an immigrant family, early manifestations are likely to appear among children in school so that measures may be taken before the problems deteriorate. With the high priority given to their children and to their education, Asian immigrant families have a concomitant high regard given to a school system. In fact, they are often more willing to accept services provided through this institution than those offered by some other governmental or nongovernmental agency.[55] Some immigrants may even refuse to approach their own ethnic organizations for help because of a loss of face within their own community.

Despite their multiple needs, there have been very few referrals for services for Asian immigrant children, and the conditions among the referred Asian children tend to be more severe cases of emotional and/or behavioral disturbances than those of non-Asian children.[56] Invisibility of the children, expectations of passivity by the teachers, inadequate educational policies, and limited availability of qualified bilingual and bicultural staff are conceived as some of the factors that have been implicated in deterring Asian children and families from using mainstream services.[57] Fortunately, the compulsory period of school attendance in our society makes it possible to have a continuity of contact with immigrant families while their children are enrolled in the educational system.

An often-expressed sentiment of immigrant parents is that they have come to the new country seeking a better future for their children, and they come prepared to sacrifice their own happiness for the sake of their children's future. However, immigrant parents are often unaware of their rights and obligations in demanding that the school provide their children with a quality education. In order to provide support and encouragement to overcome their anxieties and fears, parent education groups can be useful. The group focuses on helping parents gain knowledge that leads to the acquisition of improved parenting skills. In this group, parents are informed of the nature of the education system, of their rights as parents and citizens, and of their responsibilities in the education of their children. The parent education group is particularly beneficial for immigrant parents, who, because of their cultural background, may not understand the role of the school in American society or the responsibilities of parents in the educational process. The parent education group can also evolve into a natural support group for the immigrant parents who are often at risk of social isolation. For example, group support experience for immigrant mothers and their young children may include regularly scheduled meetings that provide such programs as social and cultural activities; individual, family, and group counseling services; community orientation; English instruction for adults and young children; social support services; and school orientation.

One of the problems that many immigrant families face is that children come to have power over their non-English-speaking parents. As children tend to be quicker in learning the language of a new society, they may control the communication between home and school, and the parents may be excluded in the process. Therefore, information for immigrant parents and culture-based parenting materials should be made available in their own languages whenever possible. Further, parent-child collaboration needs to be developed and parental involvement in the school program should be strongly encouraged.

Traditionally the mode of parent-school interaction has been to change either the parent or the child. The former mode is based on the assumption that the child's problems are the result of the parent's inadequacies. C. M. Schraft and James Comer criticized the traditional mode, arguing that by focusing on the parent's failings, the school can be diverted from examining its own role in perpetuating poor parent-school relations.[58] The school administrator and teachers should be sensitized to the variety of educational and psychological needs of children from different cultural backgrounds through in-service education that focuses not only on attitude change but on techniques for fostering healthy peer interaction between immigrant children and the native-born. The teacher education program must include immigration and cultural diversity issues in their core curriculum. Cultural-exchange programs between immigrant children and the native-born to facilitate an understanding of cultural and ethnic differences can be educationally as well as emotionally rewarding for both groups of children. Finally, there should be conscious efforts on the part of the school to hire and retain bilingual teachers and counselors. In addition, teacher education programs in colleges need to actively recruit bilingual/bicultural students as future teachers in public school systems. Immigrant children then have an adult they can talk to who shares their common culture and experiences. Teachers, on the other hand, have someone they can refer to for information and advice on problems they have not previously encountered in their teaching careers. If bilingual teachers and counselors are not available, the school may be able to draw help from parents with language capacities, and peer interpreters among students.

The school and the community are interdependent systems. Mobilizing the cultural strengths and resources of the ethnic community for its members helps ethnic families cope more effectively with the larger culture. Natural helping networks are largely perceived as preventive forces or buffers, which help people effectively work through and cope with transition, stress, physical problems, and social emotional problems without resorting to the somewhat stigmatized formal social services and mental health system. Thus, identification and evaluation of ethnic community resources should be done and the school must develop working relationships with these ethnic community agencies.

CONCLUSION

Immigrant children tend to come from families occupying a lower socioeconomic position and their parents are often poorly educated and somewhat mystified by the educational system and its process. These children generally find entry into the public school difficult because they lack the family resources and experiential background that usually lead to successful achievement in what has been called a middle-class institution. The shortage of resources, unfamiliarity with the existing educational system, and culture shock, coupled with language differences, put the immigrant children in a very vulnerable position. Therefore, these children are a high-risk group who deserve special attention from school personnel. The school-based programs have an opportunity to prevent potentially problematic situations, to reduce the duration of a concern by intervening at an early stage, and to reduce the severity of a problem that has existed over time by developing intervention strategies that utilize the resources available. In doing so, one can help the immigrant families as well as their children to cope more effectively with the stresses involved in adjusting to a new, unfamiliar environment.

NOTES

1. U.S. Census Bureau, *United States Department of Commerce News* (Washington, DC: U.S. Census Bureau, June 1991).

2. William P. O'Hare and Judy C. Felt, "Asian Americans: America's Fastest Growing Minority Group" (Washington, DC: Population Reference Bureau, February 1991).

3. Paul Ong and Suzanne J. Hee, "Twenty Million in 2020," in *Policy Issues to the Year 2020* (Los Angeles: LEAP Asian Pacific American Public Policy Institute and UCLA Asian American Studies Center, 1993), pp. 11–23.

4. U.S. Census Bureau, *Department of Commerce News.*

5. W. Caudill and G. DeVos, "Achievement, Culture, and Personality: The Case of the Japanese Americans," in G. DeVos (Ed.), *Socialization for Achievement: Essays on the Cultural Psychology of the Japanese* (Berkeley: University of California Press, 1973), pp. 220–247; see also William P. O'Hare, "A New Look at Asian Americans," *American Demographics*, 12 (October 1990): 26–31; W. Peterson, "Success Story, Japanese American Style," *New York Times Magazine* (January 9, 1966); Stanley Sue and Sumie Okazaki, "Asian-American Educational Achievements: A Phenomenon in Search of an Explanation," *American Psychologist*, 45 (August 1990): 913–920.

6. O'Hare and Felt, "Asian Americans: America's Fastest Growing Minority Group."

7. U.S. Census Bureau, "1990 Census of Population: Race and Hispanic Origin for the United States and Regions" (Washington, DC: U.S. Census Bureau, 1990).

8. Ibid.

9. U.S. Department of Education, Office for Civil Rights, "Enrollment in Public Elementary and Secondary Schools, by Race or Ethnicity and State: Fall 1986 and Fall 1991," Table 47, *Digest of Education Statistics*, 1993, p. 61.

10. Urie Bronfenbrenner, *The Ecology of Human Development: Experiments by Nature and Design* (Cambridge, MA: Harvard University Press, 1979).

11. Betty L. Sung, *Mountain of Gold* (New York: Macmillan, 1967); see also Morrison G. Wong, "Post-1965 Asian Immigrants: Where Do They Come From, Where Are They Now, and Where Are They Going?" *Annals of the American Academy of Political and Social Science*, 487 (September 1986): 150–168.

12. Victor G. Nee and Brett de Bary Nee, *Longtime Californ': A Documentary Study of an American Chinatown* (New York: Pantheon Books, 1972), pp. 30–60; see also Alexander Saxton, *The Indispensable Enemy: Labor and the Anti-Chinese Movement in California* (Los Angeles: University of California Press, 1971).

13. Wong, "Post-1965 Asian Immigrants."

14. Roger Daniels, *The Politics of Prejudice: The Anti-Japanese Movement in California and the Struggle for Japanese Exclusion* (Gloucester, MA: Peter Smith, 1966).

15. Wong, "Post-1965 Asian Immigrants."

16. Lee Houchins and Chang-su Houchins, "The Korean Experience in America, 1903–1924," in Norris Hundley, Jr. (Ed.), *The Asian American* (Santa Barbara, CA: ABC-Clio, 1976), pp. 129–156.

17. Wong, "Post-1965 Asian Immigrants."

18. Ibid.

19. Steven P. Shon and Davis Y. Ja, "Asian Families," in Monica McGoldrick, John K. Pearce, and Joseph Giordano (Eds.), *Ethnicity and Family Therapy* (New York: The Guilford Press, 1982), pp. 208–228.

20. Ibid.

21. Larke Nahme Huang and Yu-Wen Ying, "Chinese American Children and Adolescents," in Jewelle Taylor Gibbs, Larke Nahme Huang, and Associates (Eds.), *Children of Color* (San Francisco: Jossey-Bass, 1989), pp. 30–66.

22. Ibid.

23. Shon and Ja, "Asian Families."

24. Ibid.

25. Huang and Ying, "Chinese American Children and Adolescents."

26. K. K. Hirayama, "Asian Children's Adaptation to Public Schools," *Social Work in Education*, 7(4) (Summer 1985): 213–230; see also Bok Lim Kim, M. R. Sandy, and B. C. Meilhoefer, "Facilitation Roles with Non-Native Korean American Children," *Social Work in Education*, 4(2) (January 1982): 17–33; Carlos Sluzki, "Migration and Family Conflict," *Family Process*, 18 (1979): 379–390; Betty L. Sung, *Transplanted Chinese Children*, a report made to Department of Health, Education and Welfare (The City College of New York, 1979).

27. S. S. Peng, J. A. Owings, and W. B. Fetters, "School Experiences and Performance of Asian American High School Students," paper presented at the annual meeting of the American Educational Research Association, New Orleans, 1984.

28. B. I. Stockfelt-Hoatson, "Education and Socialization of Migrant's Children in Sweden with Special Reference to Bilingualism and Biculturalism," in Richard C. Nann (Ed.), *Uprooting and Surviving* (Dordrecht, Holland: D. Reidel, 1982), pp. 71–76; see also Sung, *Transplanted Chinese Children*.

29. L. H. Ekstrand, "Adjustment Among Immigrant Pupils in Sweden," *International Review of Applied Psychology*, 25(3) (1976): 167–188.

30. Ibid.

31. Kim, Sandy, and Meihoefer, "Facilitation Roles with Non-Native Korean American Children."

32. Ibid.

33. Carole Ruth Harris, "Identifying and Serving the Gifted New Immigrant," *Teaching Exceptional Children*, 23(4) (Summer 1991): 26–30.

34. Urie Bronfenbrenner, "Ecology of the Family as a Context for Human Development: Research Perspectives," *Developmental Psychology*, 22 (1986): 723–742.

35. Bok Lim Kim, *The Korean-American Child at School and at Home*, Project Report (Washington, D.C.: U.S. Department of Health, Education and Welfare, 1980).

36. Laurence Steinberg, Sanford M. Dornbusch, and B. Bradford Brown, "Ethnic Differences in Adolescent Achievement," *American Psychologist*, 47(6) (June 1992): 723–729.

37. Ibid.

38. Esther Lee Yao, "A Comparison of Family Characteristics of Asian-American and Anglo-American High Achievers," *International Journal of Comparative Sociology*, 26(3–4) (1985): 198–208.

39. Ibid.

40. Larke Nahme Huang, "Southeast Asian Refugee Children and Adolescents," in *Children of Color*, pp. 278–321.

41. Sung, *Transplanted Chinese Children.*

42. K. H. Yu and Luke I. C. Kim, "The Growth and Development of Korean-American Children," in Gloria Johnson Powell, Joe Yamamoto, A. Romero, and A. Morales (Eds.), *The Psychosocial Development of Minority Group Children* (New York: Brunner/Mazel, 1983), pp. 147–158.

43. Kim, *The Korean-American Child at School and at Home.*

44. Harris, "Identifying and Serving the Gifted New Immigrant."

45. Betty L. Sung, *The Adjustment Experience of Chinese Immigrant Children in New York City* (Staten Island, NY: Center for Migration Studies, 1987).

46. J. Kirk Felsman, Frederick T. L. Leong, Mark C. Johnson, and Irene Crabtree Felsman, "Estimates of Psychological Distress Among Vietnamese Refugees: Adolescents, Unaccompanied Minors and Young Adults," *Social Science and Medicine*, 31(11) (1990): 1251–1256; see also Huang, "Southeast Asian Refugee Children and Adolescents."

47. P. J. Graham and C. E. Meadows, "Psychiatric Disorder in the Children of West Indian Immigrants," *Journal of Child Psychology and Psychiatry*, 8 (1967): 105–116; see also M. P. Haditch and R. F. Morrissey, "Role Stress, Personality, and Psychopathology in a Group of Immigrant Adolescents," *Journal of Abnormal Psychology*, 85(1) (1976); W. P. Osborne, "Adjustment Differences of Selected Foreign-Born Pupils," *California Journal of Educational Research* 22 (1971): 131–139.

48. M. Rutter and others, "Children of West Indian Immigrants: I. Rates of Behavioral Deviance and of Psychiatric Disorder," *Journal of Child Psychology and Psychiatry*, 15 (1974): 241–262.

49. P. Hishiki, "The Self-Concepts of Sixth Grade Girls of Mexican American Descent," *California Journal of Educational Research*, 20 (1969): 56–62.

50. R. L. Derbyshire, "Adaptation of Adolescent Mexican Americans to United States Society," in Eugene Brody (Ed.), *Behavior in New Environment* (Beverly Hills, CA: Sage Publications, 1969); see also Richard C. Nann, "Uprooting and Surviving—An Overview," in *Uprooting and Surviving*, pp. 1–10; Naditch and Morrissey, "Role Stress, Personality, and Psychopathology."

51. William T. Liu, Elena S. H. Yu, Ching-Fu Chang, and Marilyn Fernandez, "The Mental Health of Asian American Teenagers: A Research Challenge," in Arlene Rubin Stiffman and Larry E. Davis (Eds.), *Ethnic Issues in Adolescent Mental Health* (Newbury Park, CA: Sage Publications, 1990), pp. 92–112.

52. Michael Aronowitz, "Adjustment of Immigrant Children as a Function of Parental Attitudes to Change," *International Migration Review*, 26(1) (Spring 1992): 89–110.

53. Heather Munroe-Blum, Michael H. Boyle, David R. Offord, and Nicholas Kates, "Immigrant Children: Psychiatric Disorder, School Performance, and Service Utilization," *American Journal of Orthopsychiatry*, 59 (October 1989): 510–519.

54. Khanh-Van T. Bui and David T. Takeuchi, "Ethnic Minority Adolescents and the Use of Community Mental Health Care Services," *American Journal of Community Psychology*, 20(4) (1992): 403–417.

55. Nann, "Uprooting and Surviving."

56. Yang J. Kim, "Problems in the Delivery of the School Based Psycho-Educational Services to the Asian Immigrant Children," *Journal of Children in Contemporary Society*, 15(3) (Spring 1983): 81–89; see also Mikyong Kim-Goh, Joe Yamamoto, and

Chong Suh, "Characteristics of Asian/Pacific Islander Psychiatric Patients in a Public Mental Health System," *Asian American and Pacific Islander Journal of Health* (in press).

57. Kim, "Problems in the Delivery of the School Based Psycho-Educational Services."

58. C. M. Schraft and James P. Comer, "Parent Participation and Urban Schools," *School Social Work Quarterly*, 1(4) (Winter 1979): 309–325.

PART IV

PROBLEMS AND POSSIBILITIES

Chapter 12

Effective Teacher Preparation for Diverse Student Populations: What Works Best?

Carmen Zuniga-Hill and Carol Barnes

INTRODUCTION

One of the major problems facing teacher education and staff development personnel is the effective preparation of teachers for diverse student populations. The demographic data are well known and clearly point to our need to address the issue in a serious, focused manner. Let us look at California as an example. According to the 1990 Census, California has a population of about 30 million, and by 1988 there was no ethnic majority in the California public schools. Latinos comprised 30.7 percent, African Americans 9.0 percent, Asians 7.6 percent, Filipinos 2.2 percent, American Indians or Alaskan Natives .8 percent, and Pacific Islanders .5%. Thus the total population of ethnically diverse students was 50.8 percent and of whites (non-Latino), 49.2 percent. Approximately one-sixth of the students are foreign-born, and at least 30 percent have limited English proficiency.[1] Nationwide by the year 2000 between 30 and 40 percent of the total school enrollment will be people of color.[2] Yet by the late 1980s, only 12 to 14 percent of the teaching force was nonwhite.[3] What faces us then, is a true mismatch between the nature of the teacher and student populations, who each bring very different backgrounds and experiences to the teaching and learning process: our teacher population is primarily white and middle class; our student population is increasingly nonwhite.

Compounding the challenges facing teachers are the problems revealed in the following statistics: for every 100 students in public schools in California, 23 live below the poverty level: 7 live in families in which child abuse has been suspected; and 10 have learning or physical disabilities.[4] In addition, nationwide both poverty and dropout rates are higher among the nonwhite population.[5] The interconnections among the demographic variables and poverty have been consistently reported. J. L. Brown states: "Poverty will be the rule rather than the exception for the two largest racial and ethnic minorities in the country."[6]

How can we possibly prepare teachers to deal with these phenomena? The Tomas Rivera Center report, *Resolving a Crisis in Education: Latino Teachers for Tomorrow's Classrooms*, part of a five-year research project funded by the Exxon Educational Foundation, addresses the issue of teacher preparation and recruitment specifically for the Latino population. It suggests that the best way to meet the challenges of teaching the nation's diverse Latino student population is first to dramatically increase the number of Latino teachers and second to better prepare teachers of all ethnic backgrounds to meet the needs of Latino students.[7]

Clearly one could extend these recommendations to each underrepresented ethnic group in the United States. The recommendation to dramatically increase the number of Latino teachers, while certainly a lofty goal, is very likely unreachable in the foreseeable future. According to a 1991 report by the former California superintendent of schools, California has approximately 8,000 bilingual teachers and needs an additional 14,332, a number that will surely grow if the demographic trends follow all predictions. Projections for the nation by 2000 are for a need for 97,000 bilingual teachers.[8] Yet colleges and universities, with rare exceptions, are preparing only a fraction of these needed teachers, and district intern programs, while attracting minority teachers at a higher rate than universities, often suffer from a higher attrition rate after the third year of teaching.[9] The second recommendation, better preparation for teachers of *all* ethnic backgrounds, is perhaps even more crucial because it is more realistic; it will be the focus of this chapter. We will discuss how we prepared teachers to work with diverse populations in the past, and what teachers will need to know and be able to do to be effective with today's diverse students.

HISTORICAL PERSPECTIVE

Until the 1970s, teacher preparation programs devoted relatively little time to preparing teachers to work with students from diverse populations.

> Reflecting the prevailing goals of the nation as articulated by its powerful and economic leaders, the schools and colleges promoted and embraced Americanization and blind loyalty to the nation during the turn of the century and World War I periods. In this atmosphere of virulent nativism, government-sponsored propaganda, and emphasis on blind patriotism and Americanization, the idea of cultural pluralism in education would have been alien and perhaps viewed as seditious as well as un-American.[10]

Teacher preparation, done mainly in normal schools and colleges, reflected this view, and the teaching of diverse populations was a nonissue. America, after all, was a melting pot.

James Banks presents an interesting review of the trends in education of American Indian, Black American, and Mexican American education from the 1920s to the 1940s.[11] He notes that debates were common between assimilation versus self-determination and between practical, industrial education versus a traditional education. As early as the 1940s, pioneer educator George Sanchez recognized the challenge posed to teachers when their students' native languages were other than English. He advocated instruction geared to this diversity and urged educators to consider the unique cultural and linguistic characteristics of the students as they prepared for instruction.[12]

During and after World War II, as racial tensions increased, projects such as the Intergroup Education in Cooperative Schools and the College Study in Intergroup Relations emerged to effect changes in teacher preparation and school curriculum. While most of the reforms failed to remain part of the formal curriculum, they did contribute to the knowledge base of teacher preparation, and many institutions continued some portions of the project. (For an analysis of why these reforms failed, for the most part, to become institutionalized, please refer to Banks.)[13] It is interesting to note that the reasons that the reforms did not remain part of the curriculum are almost identical to those describing failed educational reforms today: the mainstream never internalized the underlying assumptions nor understood how the effort contributed to the major goals of the schools; the need for reform was seen as less critical; the reform remained on the periphery of educational thought.[14]

The teaching of assimilation remained the goal of most teachers in the 1950s and 1960s, in spite of the fact that it wasn't working very well in society. At best, teachers were taught to focus on the heroes and holidays of the various ethnic groups, and Booker T. Washington and piñatas became a prominent part of the social studies curriculum.

By the 1960s the black civil rights movements had legitimized being proud of one's heritage, and groups began to search for their ethnic identities.[15] Ethnic studies courses and departments began to appear with great frequency on college campuses, but the enrollment in these studies tended to be mainly the students of the ethnic group under study, and the coursework did not have the widespread impact that many had hoped it would.

After the Immigration Reform Act of 1965 was passed, the United States experienced its largest wave of immigrants since the turn of the century. Nearly 80 percent (78.6%) more immigrants entered the United States in the decade between 1971 and 1980 than had entered in the years between 1951 and 1960.[16] Only a few (18%) of the legal immigrants were from Europe; most were from Asia or Latin America. Racial and ethnic problems increased in the urban schools; parents blamed teachers for not doing enough, and teachers blamed their university preparation programs for not teaching them how to cope. Ethnic revitalization was occurring at a rapid rate in the 1970s and 1980s, and teacher educators were making major changes in their curricula, both as response to changing accreditation standards and to society as a whole. By the late 1980s many teacher education students were being exposed to James Banks' levels of Integration of Ethnic Content in the Curriculum and were encouraged and required to incorporate levels two, three, and four (described in detail later in this chapter) in their lesson and curriculum planning.

By 1977 the National Council for the Accreditation of Teacher Education had developed standards for the inclusion of courses and programs in multicultural education for teachers, and these standards have continued to be refined and strengthened. In addition, many states now require that teacher preparation programs include coursework, and in some cases fieldwork, in the education of culturally and linguistically diverse populations. However, as Sheryl Santos notes, teacher education students are not "beating down the doors" to enroll voluntarily in courses dealing with multicultural education, so strong enforcement by the state licensing boards and accreditation agencies will be needed to ensure that teachers have the knowledge base to teach children from diverse backgrounds.[17]

Other recent pressures on teacher education and staff developers to reform their programs have come from the textbook publishers (and, of course, from the Departments of Education in those states whose statewide textbook adoptions often drive national curriculum content). Newer texts, particularly in the social studies, takes a more pluralistic view of the field, and teachers not recently prepared may be ill-equipped to teach this curriculum.

What we are beginning to see now in teacher preparation is a move away from the generalized stereotypes of "all African American children do..." and "all Latino students learn best by..." and away from the attitude that "these poor little minority children need to be brought up to speed." The most recent approach in teacher preparation curriculum draws on the generalizations that anthropologists have used as a lens—family structures, use of time, and kinship—as a means of helping future teachers develop a better understanding of children of diverse backgrounds and therefore more effective teaching strategies for all children. The goal of such teacher preparation programs is to develop teachers who can implement effectively the five dimensions or components described by James Banks: (1) content integration—the use of examples, data, and information from a variety of culture groups to illustrate key concepts, principles, generalizations, and theories; (2) knowledge construction—the use of data about the implicit cultural assumptions, frames of reference, perspectives, and biases within a discipline influence the construction of knowledge; (3) prejudice reduction; (4) equity pedagogy; and (5) development of an empowering school culture and social structure.[18]

Unfortunately most teacher preparation programs have not yet incorporated these components of instruction. Furthermore, teacher preparation programs usually examine separately how the issues of language and culture impact the teaching of linguistically and culturally diverse students; the dichotomy is an artificial one, however, in that the two issues are inextricably bound when it comes to addressing the learning needs of diverse students. We, as teacher educators, tend to discuss them separately, because in so doing we can explore the extensive body of research that has been generated in each domain, but we are probably doing a disservice to our students who will need to integrate these issues in their classrooms. Also, typically all prospective teachers receive instruction on issues of culture, yet only bilingual teachers will receive instruction in teaching the linguistically diverse students. This, too, is not serving our students well. The reader will note that under the sections of this chapter that discuss language and culture, direct reference is made in each section to the other one, underscoring the interrelated nature of the two. Effective teachers and teacher preparation programs incorporate findings from both areas in addressing the needs of students of diverse backgrounds.

CREDENTIALING SNAPSHOT

One area for serious attention if we are to ensure the best preparation for teachers of diverse populations is the instituting of strong credentialing requirements. Given the crucial skills and knowledge needed by teachers of diverse populations, one would expect to see very specific laws to ensure the teaching of these skills and knowledge, particularly in the states with highly diverse student populations. To test this assumption we reviewed in detail the credentialing requirements of the following states: *Highly Diverse Populations (HD)*— California, Florida, Illinois, Massachusetts, New York, and Texas, and *Less Diverse Populations (LD)*—Rhode Island, Iowa, Kansas, Minnesota, and Ohio.

We asked the following questions:

1. Is a separate ESL (English as a Second Language) credential offered? Are advanced ESL programs offered? Is a specific language required in these programs? We found that there were few differences among the HD and LD states. Two HD states and one LD state had either separate credentials or had endorsements or validations to existing credentials. In all states, advanced ESL programs were offered by at least one and usually many colleges and universities and there was no specific language required for the study or for the credential; however, in states with high Latino concentrations, the language of choice was often Spanish, though not required.

2. Is there a state requirement that all credential candidates have coursework in multicultural education: If so, how much? How many units of coursework are required for bilingual or ESL certification beyond the basic program? All states except one HD have a multicultural requirement. In that state it exists only for teachers of English to speakers of other languages (ESOL) or to teachers of limited English proficiency (LEP). Interestingly, two LP states call their requirements "human relations." In every case, the number of semester units in multicultural education required of all students was determined by the individual universities, not stipulated by the states.

Eugene Garcia examined certification requirements in the subset of six states that, when taken together, educate almost two-thirds of the language-minority students in the nation: California, Florida, Illinois, New York, New Jersey, and Texas. He notes that

> in these states, bilingual credentialing and ESL or some other related credential/ endorsement is available. However, in only three of the six states is such credentialing mandated. Therefore, even in states that are highly affected by language minority students, there is no direct concern for the specific mandating of professional standards.[19]

California currently has a bilingual emphasis within the basic credential program, and is in the process of implementing separate basic credentials in Bilingual Cross Cultural Language and Academic Development and Cross Cultural Language and Academic Development. These do not necessarily require more units of coursework than the standard teaching credential but may have more prerequisites for admission. The other states require from 9 to 30 additional units for teachers of bilingual or ESOL certification. There is no pattern of fewer units being required in LD states as one might predict, and in all states but one LS, ESOL certification is either an endorsement to the basic credential or a certificate. Some states require statewide examinations for working with LEP or bilingual students (e.g., California). Others have field experience requirements. The National Teachers Examination also now includes ESL as a subject area for testing.

Consequently we found our initial assumption—that states with highly diverse student populations would have more stringent requirements in bilingual and multicultural education—inaccurate. In fact, there is remarkably little difference among the states. This bodes well as we look toward possible national certification standards, and probably indicates the substantive influence that such national accreditation bodies as the National Council of Accreditors of Teacher Education have had and could continue to have on state and university requirements, but it raises serious questions about whether the new teachers in states with highly diverse student populations are receiving adequate preparation to deal with this diversity.

What types of preparation programs would be ideal for teachers to ensure that they are prepared to deal with the student populations they teach? What should they know and be able to do? How much fieldwork is optimal and in what settings? Teacher educators are beginning to address these questions and must reach some degree of consensus in order to establish effective program models that can be replicated. The following sections of this chapter will address the knowledge base upon which good preparation programs for teachers of diverse populations should be built and the best practices that we believe teachers should implement.

ADDRESSING THE NEEDS OF SECOND LANGUAGE LEARNERS

What do teachers need to know and be able to do? Does teaching second language mean teaching the curriculum in English using modified approaches and techniques? Does it mean using native and English language instruction— bilingual education? Each of these represents opposite ends of the continuing debate on how best to address the needs of second language learners. For the classroom teacher, working with second language learners ultimately means using principles and practices of good education *and* good second language instruction, with the minimum goal being to develop students' English language and literacy skills so as to allow their full participation and academic success in mainstream English language classes.

This section will first address key concepts of English language development approaches and bilingual education, the two most common means to teach English-as-a-second-language students. This is followed by a list of eleven principles with supporting examples that help teachers promote second language learning.[20]

English Language Development Approaches

There are various approaches or models of English language development instruction: English as a second language instruction, immersion, structured English immersion, and modified or sheltered English. While some descriptions include submersion (also known as "sink or swim") as a model or approach, it is not deemed a model here because it means that second language learners do not receive any assistance either through second language instruction or modified content learning instruction to help them learn English or learn in English.

The best of these models *teach* English and teach *in* English so as to simultaneously enhance cognitive development and English language learning. ESL focuses largely on formal aspects of language development, while immersion, structured English immersion, and sheltered English refer to specially designed academic instruction in English and provide access to the core academic curriculum through linguistically modified instruction that suits the students' level of second language comprehension. The use of these models is not mutually exclusive. For example, many schools provide ESL instruction as well as specially designed English language instruction in the content areas. With structured English immersion, prior knowledge of English is not assumed, whereas specially designed English language instruction assumes that the students have minimum second language skills. Monolingual English-speaking teachers can be taught to use all of these approaches. Key guidelines for developing specially designed English language lessons include:

Designing appropriate lessons

- ''frontloading'' instruction as much as possible through vocabulary and concept lesson previews and through building prior knowledge
- providing advance reading assignment information such as graphic organizers
- providing paired or cooperative group work
- aligning ESL instruction with content or thematic units

Simplifying linguistic input

- slowing the speech rate
- pronouncing language clearly
- using standard English
- repeating key words and phrases

Using contextual clues

- hand gestures
- facial expressions
- dramatizing meaning
- using hands-on material and manipulatives
- placing language in a physical ''here and now'' context to the greatest extent possible

Research has shown that another practice, small group work, is effective because it provides the potential for multiple opportunities for second language learners to negotiate meaning in a nonthreatening peer-supported context that enhances cognitive development. Indeed, research suggests that second language learners make the most gains when they are engaged in extensive student-student and student-teacher interactions that involve feedback and negotiating meaning, and that second language learners may never develop full second language skills in the absence of extended opportunities to interact with native speaking peers.[21] Literacy development for second language learners can include the use of literacy scaffolds—temporary structures that provide support for language or literacy support in attaining a more complex level of proficiency.[22] These include journal wiring, retellings, read alouds, paired reading, patterned writing, and mapping. General approaches to second language learning call for comprehensible input, student linguistic support, and whole language strategies to support second language learning.[23]

Classroom-based studies point to the effectiveness of combining content learning and second language learning.[24] In one study, ESL students were asked to draw from what they had learned about missions and Spanish settlements in social studies to collectively give short summaries both in oral and written form, to clarify what they did not understand, and to develop a list of questions for which they sought answers. A second study reported that classroom teachers successfully guided ESL students to classify information of a particular body of knowledge, basing new information on students' prior knowledge. The researcher suggests that "with a little conscious planning, teachers can integrate 'good' language teaching and 'good' content teaching."[25]

Bilingual Education

Bilingual education provides instruction in two languages: the home language and the ones to be acquired. Bilingual education uses native language instruction in combination with second language instruction to support the student's *learning* and, ultimately, *second language learning*. James Cummins has provided much of the theory supporting this educational approach in six key points:

1. Children learn best when they are taught in the language they function in the best—their native language.
2. Children should therefore develop a high level of native language proficiency in order to maintain normal cognitive and academic development.
3. Developing cognitive and academic abilities in the native language serves as the basis for second language development, for what is learned in the native language can be transferred and expressed in the second language, given sufficient proficiency.
4. A high level of native language proficiency must be developed before deriving benefit from second language instruction. Cummins refers to this as the *threshold* level.
5. Time spent developing native language proficiency therefore does not impede second language development.
6. Time spent developing native language proficiency eventually significantly improves second language development.[26]

Cummins further clarified the theory by distinguishing between two types of language: that used for everyday face-to-face oral communication and that which is required for understanding and talking about academic concepts. He referred to the first type as Basic Interpersonal Communication Skills (BICS) and the second as Cognitive and Academic Language Proficiency (CALP). This is a useful distinction to recall when students seem to communicate well in English at recess or lunch, but are lost during a social studies or science lesson. Two to three years is required to develop BICS and five to seven years for CALP. Thus, developing proficient second language skills is a process that occurs over some period of time.

There are two basic bilingual education models: maintenance and traditional. The goal of a maintenance bilingual education model is to preserve the native language while adding the second language. Thus some level of native language instruction is maintained throughout a bilingual education program, while English is also added. Maintenance models have not been the preferred vision, although Garcia notes a recent increase in the number of programs whose goal it is to produce bilingual and biliterate students.[27]

The goal of a transitional bilingual education model is for students to become fully functional in English. The native language is used as a vehicle by which to help students develop academically until it can be supplanted by instruction in English. This model is the most commonly used in the United States. The typical amount of time allotted for students in a transitional bilingual education program in the United States is from two to four years, clearly an inadequate time frame, given research findings by Cummins and others (see above under the discussion of BICS and CALP). Research results frequently indicate that students coming from "early exit" bilingual education programs neither develop high levels of native language proficiency nor adequate levels of English to benefit from second language instruction. In contrast, students in a well-implemented "late exit" transitional bilingual education program *do* demonstrate English language proficiency over time. The first two to three years the students learn in their native language, and receive English-as-a-second-language instruction daily. In the third, fourth, and sometimes fifth years, English replaces the native language for some content instruction. In the fifth, sixth, and seventh years, instruction is largely in English, for by this time the students will have developed a threshold level in the native language and sufficient English to derive full benefit from second language instruction.

Both maintenance and transitional models require students to transition to second language instruction. Eleanor Thonis provides four workable and straightforward guidelines that many school districts have adapted for use in transitioning students, especially the first two: (1) a high level of academic ability (CALP) in the native language, usually demonstrated by well-developed literacy skills; (2) a high level of oral language proficiency (BICS) in the second language; (3) adequate pronunciation and ear-training in the second language; and (4) a high level of interest in learning the second language.[28]

A well-implemented bilingual education program of either model must include the following minimum elements: (1) a teacher who is fully bilingual in English and in the language of the students, (2) a full class of students who share the same home language, (3) an adequate supply of quality educational materials to support the native language instructional program, and (4) a consistent program with schoolwide commitment. When all of these elements are in place, bilingual education is the preferred mode of instruction. However, the absence of any one of these elements necessarily means inadequate implementation, underdeveloped native and English language skills, with resulting poor student performance on academic measures. Results like these further call to question the positive benefits of bilingual education. Regardless of the aspect of the curriculum, failure is the predicted and logical outcome for program implementation that is inconsistent across the grades, carried out by inadequately trained teachers who may turn instruction over to instructional aides, and poor or unavailable instructional materials.

Research supports positive student outcomes in well-implemented "late exit" transition bilingual education programs.[29] Students who learn only in English initially show the most academic and linguistic growth, but students with native language instruction academically surpass them, typically in about grade three. Also, students with primary language fluency engage in rich meaning making in both languages. These findings support Cummins' theory that time spent in developing the native language serves as the basis for and eventually improves second language development.

Eleven Principles of Second Language Learning

The Foreign Language Section of the *Association for Supervision and Curriculum Development Handbook* offers eleven principles that promote effective second language instruction in the public schools.[30] These are provided below. For each principle the reader is provided with additional background explanation and examples of good practice that promote language learning for English-as-a-second language learners.

Principle 1: Second language learning should emulate authentic language use. Teachers must engage students in a communicative approach to language. This means establishing an environment and a curriculum that is based on authentic language models, real-life tasks, and that naturally draw students to communicate. For example, past tense pattern practice drills and verb conjugations are not authentic uses of language, but having students explain an amusing event that occurred is.

The concept of authentic language fits well within the classroom context because of the natural ways in which it can be used for social and academic learning purposes. Teachers should organize for instruction in ways that encourage students to communicate with each other in small groups and pairs. This permits second language learners multiple opportunities to receive meaningful input from their peers as well as to engage in linguistic output as they negotiate for meaning in completing academic activities and assignments.

Teachers and English-speaking peers can promote understanding for second language learners by providing contextual clues (hands-on material, hand gestures, facial expressions, and other ways that place language in a physical ''here and now'' context) that guide students to understand the concepts and the language that accompany them. Thus, effective teachers of second language learners provide authentic ways for developing their students' second language abilities by helping them develop cognitively, and by promoting language use that allows them to express their new knowledge.

Principle 2: The goal of language learning is performance with language rather than knowledge about language. Grammar used to be the keystone upon which second language learning was based. The preferred focus is now learning how to use language, or performance-based competence. Because performance is the ultimate goal of instruction, teachers should provide instructional time for students to practice skill development in the classroom, but it must be in the context of communicative language, not in isolation such as practice drills.

Stephen Krashen suggested that a theoretical construct he called the "monitor hypothesis" is what some second language learners use to "filter" their second language through to ensure it is correct.[31] He suggests that rule-governed language use is not as natural as language that has been learned unconsciously, nor is it learned as efficiently. However, teachers should expose students to some formal aspects of language, especially older students who often want to learn the rules of a language; but younger students often learn much better in natural contexts of the classroom. Therefore formal knowledge about a second language should have a small part in the language learning process, but engaging students in performance and communicative processes is much more effective in promoting second language learning.

Principle 3: Language learning is not additively sequential but it is recursive and paced differently at various stages of acquisition. Many factors affect rate of language acquisition: developmental factors, native language, exposure to meaningful language input, universal patterns of language acquisition, and affective influences such as motivation, self-esteem, and attitude toward the second language. Clearly, meaningful language input is a necessary component of language learning. Learner ability to receive meaningful input varies across circumstances and students. For example, a student who is motivated and at ease in a second language learning situation is receptive to language input. Krashen refers to a learner's affective predisposition as the "affective filter."[32] Low student interest and excessive error correction are discouraging and frustrating and generally cause the learner to be less enthusiastic about learning the language. Consequently, teachers should engage in minimal error correction and provide interesting and developmentally appropriate material for students.

Despite the fact that there is a great deal of variation in rate of acquisition across learners, general stages of development are helpful markers for teachers to know about. Tracy Terrell developed the Natural Approach, four stages of language development that teachers who work with second language learners can use in guiding them to develop specially designed academic instruction, or sheltered language instruction:[33] preproduction, early production, speech emergence, and intermediate fluency. In the first stage, student listens a great deal and can answer yes-no, and there are other simple questions requiring short answers. In the second stage, the student can manage to respond to questions with short sentences and has an expressive vocabulary of about 100 words. In the third stage, the student can engage in conversations and narratives, and has an expressive vocabulary of about 2,500 words. In the fourth stage, the student achieves native-like oral fluency but requires a great deal of assistance in literacy development.

Principle 4: Language develops in a series of approximations toward native-like norms. Language learning is not the accumulation of perfectly mastered elements of grammar and vocabulary. Thus, learner errors are unavoidable. This principle addresses the incredibly creative process that language learning is. Speakers never reproduce language exactly as modeled. Errors play an important role in second language learning as speakers approximate native-like speech. Errors are a natural, expected, and necessary part of language learning as the learner progresses toward native-like competency.

It serves little purpose for teachers to insist that second language learners repeat phrases until they are perfect. Through repeated exposure and practice in natural settings, students will learn standard forms and pronunciation. Additionally, it is important for teachers to realize that students who are first exposed to the second language may say very little in the first several weeks or months, despite encouraging or downright prodding. Terrell refers to this as the ''silent period,'' when the learner is processing a great deal of receptive language.[34] This is a natural stage of language development. Teachers should not worry about a new and very quiet second language learner. Language will emerge in its own time as long as the student is provided with meaningful language input.

Principle 5: Language proficiency involves comprehension and production; comprehension abilities tend to precede and exceed productive abilities. Comprehension is a key factor in language development. Receptive abilities—listening and reading—typically develop in advance of the productive or expressive abilities—speaking and writing. It is critical to continue to provide the learner with comprehensible input and authentic language models, and important to realize the benefit that the learner receives from the input may not be immediately observable.

Teachers should provide comprehensible input and authentic models of usage, both in oral and written forms. These include journal writing, retellings, read alouds, paired reading, patterned writing, and story mapping. Additionally, small-group work provides the necessary format for students to engage in language output. Peer interaction is key to providing opportunities for meaning negotiation and repeated practice in a social context. Thus it is critical that teachers provide frequent and extended opportunities for second language learners to interact with native-speaking peers.

Principle 6: Language is inextricably bound to culture; language use requires an understanding of the cultural context within which communication takes place. Language teachers have long recognized that language and culture are interrelated. To learn a second language is to learn a new culture. Therefore, total language competence requires that the second language be taught in a culturally sensitive way. For linguistically diverse students, teachers must attend to the distinctions between home and school and language and culture if educational endeavors are to be successful.

Language and sociolinguistic conventions are used differently across cultures. For example, how we respond to and interpret situations and how we accomplish things with language are all bound with culture. Does a second language learner initiate conversation with an adult in the home culture and language? Offer an opinion or suggestion to a group? What are the linguistic norms of the home? What are the discourse patterns, the nonverbal communication, patterns of socialization and learning styles of the home culture? These are likely to differ for the language and culture of the school. Thus, second language learners must not only learn the language of the school but also the new culture in which it is embedded.

A specific way that teachers can help students bridge cultural and linguistic learning is to teach them how to "do things" with language. Linguists call these speech acts. For example, inviting, accepting, refusing, complementing, thanking, greeting, and leave-taking are all ways we accomplish things through language and that are culturally bound. Teaching second language learners how to accomplish these things can be done through role playing and short dramatizations. These provide the student with an important way of becoming comfortable and proficient in the second language and the second culture.

Principle 7: Language learning is complex; instruction takes into account individual learning styles and rates, and also attends to teaching process strategies for successful learning. Many factors affect a student's ability to learn a second language. While some of these such as age and native language are beyond a teacher's control, teachers can successfully address other factors such as strengthening motivation, lessening anxiety, and improving learning strategies.

It is especially important for teachers to consider interests and developmental ages of their second language learners in order to maintain high levels of motivation while they are engaged in the challenge of learning in a second language. It is also important that teachers of students who demonstrate observable levels of anxiety do not overcorrect these students or insist that they verbally "perform" on command, but rather encourage communication in pairs, small groups, or even in written format until the anxiety level is reduced. It is also helpful to specifically teach a variety of social, affective, and comprehension strategies that enhance language learning. Examples of these are asking questions, cooperating with peers, taking linguistic risks, encouraging oneself, using sounds and mental images, and using context to make guesses.[35]

Principle 8: The ability to perform with language is facilitated when students actively engage in meaningful, authentic, and purposeful language learning tasks. Meaning and purpose in authentic situations result in proficient language learners. This means that teachers must engage students in the use of real language to communicate in real-life situations. Regardless of the type of second language classroom, teachers who offer active language environments enhance their students' abilities to engage in high-level language and thinking skills, and in meaningful, authentic language use. It is critical for teachers of second language learners to engage in less teacher talk and provide ample opportunities for their students to develop oral and literacy skills in authentic contexts. Again, structuring paired and small-group work around tasks that students must complete together provides meaningful language engagement for second language learners.

Principle 9: Assessment reflects instructional goals and is performance-oriented. Assessment should measure a student's ability to perform authentic communication tasks. Assessment procedures and materials should come from a variety of sources, including formal tests and a student portfolio that documents growth in listening, speaking, reading, and writing.

Portfolios lend themselves well to assessing second language learners in all of the language modes, as well as for content area assessment. The latter is of great concern to teachers in that second language learners often know and understand more than standard content assessment measures indicate. Engaging students in oral and written retellings and measuring them with open-ended rubrics, periodic taped oral interviews using the same questions across interviews, and writing samples from across the curriculum that include content area journals are all measures that teachers can use both for diagnosis and evaluation of student progress and to profile a student's changing abilities and needs.

Principle 10: Technology and textbook materials play a support role for language learning goals: they should not determine curriculum. This principle speaks to the need for language teachers to integrate various forms of teaching materials, media, and technology into the foreign language curriculum. The caution is that these should be included in a planned and organized manner that is integrated with the curriculum in order to avoid a smorgasboard approach to language learning.

Teachers who work with students of diverse backgrounds are encouraged to go beyond textbooks to use authentic and high-quality literature, whole language strategies, and thematic instruction. Thematic instruction creates a meaningful conceptual framework that allows students to use oral and written language for learning content. The theme establishes a context that supports comprehensible input, which in turn increases both content learning and second language development. Theme-based collaborative projects also create student interest, motivation, involvement, and purpose. Further, there are an increasing number of technological innovations appropriate for use with second language learners. The extent to which teachers are able to include thematic instruction and a variety of support material and technology will enhance learning for students of linguistically diverse backgrounds.

Principle 11: Teachers are qualified in the languages they teach. This implies proficiency in the language, experience with the cultures represented by the language, and pedagogical expertise specific to the language. Schools are encouraged to consult teacher standards developed by relevant professional organizations.

This principle especially pertains to foreign language teachers and teachers in bilingual education programs. While we realize the improbability of ever having a sufficient quantity of qualified bilingual teachers, it is critical that those who *are* teaching in bilingual classrooms be highly proficient in both languages. Data from bilingual education classrooms show that students who develop high levels of native language proficiency ultimately show positive achievement levels in English.[36] Teachers must therefore provide correct and appropriate oral and literacy modeling and must engage students in discourse to help them develop high levels of thinking skills in that language. In order for teachers to accomplish this, they must possess fully developed other-than-English language skills. Language assessment for prospective bilingual education teachers must also be appropriate and adequate to determine levels of proficiency.

ADDRESSING THE NEEDS OF CULTURALLY DIVERSE STUDENTS

Several researchers have provided frameworks or typologies as a means of organizing and understanding the growing array of literature in the field of multicultural education.[37] The challenge of developing a single framework or typology that encompasses the broad range of literature related to multicultural education lies in the inconsistencies and multiple meanings of terms across researchers, lack of clarity, and omitted or interrelated categories. Despite differences in nomenclature or overarching organization, researchers and practitioners hold the common vision that the intent of the study of multicultural education is to reform practices to provide all students equality in education, and to empower all students to become full participants in our society.

In this section, we will examine the research that best supports classroom practice and will discuss the implications of this research for teacher preparation programs. To do so, we borrow from Banks' conceptualization of multicultural education, which includes content knowledge and integration, knowledge construction, prejudice reduction, equity pedagogy, and empowering school culture.[38] While this framework is very useful in terms of conceptualizing the key issues, the categories are not mutually exclusive. Overlap does exist. We suggest that all of these elements must be present in order for ''best practice'' to occur and to bring about equity for all students.

Content Knowledge and Integration

This dimension addresses specific content knowledge about diverse groups for teachers as well as students, and where this knowledge should be located. It also asks the question ''who should the audience be?''

Content knowledge integration is a key element of multicultural education. Researchers assume that there is a link between how much teachers know and how much they utilize what they know in their teaching. This assumption is also evidence in preservice and in-service professional development. Wayne Wayson examined how much factual information prospective teachers have about specific ethnic or cultural groups to establish teacher preparedness for multicultural education, and found that 40 percent felt inadequately prepared to teach children of diverse backgrounds.[39] Gary Moultry suggested that ethnic studies (content knowledge) help prospective teachers develop empathy toward the students whom they will teach and that preservice teachers should therefore be required to take one university course whose content addresses a specific cultural group.[40] Patricia Avery and Constance Walker state that "preservice teachers who have not had the opportunity to develop their awareness, knowledge, and skills at working with diverse populations will be inadequately prepared to meet the classrooms of a diversity society."[41]

It stands to reason that teachers must have background knowledge in order to implement it in the classroom. Typically, preservice and in-service teachers acquire this knowledge through single-group studies courses. The assumption of requiring single-group ethnic studies courses in teacher preparation programs is that knowledge should be taught separately from methods courses to provide in-depth understanding and knowledge. On the one hand, single-group ethnic studies courses develop a knowledge base and a better understanding of the children of a particular cultural and/or linguistic background. On the other hand, these in-depth studies often leave teachers wondering how to utilize this information in appropriate and meaningful ways in the classroom context. Furthermore, prospective teachers will likely take only one such course and thus will become well-versed with only one ethnic group. This is problematic in states with highly diverse populations. In such cases, a more general ethnic studies course that focuses on two or three ethnic groups may be more useful. Teachers must realize that some information is for professional development and is critical to helping them view their students through a broader lens to understand students of diverse backgrounds. Additionally, however, ethnic study courses should assist teachers in developing ways to integrate this knowledge into content areas. If not, this valuable knowledge too often becomes a useless artifact.

An effective way to integrate information across the curriculum is to embed into any course or content area examples, information, data, and knowledge in general from a variety of cultural and ethnic backgrounds to illustrate principles, generalizations, or concepts particular to a specific course of study. This approach is valuable because it addresses the unique needs of ethnic minority students, allows for a broad view of a variety of cultures and ethnic groups by a cross-section of the student population, and helps all students develop democratic attitudes. However, this approach requires that teachers have a considerable knowledge base. A caution with this approach is that teachers may excuse themselves from the responsibility of integrating content knowledge into all subject areas, perceiving multicultural education as relevant only to certain subjects.[42]

Knowledge Construction

A key element in multicultural education is developing perspectives and understandings that take us beyond our understandings and assumptions about how things are. Knowledge construction helps students and teachers examine how we come to know something, what the points of reference are, what our biases are, and what governs what we value. To illustrate the point of perspectives, Hugh Price, having grown up in Washington, D.C., recalls learning about the

Civil War—the southern version—and learning later in life that there was a northern version of the same war.[43] In applying knowledge construction to classroom practice, teachers engage students in examining events and issues from multiple perspectives and guide them in considering ethical, social, and racial or ethnic aspects, as well as social and political contexts in which events occur. Knowledge construction enables students to draw their own conclusions, and ultimately to become agents for social change. Teaching practices that promote knowledge construction are not self-evident, and teacher preparation programs should be designed to help prospective teachers develop and implement specific strategies to help their students develop multiple perspectives.

Textbooks are the most common teaching tool. Aside from textbooks that may not offer students opportunities to question issues or to develop a broad view of the society, teacher modification of the curriculum offers a viable approach. Banks provides an approach to multicultural curriculum development that is practical and provides teachers a means of self-assessment ("I am here in terms of my curriculum development vis-a-vis multicultural education") and a way to become more skilled and sophisticated at integrating multiple perspectives.[44] Banks' four levels of multicultural curriculum development are the contributions approach, the additive approach, the transformation approach, and the social action approach. If taught to develop curriculum that reaches the higher levels of this scheme, teachers will be most likely to engage students in developing multiple perspectives.

The *contributions approach*, referred to by some as "heroes and holidays," provides a means for teachers to include elements such as a celebration, a typical food, or other discrete aspects of culture. While this approach is commonly used because it is easy and allows for content knowledge and curriculum integration, it does not encourage students to develop an understanding of these discrete elements in a broader cultural context. The *additive approach* adds a unit of study about a cultural or ethnic group, and permits more inclusion of specific content knowledge, typically through a unit of study about a particular group as, for example, the Native Americans of the Northwest.

The remaining two levels, the transformation approach and the social action approach, guide students in constructing other-than-mainstream understandings and perspectives. The *transformation approach* requires that teachers modify the standard curriculum by including divergent views and complexities of any event that shapes history and who we are. For example, studying the American Revolution by infusing perspectives of the Loyalists faithful to the crown, or of the French who had just lost a war to the British, provide students with a richer, multidimensional view of the war. Similarly, a transformation approach in studying the Sioux Nation might include an examination of the role of the buffalo as seen from each of the worldviews of the European American and the Sioux in the film *Dances With Wolves*, thus guiding students to develop a broader way of seeing and understanding.[45]

The *social action approach* moves students into the realm of acting upon a belief or understanding. In this approach, students define a concern or problem, gather data, draw conclusions, and decide upon a course of action to take in an attempt to bring about change. A key component is to help students develop social and efficacy tools that they can utilize beyond their public schooling years. This approach takes considerable commitment from a teacher, but there is support for positive effects resulting from this approach. For example, George Wood describes a teacher who effectively engaged students in social action by adapting an English curriculum to meet the students' needs and interests, which ultimately resulted in a community-based project to provide assistance to needy teens.[46] Again, a social action approach prepares students to work toward social equity and improving the social condition while helping them develop skills that will serve them throughout their lives.

Carl Grant and Christine Sleeter's *Turning on Learning* is a text devoted to helping teachers develop specific lessons and units in all areas of the standard school curriculum that connect with students' interests and develop students' abilities to examine from multiple perspectives common occurrences from everyday life, capitalize on diverse in-class resources, and expand their understandings to include broader social contexts.[47] For example, a lesson on the importance of math in everyday life becomes "multicultural" and helps students develop multiple perspectives when, in addition to identifying jobs and tasks that involve mathematics, they are asked to develop a chart indicating how many people of color and which gender most commonly hold these jobs/complete these tasks, which of these jobs pay the most, and how much education and how much and what kind of math training is necessary to do these jobs. A social studies unit on the Hmong and Khmer suggested by Grant and Sleeter does not begin with a lecture or readings about Cambodian and Hmong people, but from *within* that culture by having students view a film on the refugee camp experiences of a family and their subsequent adjustment to life in the United States. Other procedures include an interview with a member of the Hmong culture (possibly a fellow classmate) and viewing and discussing a video on Cambodian health care and practices. The latter assignment again begins from within the Cambodian culture, providing students the opportunity to build an understanding of values, beliefs, and understandings from a non-Western perspective.

Prejudice Reduction

This dimension of multicultural education supports the examination of our values, beliefs, and biases as a means of becoming more open and accepting of others, and of developing more democratic attitudes, values, and behaviors. Prejudice reduction pertains both to students and teachers and is a crucial element of teacher preparation. Teachers who do not recognize and examine their own beliefs, values, and biases will not be successful in engaging students in examining *their* views and beliefs.

As with content knowledge, many researchers assume that there exists a direct relationship between teachers' beliefs and attitudes toward children of diverse backgrounds and how effectively they will be able to teach these students. It is clear from the studies that have investigated this issue that teacher preparation programs must devote time and attention that allow and challenge teachers to examine their attitudes and beliefs about students of diverse backgrounds, and to help them develop an awareness of the multiple factors that influence students' ability to perform well on school tasks.

The desegregation efforts of the 1970s mandated that changes occur in how we group children across school districts; however the schools did not develop models or resources to help children or teachers find ways of addressing students' attitudes and beliefs once the students were regrouped. Cooperative learning provides one such vehicle. Findings from studies on cooperative learning generally reveal that it improves academic performance of ethnically diverse students and that it improves attitudes of all students toward members of other ethnic groups.[48] Thus, teachers would do well to implement some cooperative learning strategies as one means of improving students' attitudes toward each other.

Other research, however, points to the importance of teaching students how to share equitably in the tasks and responsibilities to be accomplished, because when this is not done, mainstream students tend to dominate.[49] Children do come to school with misconceptions about other groups outside their own, but these views can change over time with the help of carefully implemented cooperative learning strategies. Children can learn to espouse more democratic and inclusive views and attitudes necessary to survive in an increasingly multicultural society. Many professional preparation programs teach prospective teachers how to implement a variety of cooperative learning strategies, and should continue to do so, since this is a viable way to reduce prejudice among students.

Equity Pedagogy

Children of diverse ethnic and cultural backgrounds have experiences in their early preschool lives that are significantly different from those of middle-class European American children. Indeed, their life experiences in their formative years often place them at odds with mainstream American school culture. They often do not easily enter into the public school institution that reflects norms, values, and knowledge that are consonant with European American middle-class America. As a consequence, students of diverse ethnic, cultural, and linguistic backgrounds often experience home-school discontinuities early in their schooling and if not addressed by appropriate teaching result in getting them off to a bad start that spirals downward as they move through their public school experience. Thus it is critical that teachers, 83 percent of whom are culturally different from the students they teach, utilize approaches that maximize these students' cultural and linguistic capital and that help them mediate school knowledge so as to expand their cultural and linguistic boundaries. Equity pedagogy focuses on teaching strategies, techniques, methods, and approaches that allow teachers to make learning available and equitable for all students. Knowing how to utilize these approaches does not come intuitively. Prospective teachers must be provided with examples of approaches used by exemplary practicing teachers that embody equity pedagogy. Student teachers must be encouraged in their fieldwork to implement similar approaches.

An important research focus of the 1970s was that of valuing the home dialect or language. As Grant and Sleeter state, "teachers must be careful not to punish or criticize students for having mastered their home dialect; rather they should view it as a language base on which mastery of an additional dialect can be built."[50] This view of the home language or dialect developed in the 1970s through the work of linguists such as Stephen and Joan Baratz, William Labov, and Geneva Smitherman.[51] Their work established black English as a language system in its own right that is closely related to standard English, but governed by its own systematic rules for usage. This resulted in the firm belief that carries through until today that effective teachers find ways to both validate the language that the child brings to school and to assist the child in adding to that linguistic repertoire.

The ethnographic studies that emerged in the 1980s utilize the richness of careful, detailed description to help teachers understand children's cultural environments and realities in which children spend the first five years of their lives. This research helps teachers understand their students' home-school discontinuities as they move between the home culture and the mainstream culture of school that often negatively impacts on students' abilities to become full participants in mainstream schools.[52] Teachers can use the careful and detailed descriptions provided by ethnographic researchers who explore modes of cultural transmission, socialization practices, and ways of learning and knowing to inform educational practice. Teachers whose instructional approaches reflect a sensitivity to a student's home culture provide their students with a solid foundation on which to build school success.

On the basis of ethnographic research, several specific recommendations have been made to modify the teaching-learning process in multicultural contexts. For example, the work of Kathryn Au et al. demonstrates that when teachers were trained to use "talk story" (a Hawaiian way of story telling) in conjunction with reading instruction, reading comprehension of Hawaiian students improved substantially.[53] Henry Trueba and Concha Delgado-Gaitan examined the concepts of sharing and cheating among Latino students as viewed by Latino and mainstream teachers and found that the views held by each group of teachers greatly affected how they interpreted their students' actions in the classroom.[54] The researchers suggest that if teachers understand that the line between sharing and cheating is drawn differently for Latino students, they may interpret students' classroom behavior differently. Esteban Diaz, Luis Moll, and Hugh Mehan describe a project in which writing modules were developed, based on community data gathered by trained parents and other community residents.[55]

The data then served as the basis for the writing modules the teachers used to help middle school students develop literacy skills.

Thus, through knowledge of a particular culture based on ethnographic studies, teachers can incorporate diverse ways of organizing for instruction and teaching. They can accept diverse patterns of interaction and ways of learning and expressing knowledge. Further, teachers who understand their students' home culture can advocate for their students in ways that may not be understood or appreciated by other teachers because they possess a broader cultural context in which to understand and value their students.

Empowering School Culture

As a result of declining student achievement and lack of public support, schools have begun to change their fundamental ways of operation. Occurring under the broad heading of "restructuring," these efforts to revamp how schools look and behave have taken many different forms. Clearly, one area that should be of major concern in these plans to restructure is helping teachers meet the needs of their diverse student populations by empowering the school culture— that is, creating a school environment that is inclusive of and meaningful for all students. Most frequently, beginning teachers learn how to teach specific subject matter, but they receive little training in how to change educational environments, in how to "shake up" the system.

There are competing forces in this particular aspect of the reform movement: those who believe that the role of schools today is to continue to try to assimilate students in the mainstream American culture, and those who believe that schools should be charged with empowering people of color as well as educating well the mainstream. Until there is a fundamental agreement as to which role is paramount, the education of teachers will continue to be the whipping post for what is wrong with schools. As Cherry Banks states, "even though the recent national focus on education has put school reform on the front burner, much of today's discussion resurrects old approaches and does not address the complexity of urban schools."[56] She notes that school choice, new kinds of testing, and more rigorous high school graduation standards are largely silent on the issues of equity. They abandon the issues of high quality education for all but, more importantly, for the most part they ignore the fundamental knowledge, attitudes, and skills that teachers bring to the classroom.

Those of us in teacher education are confident that we can help teachers construct the technical knowledge needed to build curriculum and teach linguistically and culturally diverse student populations. What has proved to be the greatest challenge is changing attitudes and belief systems about diversity, language, color, parent-participation, testing, and eliminating the "us" versus "them" mentality of both prospective teachers and the current teaching force that will be needed if we are truly to empower the school culture.

Some of the critical elements necessary to bring about school empowerment for students of all backgrounds that can be addressed through school restructuring include changing grouping practices, structuring time for on-going professional development, and promoting the importance of teacher expectations for student achievement. Programs to prepare school administrators will need to deal in depth with these issues if real change is to occur. We can also learn from the promising practices in schools that have successfully met the needs of their students over a period of time.

Prime among these promising practices is attention to grouping and tracking. Grouping practices that segregate students do not promote an empowering school culture and must be eliminated. Such practices can occur either within an elementary classroom or structurally throughout an entire school, typically a high school. Jeanne Oakes' work on student placement and tracking showed that students of color and low-income students are typically counseled into non-academic classes and into classes that take them off-campus and away from systematic contact with core academic programs. She also found that women and students of color are considerably underrepresented in university programs in mathematics and the sciences.[57] Discriminatory grouping practices frequently expose students to less demanding content and undermine students' confidence in their own abilities. Additionally, students who are placed in "ability groups" tend to remain in the same groups and fall farther behind each year. Counseling students of color and low-income students into vocational rather than academic classes and placing them on the basis of perceived ability are practices that put them in jeopardy of academic success and achieving to their capacity. Teachers must be mindful of groups or classes in which an overrepresentation of a particular ethnic group exists. Examining and changing student placement practices and counseling practices wherever inequities exist is critical for empowering school culture.

An issue that positively impacts school culture is establishing schoolwide staff development. Teachers feel the enormous pressure of time constraints, and as more professional demands are made on them, it becomes critical for schools to structure time and provide useful ways to help teachers examine their own attitudes and beliefs and develop more background knowledge and related teaching strategies and approaches. This structured time for teachers is a key element in promoting an equitable school culture. Teachers also benefit from demonstrations, practice, and peer coaching as well as coursework and on-going in-service training rather than single-session in-services.[58]

Teacher preparation programs must also underscore the importance of teacher expectations in student achievement as one of the most powerful determinants of how students perform academically. Examples from educational research and from the popular media that include books and films (such as *Stand and Deliver*) attest to the power that teachers hold in expecting and receiving the best from their students.[59] One of the most compelling examples is Marva Collins' personal story of how she refused to accept that the children in her housing project neighborhood school were any less capable and competent than children from

different racial backgrounds and different neighborhoods.[60] Her successful academy with its years-long waiting list and the success of its graduates epitomize
the power that teacher expectations hold in academic achievement for students
of color.

What, then, are elements that should be developed in schools seeking to establish an empowered school culture for all students? James Comer and colleagues developed a model of education to help address the learning needs of
students of color of a low socioeconomic background.[61] Most notably, the
Comer model includes restructuring a school to establish participatory policy
and decision-making processes that include all school staff and parents, and
developing immediate solutions to problems rather than placing blame on the
students. These elements operate within the underlying assumption that all students can and will learn. The Comer model was successfully implemented in
two inner-city schools in the late 1960s and is currently yielding positive results
in similar settings. Tamara Lucas, Rosemary Henze, and Ruben Donato examined schools throughout the United States to determine what promoted success
for language-minority students.[62] They found the following common elements
among six schools that best promoted success for their language minority students:

- Value is placed on the students' languages and cultures.
- High expectations of language minority students are made concrete.
- School leaders make the education of language minority students a priority.
- Staff development is designed to help all school personnel serve language minority
  students more effectively.
- A variety of courses and programs for language-minority students is offered.
- A counseling program gives special attention to language minority students.
- Parents are encouraged to become involved in their children's education.
- School staff members share a strong commitment to empower language minority stu-
  dents through education.[63]

Drawing from research on the common elements among schools that have
established empowering environments for all students, we know that the following are very important: basic skills and content that students are expected to
master, whole staff accountability, parent/school contact, a counseling program
with special attention given to the needs of students of color, value placed on
students' language and culture, and principals as instructional leaders, disciplinarians and evaluators.

In addition to examining issues of language and culture as they impact on
students of diverse backgrounds, another means of providing insight that can
inform teacher preparation is to look at studies that focus on teachers who are
deemed especially successful by other teachers, parents, administrators, students,

or by a combination of these. In the next section we will examine findings from several case studies to add another dimension to effective practice.

CASE STUDIES

A number of case studies have examined the classroom practices and environments of teachers who have been particularly successful in promoting academic success among linguistically and culturally diverse students.[64] Case studies are useful in that they provide insight on what are effective practices, and they often reveal common practices and attributes across these teachers and their classrooms. The following are the case study findings of effective teachers of culturally diverse students. Student teachers should be encouraged to engage in similar approaches.

1. The teachers in these studies create learning environments so that students can develop cognitively and linguistically. They engage in strategies and approaches that promote communication between the students and themselves as well as among the students. These teachers often organize instruction thematically. Themes and topics may be student selected or negotiated with the teacher. The teachers, however, see themselves as ultimately responsible for ensuring that the students learn the appropriate skills and content knowledge.

2. These teachers activate students' prior knowledge and engage them in ways to use and expand what they know. Their students frequently engage in small collaborative group work that promotes student discourse. Students seek and obtain information from each other, support and encourage each other, ask each other hard questions, and challenge each others' answers. Through these strategies and approaches, the teachers promote social learning processes that in turn enhance all aspects of language and cognitive development.

3. These teachers are current in their knowledge and use of language arts instructional strategies. This is a critical area because these strategies and approaches are also relevant to instruction in many of the content areas. They engage their students in literature study groups, various types of journal writing, classroom publication ventures—in short, reading and writing for a variety of authentic purposes. They also assess their students' abilities in a variety of ways, including the use of sampled work across time to note areas of growth and weaknesses.

4. These teachers participate in professional activities, often as leaders. Many of them see themselves as well-informed instructional innovators in their schools. They are frequently sought out by other colleagues for ideas and advice. Many of them conduct professional development workshops and in-services in their districts or through professional organizations. They also continuously seek professional development for themselves. Related to this, they are reflective practitioners. They think about and communicate their philosophies, which are consistent with their teaching practices. They are professionally well-grounded

and knowledgeable, and they easily articulate their knowledge base and beliefs about teaching.

5. These teachers embed instruction in a context that fosters mutual accommodation. They realize that their students of diverse backgrounds are often required to adapt to the school environment in ways that mainstream students often do not even consider. Thus these teachers seek ways to develop a mutually respectful environment. The following quote from a case study on exemplary teachers of second language learners exemplifies the accommodation that teachers of diverse students make:

> I grew up in an anglo-centric environment where you sit down, you think things through, and you do your work. It worked for me. When I came here to teach, I found I had to re-orient my thinking, and it is a different way of doing business.[65]

6. Some teachers specifically include culturally relevant material and perspectives—for example, a thematic unit on monsters that includes Mexican legends and folktales that deal with the supernatural.[66] Another example comes from a predominantly Latino classroom that also included students from other ethnic and racial backgrounds. We quote the same teacher as above:

> We also try to develop different perspectives. Our Vietnamese student believes in ghosts. On *Dia de los Muertos* [Day of the Dead, a day celebrated in Mexico and Central America to honor deceased relatives], we discussed ghosts. Could they exist? Who believes in them? We talked about this.[67]

As a result of this and other classroom conversations about different beliefs and understandings, the students grew to have a broader understanding of their world, and as the teacher stated, "a lot of respect has emerged."[68]

7. For teachers of students of diverse backgrounds, mutual accommodation extends into the community. Teachers in these case studies seek innovative ways to foster home-school communication, include parents as resources in their instruction, have high levels of parent involvement, work hard to understand their students and the community, and advocate for students and their families in ways that often go beyond the level of engagement of their counterparts in classes with mainstream culture students. These teachers are highly committed to the academic success of their students, and know that parent communication and support is of key importance in this effort. The parents of these teachers' students often speak of the strong caring relationship between teacher and students. This is in contrast to Anglo parents, who may question the school's interest or authority to carry out instruction and activities in the students' best interest.[69] The parents view these teachers as trusted, respected, and honored for their efforts they make for their children.

These common elements across various case studies help us understand in real and workable ways what effective instruction is for students of diverse backgrounds. We need to ensure that this information is consistently infused into the teacher education curriculum and that student teachers receive support in implementing these approaches in their fieldwork. In the following section, we will synthesize the discussion so far regarding findings pertaining to the needs of second language learners, of culturally diverse learners, and of the case studies, and we will suggest commonalities of knowledge, skills, and experiences that best prepare teachers to work with students of diverse backgrounds.

INITIAL PREPARATION, CONTEXT-BASED PRACTICE, AND CONTINUED SUPPORT FOR TEACHERS WHO ADDRESS THE LEARNING NEEDS OF ALL STUDENTS

We have discussed various aspects of professional preparation for teachers who will work with diverse student populations, as well as what practices teachers should engage in to promote success for all their students. What, then, would be the key aspects for inclusion in teacher preparation programs, what should teachers do in the context of their schools, and what support would teachers need to ensure continued growth?

1. Teachers should demonstrate a broad acceptance of diversity and incorporate it into all aspects of their teaching and the curriculum. One of the best ways to accomplish this is to ensure that preservice teachers in professional preparation programs are continuously required to examine their own beliefs, to consider issues that impact on their teaching when working with students of diverse backgrounds, to adapt approaches, strategies, and techniques that will assist them in addressing the learning needs of students of diverse backgrounds, and to incorporate knowledge in all instruction that will prepare all students to live and work in a multicultural society. In-service follow-up to university coursework once teachers begin to work in their classrooms is even more effective in ensuring that teachers continue to use and build upon existing knowledge and best practice.[70] A collaborative, teamwork approach through pairing new and established teachers also provides modeling for different purposes that benefit both parties.

2. Student teachers should have ample exposure through fieldwork to students of diverse backgrounds and teachers who can model appropriate teaching approaches. University coursework alone is not enough to adequately prepare prospective teachers for working in diverse settings. Student teachers should experience a substantial amount of fieldwork simultaneously with supportive university coursework in settings with students of diverse backgrounds and with master teachers who are appropriately certified and can model the best practices.[71] Support in the field from master teachers and field supervisors is crucial, as is the need for being shown specific ways to implement what teachers learn in the university setting.[72] Theory, demonstration, practice, and peer coaching provide the best possible combination for guiding teachers to develop professional skills and abilities to address the needs of all students.

3. All school personnel should find multiple ways to make school-home-community connections. In the flow of a busy schedule, teachers and other school personnel sometimes lose track of the fact that both home and school are important environments and that the child's best interests are served when good communication occurs between both of these environments. Communication becomes especially important with families who are typically not a part of school life because they may feel uncomfortable or alienated in an environment with which they may have little experience. Effective teachers find ways to make connections with their students' families by establishing lines of communication and by finding a variety of ways to involve them in the life of the school. Teacher preparation programs must therefore help student teachers develop ways to reach out to their students' families, help them develop ways to capitalize on interests and talents that exist in the community and bring them into the school.

4. There should be a shared schoolwide commitment to continued professional development that helps teachers meet the educational needs of all students. Teachers should engage in staff development that is explicitly designed to develop strategies, techniques, and approaches that help them provide linguistically and culturally appropriate teaching, and to help teachers understand ways to value the languages and cultures of their students. Support through modeling and peer coaching should also be made available. Teachers should be offered incentives and compensation for their participation in this staff development.

NEEDED RESEARCH

We recognize that the schooling vulnerability that students of linguistically and culturally diverse backgrounds face is often caused by economic, social, and psychological challenges. Clearly, education is not the exclusive solution to bringing about change, but it is a key factor and our most optimistic one, because it is where we in the field of education have the greatest opportunity to bring about change. Yet many questions remain as we continue our efforts to prepare sufficient numbers of new teachers for our increasingly diverse student populations and as we attempt to provide staff development for our existing teacher force.

Much research is needed about the large questions relating to teacher preparation. One concern has to do with examining prospective teachers' beliefs. We know that beliefs are not the same as knowledge, that they drive decisions that people make, and that they are deeply ingrained and resistant to change.[73] Consequently, changes in prospective teachers' beliefs are not likely to occur within the duration of a teacher preparation program. Thus it becomes critical to select those candidates who either already hold the desired beliefs about issues relating to diverse students or who are likely to be amenable to change. Further research is needed on ways to examine prospective teachers' beliefs regarding issues of diversity and ways of guiding the selection process for teacher education programs. Research is also needed about successful ways to modify values and beliefs of new and existing teachers who *are* most likely to change their attitudes about students from diverse backgrounds.

Other questions also face us regarding the preparation of teachers to work with students of diverse populations. We know the field experiences in appropriate settings with appropriate modeling are crucial, but we do not know how long and how intense these should be. We also need more follow-up research on which practices teachers take from their university preparation and actually implement in the classroom. We must also come to some agreement on the basic knowledge and skills needed by teachers of diverse populations. S. Ana Garza and Carol Barnes, among others, have attempted to address this issue, but they have no empirical data to support their recommendations.[74] Professional preparation models for teachers who will work with students of diverse populations need to be carefully documented, field tested, compared, and the results disseminated.

This chapter has focused on teacher preparation, but it is important to examine which strategies and approaches work best with students in the classroom. There is a growing amount of descriptive data and recommendations regarding what teachers should do, but there is little empirical data on what, in fact, are effective practices in teaching students of diverse backgrounds. Related to this is the issue of examining various forms of student assessment. What are the most authentic forms of language assessment? Of content assessment? What kinds of assessment are culturally appropriate? We need this information in order to learn what is effective practice with students and therefore what is important to include in teacher education programs.

We also need more data that explore the relationship between cognitive development and bilingualism, as well as research that examines language development of younger versus older language learners. This information is crucial for teachers in implementing sound classroom practices.

Finally, we need to examine ways that prepare educators to interface with other professionals whose work directly impacts on students and their families. We speak of the importance of making home-school connections. Taken seriously, these connections cannot be seen only as how the school chooses to define the relationship, but rather what contributes to the students' overall well-being. We must cease to see our work as separate from the work of other professionals, because no single profession or institution working in isolation can address the various needs of students in ways that make a lasting difference. Successful schooling goes hand-in-hand with students' general well-being. Developing and examining ways of preparing teachers to work with other professionals in providing integrated services is also a critical component in moving us toward addressing the needs of all our students.

Clearer answers to these issues and questions can begin to help us refine accreditation standards, state credentialing requirements, and teacher preparation and staff development curriculum. Just as K–12 schools need major restructuring to serve the needs of all students, teacher education needs systemic reform to do a better job. At a time when research budgets are declining precipitously, this will be difficult to accomplish. We can only hope that the dire need for reform will overcome the obstacles.

CONCLUSION

We recognize that the issues surrounding the best preparation for teachers of linguistically and culturally diverse students is complex. This chapter has looked at the issue from an educational standpoint. In reality, the issues are embedded in a broader context. Academic success must be supported by students' physical, emotional, psychological, and social well-being. Oftentimes, in mainstream culture middle-class families, these are givens and they exist in ways that the school recognizes, legitimizes, and validates. With students of diverse backgrounds, these may be present in ways that mainstream culture does not recognize and that therefore create a home-school mismatch. The absence of any of these elements can cause school vulnerability.

We must bear in mind three facts as we take on preparing all of our students for tomorrow's world: (1) there are no quick fixes for problems that have developed over many years; (2) these complex issues and challenges cannot be singlehandedly addressed by educators operating in isolation from other professionals whose work directly impacts these students and their families; and (3) teacher educators and teachers must cease the "business as usual" approach. Regarding this final point, as educators we must make a fundamental change in the way we prepare teachers and in the way we approach the education of our students. We have presented a summary of both the theoretical and empirical background knowledge bases as well as some tangible and workable approaches that can move us toward bringing about change. Teacher educators must ensure that this aspect of professional preparation is an integral part of teacher preparation programs, most especially where geographical location dictates this need. We need to make this the norm for teacher preparation so that outstanding practices and educational models become the standard and not the exception. We must do this as if there were not a second chance, for in reality, to do less is to shut the door on human capital that we have no right or can afford to waste.

NOTES

1. Natalie A. Kuhlman and Jane Vidal, "Meeting the Needs of LEP Students Through Teacher Training: The Case in California," *Journal of Educational Issues of Language Minority Students*, 12 (Summer 1993): 98–99.

2. Carl Grant and Jane Vidal, "Preparing Teachers for Diversity," in Robert Houston (Ed.), *Handbook of Research on Teacher Education* (New York: Macmillan, 1990).

3. Ibid., p. 403.

4. *Los Angeles Times*, October 30, 1993, "Grading the Schools."

5. Kathleen Kennedy Manzo, "Latino Student Failures Tied to Lack of Latino Teachers," *Black Issues in Higher Education*, 10 (1993): 17.

6. J. L. Brown, "Two Americas: Racial Differences in Child Poverty in the U.S.," Center on Hunger, Poverty, Nutrition Policy (Medford, MA: Tufts University School of Nutrition, 1993).

7. Yolanda Rodriguez Ingle and Raymond Castro, *Resolving a Crisis in Education: Latino Teachers for Tomorrow's Classrooms* (Claremont, CA: Tomas Rivera Center, 1993).

8. William Honig, *Remedying the Shortage of Teachers for Limited-English-Proficient Students* (Sacramento: California Department of Education, 1991).

9. Trish Stoddart, "Los Angeles Unified School District Intern Program: Recruiting and Preparing Teachers for an Urban Context, Policy Analyses for California Education (PACE) Policy (Rep. No. 91-10-1). (Berkeley: University of California, 1991).

10. James Banks, *Multiethnic Education: Theory and Practice*, 2nd ed. (Boston: Allyn and Bacon, 1988).

11. Ibid., pp. 6–7.

12. Ibid., p. 7.

13. Ibid., p. 9.

14. Ibid.

15. Ibid., p. 11.

16. Ibid.

17. Sheryl Santos, "Promoting Intercultural Understanding Through Multicultural Teacher Training," *Action in Teacher Education*, 8(1) (Spring 1986): 19–25.

18. James Banks, "Integrating the Curriculum with Ethnic Content: Approaches and Guidelines," in James Banks and Cherry A. McGee Banks (Eds.), *Multicultural Education: Issues and Perspectives*, 1st ed. (Boston: Allyn and Bacon, 1989).

19. Eugene Garcia, "Language, Culture, and Education," in Linda Darling-Hammond (Ed.), *Review of Research in Education* (Washington, DC: American Educational Research Association, 1993), p. 76.

20. *Association for Supervision and Curriculum Development Handbook*, "Foreign Language Principles" (Alexandria, VA: ASCD, 1992).

21. Merrill Swain and Sharon Lapkin, "Canadian Immersion and Adult Second Language Teaching: What's the Connection?" *Modern Language Journal*, 73 (1989): 150–159; Fred Genesee, Naomi Holowbow, Wallace Lambert, and Louis Chartrand, "Three Elementary School Alternatives for Learning Through a Second Language," *Modern Language Journal*, 73 (1989): 251–263.

22. Owen Boyle and Suzanne Peregoy, "Literacy Scaffolds: Strategies for First- and Second-Language Readers and Writers," *The Reading Teacher*, 44 (1990): 194–200.

23. Stephen Krashen, *The Input Hypothesis: Issues and Implications* (New York: Longman, 1985); Merrill Swain, "Communicative Competence: Some Rules for Comprehensible Input and Comprehensible Output in its Development," in Susan Gass and Carolyn Madden (Eds.), *Input in Language Acquisition* (Rowley, MA: Newbury House, 1985); Yvonne Freeman and David Freeman, *Whole Language for Second Language Learners* (Portsmouth, NH: Heineman, 1992).

24. Bernice Hawkins, "Scaffolded Classroom Interaction and Its Relation to Second Language Acquisition for Language Minority Children," unpublished doctoral disserta-

tion, UCLA, 1988); Margaret Early, "Enabling First and Second Language Learners in the Classroom," *Language Arts*, 67 (1990): 567–575.

25. Early, "Enabling First and Second Language Learners," p. 574.

26. James Cummins, "The Role of Primary Language Development in Promoting Educational Success for Language Minority Students," in *Schooling and Language Minority Students* (Los Angeles: Evaluation, Dissemination and Assessment Center, California State University, 1981).

27. Garcia, "Language, Culture, and Education."

28. Eleanor Thonis, "Reading Instruction for Language Minority Students," in *Schooling and Language Minority Students*.

29. Ann C. Willig, "A Meta Analysis of Selected Studies on the Effectiveness of Bilingual Education," *Review of Educational Research*, 55 (1985): 269–317; David Ramirez, Sandra Yuen, Dena Ramey, and David Pasta, "Final Report: Longitudinal Study of Structured English Immersion Strategy, Early-Exit and Late-Exit Transitional Bilingual Education Programs for Language Minority Children," *Executive Summary* (San Mateo, CA: Aguirre International, February 1991); Judith Langer, Lilia Bartolome, Olga Vasquez, and Tamara Lucas, "Meaning Construction in School Literacy Tasks: A Study of Bilingual Students," *American Educational Research Association*, 27 (1990): 427–471.

30. *ASCD Handbook*.

31. Krashen, *The Input Hypothesis*.

32. Stephen Krashen, "Bilingual Education and Second Language Acquisition Theory," in *Schooling and Language Minority Students*.

33. Tracy Terrell, "The Natural Approach in Bilingual Education," in *Schooling and Language Minority Students*.

34. Ibid.

35. Rebecca Oxford, *Language Learning Strategies* (Boston: Heinle and Heinle, 1990).

36. Ramirez et al., "Final Report." Langer et al., "Meaning Construction in School Literacy Tasks."

37. Carl Grant and Christine Sleeter, "The Literature on Multicultural Education: Review and Analysis," *Educational Review*, 37(2) (1985): 97–118; Carl Grant and Walter Secada, "Preparing Teachers for Diversity," in Robert Houston (Ed.), *Handbook of Research on Teacher Education* (New York: Macmillan, 1990); Donna Gollnick and Philip Chinn, *Multicultural Education in a Pluralistic Society*, 3rd ed. (New York: Merrill, 1990).

38. James Banks, "Multicultural Education: Historical Development, Dimensions and Practice," in Darling-Hammond, *Review of Research in Education*.

39. Wayne Wayson, "Multicultural Education Among Seniors in the College of Education at Ohio State University," paper presented at the American Educational Research Association Meeting (New Orleans, April 1988).

40. Gary Moultry, "Multicultural Education Among Seniors in the College of Education at Ohio State University," paper presented at the American Educational Research Association Meeting (New Orleans, April 1988).

41. Patricia Avery and Constance Walker, "Prospective Teachers' Perceptions of Ethnic and Gender Differences in Academic Achievement," *Journal of Teacher Education*, 44(1) (1993): 27–37 (quote appears on p. 28).

42. Banks, "Multicultural Education."

43. Hugh Price, "Multiculturalism: Myths and Realities," *Phi Delta Kappan*, 74(3) (November 1992): 208–213.

44. Banks, "Integrating the Curriculum with Ethnic Contents."

45. Orion Pictures, *Dances With Wolves*, 1990.

46. George Wood, "Teachers as Curriculum Workers," in James Sears and J. Don Marshall (Eds.), *Teaching and Thinking About Curriculum* (New York: Teachers College Press, 1990).

47. Carl Grant and Christine Sleeter, *Turning on Learning* (Columbus, OH: Merrill, 1989).

48. Robert Slavin, "Cooperative Learning: Applying Contact Theory in Desegregated Schools," *Journal of Social Issues*, 41 (1985): 45–62; Robert Slavin, "Effects of Biracial Learning Terms on Cross-Racial Friendships," *Journal of Education Psychology*, 71 (1979): 381–387; Spencer Kagan, "Cooperative Learning and Sociocultural Factors in Schooling," in *Beyond Language: Social and Cultural Factors in Schooling Language Minority Students* (Los Angeles: Evaluation, Dissemination and Assessment Center, California State University, 1986).

49. Elizabeth Cohen, "Interracial Interaction Disability," *Human Relations*, 25 (1972): 9–24.

50. Grant and Sleeter, *Turning on Learning*, p. 15.

51. Stephen Baratz and Joan Baratz, "The Social Science Base of Institutional Racism," *Harvard Educational Review*, 40 (1971): 29–50; William Labov, "The Logic of Nonstandard English," *Monograph Series on Language and Linguistics* (Washington, DC: Georgetown University Press, November 22, 1969); Geneva Smitherman, *Talkin' and Testifyin'* (Boston: Houghton Mifflin, 1977).

52. Shirley Brice Heath, *Ways With Words* (New York: Cambridge University Press, 1983); Shirley Brice Heath, "Sociocultural Contexts of Language Development," in *Beyond Language: Social and Cultural Factors in Schooling Language Minority Students*; Jose Macias, "The Hidden Curriculum of Papago Teachers: American Indian Strategies for Mitigating Cultural Discontinuity in Early Childhood Schooling," in George Spindler and Louise Spindler (Eds.), *Interpretive Ethnography of Schooling* (Hillsdale, NJ: Erlbaum, 1986); Susan U. Phillips, *The Invisible Culture: Communication in Classroom and Community on the Warm Spring Indian Reservation* (White Plains, NY: Longman, 1982); Sarah Michaels, "Narrative Presentation: An Oral Preparation for Literacy in the First Grades," in Jenny Cook-Gumperz (Ed.), *The Social Construction of Literacy* (Cambridge: Cambridge University Press, 1986).

53. Kathryn Au, Doris Crowell, Cathie Jordan, Kin Sloat, Gisela Speidel, Thomas Klein, and Roland Tharp, "Development and Implementation of the KEEP Reading Program," in Judith Orasanu (Ed.), *Reading Comprehension: From Research to Practice* (Hillsdale, NJ: Erlbaum, 1986).

54. Henry Trueba and Concha Delgado-Gaitan, "Socialization of Mexican-American Children for Cooperation and Competition: Sharing and Copying," *Journal of Education Equity and Leadership*, 5(3) (1985): 189–204.

55. Esteban Diaz, Luis Moll, and Hugh Mehan, "Sociocultural Resources in Instruction: A Context-Specific Approach," in *Beyond Language: Social and Cultural Factors in Schooling Language Minority Students*.

56. Cherry A. McGee Banks, "Restructuring Schools for Equity—What We Have Learned in Two Decades," *Phi Delta Kappan*, 9(43) (September 1993): 42–48.

57. Jeanne Oakes, *Keeping Track: How Schools Structure Inequality* (New Haven,

CT: Yale University Press, 1985); Jeanne Oakes, *Multiplying Inequalities: The Effects of Race, Social Class, and Tracking on Opportunities to Learn Mathematics and Science* (Santa Monica, CA: The Rand Corporation, 1990).

58. Grant and Sleeter, "The Literature on Multicultural Education."

59. Ronald Edmonds, "Characteristics of Effective Schools," in Ulric Neisser (Ed.), *The School Achievement of Minority Children* (Hillsdale, NJ: Erlbaum, 1986); Ly Lezotte, "Effective Schools: A Framework for Increasing Student Achievement," in Banks and Banks, *Multicultural Education: Issues and Perspectives*; Lawrence Stedman, "It's Time We Changed the Effective Schools Formula," *Phi Delta Kappan* 4(37) (November 1987): 215–224; Sylvia Ashton-Warner, *Teacher* (New York: Simon and Schuster, 1963); Marva Collins and Civia Tamarkin, *Marva Collins' Way* (East Rutherford, NJ: Putnam, 1990); Warner Brothers, *Stand and Deliver* (1988); Columbia Pictures, *Stand By Me* (1986).

60. Collins and Tamarkin, *Marva Collins' Way.*

61. James Comer, "Educating Poor Minority Children," *Scientific American*, 259 (November 1989): 42–48.

62. Tamara Lucas, Rosemary Henze, and Ruben Donato, "Promoting the Success of Latino Language-Minority Students: An Exploratory Study of Six Schools," *Harvard Educational Review*, 60 (August 1990): 315–334.

63. Ibid.

64. Christian Faltis and Barbara Merino, "Exemplary Practices of an Expert Teacher in a Bilingual Classroom and Community Setting: A Case Study," paper presented at the American Educational Research Association Meeting (San Francisco, April 1992); Eugene Garcia, "Instructional Discourse in 'Effective' Hispanic Classrooms," in Richard Jacobsen and Christian Faltis (Eds.), *Language Distribution Issues in Bilingual Schooling*, Clevendon: Multilingual Matters, 1990; Luis Moll, "Key Issues in Educating Latino Students," *Language Arts*, 64 (September 1988): 315–324; Lucinda Pease-Alvarez, Eugene Garcia, and Pola Espinosa, "Effective Instruction for Language-Minority Students: An Early Childhood Case Study," *Early Childhood Research Quarterly*, 6 (1991): 347–361; Charlene Rivera and Annette Zehler, *Collaboration on Teaching and Learning: Findings from the Innovative Approaches Research Project* (Arlington, VA: Development Associates, 1990); Carmen Zuniga-Hill and Ruth Helen Yopp, " 'Thinking Things Through in a Different Way:' Exemplary Practices for Teaching Second Language Learners," paper presented at the American Educational Research Association Meeting (San Francisco, April 1992).

65. Zuniga-Hall and Yopp, " 'Thinking Things Through,' " p. 13.

66. Garcia, "Language, Culture, and Education."

67. Zuniga-Hill and Yopp, " 'Thinking Things Through,' " p. 13.

68. Ibid.

69. Pease-Alvarez, Garcia, and Espinosa, "Effective Instruction for Language-Minority Students."

70. Robert Milk. "Responding Successfully to Cultural Diversity," in Robert DeVillar, Christian Faltis, and James Cummins (Eds.), *Cultural Diversity in Schools: From Rhetoric to Practice* (Albany: State University of New York Press, 1992); Grant and Sleeter, "The Literature on Multicultural Education."

71. Milk, "Responding Successfully to Cultural Diversity."

72. Carl Grant and Ruth Koskela, "Education That is Multicultural and the Relation-

ship Between Preservice Campus Learning and Field Experience,'' *Educational Researcher*, 79(4) (1986): 197–203.

73. M. Frank Pajares, ''Teachers' Beliefs and Education Research: Cleaning Up a Messy Construct,'' *Review of Educational Research*, 62(3) (Fall 1991): 307–332.

74. S. Ana Garza and Carol Barnes, ''Competencies for Bilingual Multicultural Teachers,'' *Journal of Educational Issues of Language Minority Students*, 5 (Fall 1989): 1–25.

Chapter 13

Ecocultural Context, Cultural Activity, and Emergent Literacy: Sources of Variation in Home Literacy Experiences of Spanish-Speaking Children

Leslie Reese, Claude Goldenberg, James Loucky, and Ronald Gallimore

INTRODUCTION

Just as language acquisition begins long before the child speaks a word, literacy begins to emerge long before formal instruction (Mason & Allen 1986; Teale & Sulzby 1986). Children's acquisition of literacy must be understood as an emergent developmental process, which includes the very earliest exposure to the uses of print and is rooted in the child's experiences in the home, community, and school. Such an emergent conception of literacy development explains why home experiences with print are associated with reading and school achievement (Hess & Holloway 1984).

However, children experience very different home literacy environments, largely as a function of social, cultural, and economic factors. Working-class families, for example, are less likely to read to their children than are middle-class families (Wells 1985; Teale 1986; Feitelson & Goldstein 1986). In working-class families of different ethnic backgrounds, A. B. Anderson and S. J. Stokes (1984) found that less than 2 percent of all home literacy activities involved story reading. Differences in home literacy activities are, then, likely to be related to social class differences in school achievement.

Although socioeconomic factors show a general correlation with children's home literacy experiences, there is considerable variability in literacy practices within social groups (Anderson & Stokes, 1984; Teale, 1986). In fact, *within-group variability* might be larger, and more significant in its consequences for school achievement, than variability *between-groups*: "It is what parents *do* [or, we might add, what goes on in the home] rather than their *status* that accounts for the learning development of their children" (Bloom 1981, p. 92).

K. R. White's (1982) meta-analysis of studies that examined socio-economic status and student achievement revealed that measures of social class and measures of achievement were highly correlated when aggregated units of analysis (such as school or neighborhood) were used. When the unit of analysis was the individual student, however, the magnitude of associations between social class and achievement dropped dramatically.

White's analysis suggests there is enormous variability from student to student and home to home within any social class. Discovery of this variability has prompted some researchers to look more closely at the literacy experiences of children in working-class and minority homes. For example, recent studies have established that children in working-class families observe and make use of print for a variety of purposes. Highly variable from one family to the next, these purposeful uses of print occur in many contexts: daily routines, religion, entertainment, and interpersonal communication (Anderson & Stokes 1984; Auerbach 1989; Goldenberg 1989a; Taylor & Dorsey-Gaines 1988).

Perhaps most telling is Teale's (1986) finding that differences in frequency and duration of literacy activities among low-income families could not be attributed to major structural or demographic variables. Socioeconomic status and ethnicity must therefore be "unpackaged" by investigating how varying social and cultural factors affect young children's literacy experiences, within various groups.

We must look beyond categorical variables such as class and culture, at least as they have traditionally been defined, if we are to understand the social influences and the cognitive effects of children's home experiences with language and literacy. Nor is it sufficient to document variability within social categories without specifying the sources of that variability. What is needed is a way of conceptualizing and analyzing the *context* of early literacy experiences so that we can simultaneously consider ecological and cultural factors, as well as individual child experiences and development, that are responsible for significant variations in children's literacy-related experiences. Ecocultural and activity setting theory is one such conceptualization.

AN ECOCULTURAL AND ACTIVITY-SETTING APPROACH TO HOME LITERACY

Our version of ecocultural theory is derived from two traditions. The first is psychocultural theory developed by the Whitings and others (Whiting & Whiting 1975; B. Whiting 1976, 1980; B. Whiting & Edwards 1988; Munroe, Munroe, & Whiting 1981; LeVine 1977; Super & Harkness 1980, 1986; Weisner 1984; Weisner & Gallimore 1985; Weisner, Gallimore, & Jordan 1988; Gallimore, Weisner, Kaufman & Bernheimer 1989). The second tradition derives from Soviet sociohistorical and activity theory (Leont'ev 1981; Vygotksy 1978), more specifically, from emergent adaptations and extensions of these similar ideas (Bruner, 1961, 1973, 1983, 1984; Cole 1985; Minick 1985, 1987; Rogoff 1990; Tharp & Gallimore 1988; Wertsch 1981, 1985; Wertsch, Minick, & Arns 1984).

The idea that each family is adapted to, or is adapting to, a niche is fundamental to ecocultural theory. In one respect, the ecocultural niche of the family retains a familiar meaning of niche as environment, setting, or habitat. It reflects the material environment and ecology as traditionally defined in social science, with features such as income, public health conditions, housing and space, transportation, and distance from kin or services. In comparative and cross-cultural studies of human development, the ecocultural niche includes as well the sociocultural environment surrounding the child and family. The niche concept implies evolution through time and adaptation by the participants to the constraints imposed by the subsistence base, the climate, and the political economy of the region (Super & Harkness 1980; Whiting & Whiting 1975; B. Whiting 1980; LeVine 1977; Ogbu 1981).

The theory is sensitive not only to variations in socioeconomic and material factors but also to the role of cultural and personal *beliefs and values* in influencing the niche. In each feature of the niche, both the material ecology and cultural system are operating, often in ways that are relatively transparent to individuals and families within the niche itself. In complex interaction, beliefs and ecology shape and are shaped by the subsistence base of the family, the domestic workload, division of labor and management of children, and exposure to alternative social and cultural information and norms, among other possibly relevant features of the econiche.

But no matter how carefully econiche features are defined, they do not necessarily offer a way to study their effects on individual children's experiences—for example, their experiences with print. A unit of analysis is needed that is intermediate between ecological and cultural presses, and individuals. Ecocultural and activity-setting theory proposes such a unit of analysis—*activity settings*, which are an observable manifestation of econiche features (interactions of ecology and culture) that can be "seen" in the everyday routines of families. The dimensions of activity settings, and hence the categories used to define and analyze them, are:

1. The personnel present and available for participation;
2. the cultural goals, values, beliefs, and attitudes that participants bring to the activity;
3. the immediate motives, purposes, emotions, and intentions guiding the action;
4. the nature of the tasks that are accomplished; and
5. the scripts, normative behaviors, and patterns of appropriate conduct used during the activity.

It is through these activity variables that the surrounding ecocultural niche influences children (and the rest of the family), and it is through these same variables that early literacy experiences are created and shaped. For example, who is with a child, what they are doing, and how they do it are variables influenced by the ecocultural niche. If mothers and fathers are involved in sub-sistence activities that take them away from the household, then young children are left in the care of others. Who these caretakers are, their values and goals, and the ways they interact with children thus become the units of analysis of the effects of the niche, including the subsistence features of the niche.

Besides subsistence, what other niche features might impact the activity set-tings of children? Beatrice Whiting and Carolyn Edwards (1988) inventoried ecocultural niche factors for which there is cross-cultural and comparative evi-dence of influence on one or more dimensions of everyday activity and therefore on child development. Weisner, Gallimore, and their associates (Weisner 1984; Weisner & Gallimore 1985; Gallimore, Weisner, Kaufman, & Bernheimer 1989) have elaborated the conceptualization of the surrounding niche in order to iden-tify the features that affect activity settings and family accommodation strategies. Weisner (1984) has grouped econiche features into five clusters, ranked roughly in order of their empirically demonstrated impact on everyday life, and on child development, beginning with the most influential:

1. Health and mortality of the child and family members (such as demographic trends, risks of disease, community and child safety, etc.).
2. Subsistence and the provision of food and shelter (such as the work cycle and timing, chores and tasks related to subsistence).
3. Domestic workload and household routine (personnel around children and available to them for interaction, and what activities those people are engaged in; division of labor, who is involved in the domestic domain, who occupies culturally recognized roles in child care, and the role of peer and play groups).
4. Child care structures, values, and practices; roles available in the community (care-takers, roles of men and women; availability and kinds of social support; domestic and spouse relations and how these affect child care).
5. Cultural alternatives available to parents and children (outside influences, information available, variability of information, etc.).

For our purposes here, we have used these five categories to look for evidence of ecocultural niche impact on activity settings of five-year-old Hispanic children that involve literacy events. We have broadly defined literacy activities as those involving any interaction (reading, writing, or the observing of reading or writ-ing) with print. These activities include more formal events, such as review of homework and reading stories, as well as more common but fleeting or informal activities such as reading an advertisement, writing a message, or leafing through a catalog.

In keeping with the ecocultural/activity approach outlined above, we focus inquiry not simply on the literacy event itself. We also examine the personnel who are available to carry out the task, the way in which the activity is carried out, the goals and beliefs underlying the activity, and the motives that drive it. In order to analyze why the activities take the particular form that they do in different family settings, we also examine ecocultural factors that shape the activities. We have employed these concepts in an ongoing study of young, Spanish-speaking children who are at risk for poor literacy development.

PURPOSE OF THE STUDY

Our study examined the home literacy environments of Spanish-speaking kindergarten children of immigrant parents. Our goal was to understand the origins of literacy experiences, the role that the school and other institutions play in shaping these experiences, and the interplay between home and school over time. By focusing on everyday activities through which children experience literacy, we also sought to identify the range and sources of variability among the families observed.

Concentrating on low-socioeconomic-status Spanish-speaking children in the United States, our research concerns a population that poses significant challenges for many schools in this country. Risk for academic underachievement of Latino compared to non-Latino students is revealed in such indicators as test scores, grade retention, early school leaving, and other indices of educational attainment. Even when instructed and tested in Spanish, these children achieve at significantly lower levels as early as first grade, and the gap progressively widens thereafter (CTB/McGraw-Hill 1982, 1988). Children of Hispanic descent continue to lag behind their majority peers throughout their school careers (Arias 1986; Orfield 1986) and are more likely to leave school before graduation (Haycock & Navarro 1988).

METHOD

Community Context

Our study was conducted with families in a small, predominantly Latino community within the Los Angeles metropolitan area. The community is located in one of the county's poorest areas and is characterized by small houses and compact apartment buildings occupied mostly by working-class families. Many residents are employed in light industry and in service jobs in hotels, restaurants, and firms surrounding the nearby international airport.

Reflecting the enormous influx of Latino immigrants into the United States and particularly Southern California in the past two decades, the local school district has undergone fundamental changes in its ethnic and socioeconomic composition at the same time it experienced an explosion in its student population. Whereas 81 percent of the 2,837 students enrolled in 1968 were white, by 1987, 97 percent of the nearly 5,000 students were minority, most of whom (88%) were Latino.

As a port-of-entry community, this is the first U.S. residence of many community dwellers, and binational ties are maintained to relatives in natal communities in central and western Mexico and Central America. For many residents the school system represents the most visible American institution and a potential bridge between cultures.

Study Sample

Initial contact with families was made by sending letters to the parents of Spanish-dominant kindergartners in four classrooms in two different elementary schools (two classrooms per school). The letters requested permission for one of two Spanish-speaking fieldworkers to contact parents by telephone. Of the 84 children eligible for inclusion in the study, the parents of 72 (86 percent) returned the permission slip indicating willingness to participant in the study.

Ten subjects were selected at random from the four classrooms, three from two classrooms and two from the other two. We contacted a total of sixteen parents in order to construct our sample of ten. Two parent contacts were not attempted due to absence of a telephone in the home. Thus our sample might be biased somewhat by self-selection or economic factors.[1]

In each family in our sample, at least one parent was employed, and in six cases both parents worked outside the home. Jobs included work in hotels, factories, maintenance, mechanics firms, and garbage collection. No family received welfare support, although eight of the ten children received free or reduced meals at school. Parents' employment ensured that no family was destitute, but the economic circumstances of most of the families were relatively precarious. In four families, parents were laid off work during the course of the study. In another, an aunt who worked as a maid in a hotel was occasionally sent home without pay when not needed. Some families supplemented their income by collecting aluminum cans and cardboard. Others worked out of their homes, doing welding, selling jewelry and clothing, and selling illegally copied cassettes (an activity that was halted by a police raid).

Parents' educational levels were generally low, even in comparison to the overall education level of Mexican-origin adults in the United States who, in 1988, had a median of less than eleven years of schooling (U.S. Department of Commerce 1988). The median years of schooling for parents in our sample was seven for mothers and five for fathers (overall mean = 6.5; range, 1 to 12).

Reflecting parental origins in the district as a whole, 79 percent of the parents in our sample were immigrants from Mexico and 21 percent from Central America. Length of residence in the United States varied from one to nineteen years (mean = ten), and many of the parents qualified for legal residence under the 1986 Immigration Reform and Control Act.

Spanish is the language of all of the homes studied; all children participated in a bilingual instructional program in which literacy instruction for the first few years is in Spanish.

Table 13.1
Definitions of Child Activities Used by Observers

Learning events with text: child is directly involved in any episode or activity
which involves the use of written text, even if a single letter or word.

Learning events without text: child is involved in an activity which involves
learning a skill or knowledge but does not make use of text. This
includes, for example, activities such as drawing, numeracy, recitation, or
learning morals.

Playing inside: all child's indoor play, alone or with others, with the exception of
learning episodes defined in #1 and #2 above.

Playing outside: all child's play outside the home, alone or with others, with the
exception of learning episodes defined above.

TV watching: child is directly and primarily involved in watching television.

Conversational acts: child participates in or listens to conversations, and is not
primarily involved in any other activity. Conversation while primarily
involved in another activity, such as playing a game or watching
television, is not included.

Chores and household obligations: includes household cleanup, running
errands, and taking care of siblings, whether or not child has been
specifically instructed.

Personal needs: child is involved in eating, bathing, dressing, shining shoes or
using the bathroom.

Sleeping or resting: child is sleeping or resting, without being involved in any
other activity such as watching television or conversing.

Miscellaneous: includes activities that cannot be placed in other categories,
such as discipline episodes, greetings, and transitions from one activity
to the next.

Procedures

The ten students in our study were visited at home once or twice monthly
during the school year. Following an introductory visit to explain the purpose
of the study, each child was observed during approximately twelve visits (range
= seven to fourteen). Visits averaged 112 minutes, and the total of 118 home
visits resulted in just under 220 hours of observation time. Most observations
were conducted during the afternoons when children returned from school, at a
time most likely to capture learning events, and at least one visit per child was
conducted on a nonschool day. In addition to the time engaged in actual observation of child activities, fieldworkers visited the families for a videotaping
session, interviews, and informal visits. The total amount of time spent with the
sample families was approximately 250 hours.

The higher incidence of learning activities during the hours we observed was
confirmed by parents' reports, with the exception of reading to children, which
a few of the parents reported engaging in at bedtime. Observations at this time
of day, however, would have been highly intrusive. In all of the homes, parents
and children slept in the same bedroom, and in half of the homes, other family
members slept in the living room or kitchen.

All observed child activities were grouped according to categories derived
during the course of our ethnographic observations. Table 13.1 presents the
categories for the full range of children's activities and their definitions. Based

on these definitions, and through close collaboration between fieldworkers, children's activities were coded according to type and duration. When children were involved in two activities simultaneously, such as eating and watching television, only the predominant activity was coded. Timing of all activities was determined with wristwatches.

The focus of data collection was on learning events involving the target child and on literacy activities in particular. Activities involving interaction with print in any way were termed "literacy events." These ranged from doing homework, copying words and letters, and pretend reading, to observing others reading and writing. Related activities involving numeracy, paper-and-pencil activities of various sorts, or explicit teaching (often oral) that did not involve print, but clearly formed part of the context in which literacy emerged, were termed "learning events." The category of learning events thus includes both those with text (literacy events) and those without text.[2] Table 13.2 provides a list of the learning event categories and their definitions.

Because learning activities were those of interest for this study, they were observed and described in as much detail as possible. The five dimensions of activity settings guided fieldworkers' recording of information about each learning event: *personnel* present and involved; *tasks* used, including where any materials came from; purposes associated with the task, including the *expressed motive* for the activity and *cultural values or goals* either implicit or explicit in the activity; *scripts* used to carry out the task, including helping or teaching strategies, the affective quality, and the nature of participant interaction. Notes also reflected other contextualizing information, such as where the activity occurred and the physical characteristics of the setting. In addition, children's learning events were coded for whether alphabetic texts were used, the type and origin of other materials in use, and who initiated the event.

Data on the duration of activities are used in this study for purposes of comparison among cases only, not to reconstruct an "average day" in the life of a kindergarten child. The timing of activities with a wristwatch provided a level of precision sufficient for this task. However, in an effort to capture and record all learning experiences of the child, however brief, any learning activity that lasted more than ten seconds was coded as lasting one minute. This resulted in a slight inflation of the amount of time spent involved in learning activities as compared to nonlearning activities. For example, if a child engaged in five brief learning experiences during a visit, these would be coded as five separate minutes, thus inflating the proportion of learning versus nonlearning event time. It should be stressed that the goal of this study was to capture and analyze the activity setting variables of child learning activities, and to reflect as accurately as possible the *full range* of possible literacy events.

Fieldworkers also talked with family members regarding their own and their child's education and learning experiences. Through both informal and more structured interviews, we attempted to elicit parent perspectives regarding children's literacy development, their views on how children learn to read, their

Table 13.2
Child Learning Event Definitions

Homework: child's or sibling's work assigned by school to be completed and returned.
  a. With text: includes papers with letters, words, syllables,
     and/or extended text. Includes papers with written
     instructions only, if these are read and/or noted. Also
     includes reading aloud when required by school.
  b. Without text: includes numbers, shapes, drawing lines. If
     there are written instructions, these are not read or noted.
Review or use of materials from school: reuse of old homework or
     classwork; reading of notes, flyers and newsletters. Does not
     include current homework.
  a. With text: see above.
  b. Without text: see above.
Playing school or church: children role play church or school activities.
  a. With text of any sort.
  b. Without text or with text which is not used or noted in any way.
Explicit teaching by someone in the household but without
     materials from school.
  a. With written text, for example, writing or copying letters,
     words or name.
  b. Without text: includes writing or copying numbers; counting
     or saying the alphabet aloud; explicit teaching of morals,
     manners, or household tasks, or any other episode in which
     the focus is on teaching the child a skill or providing him
     with knowledge or information.
Reading: reading of extended text by or to the child. Includes
     pretend reading.
Literacy-related games or toys: use of flashcards or any game in
     which text is used as, for example, in the use of written instructions or rules.
Environmental print: child interacts in some way (reading or
     writing) with advertisements, flyers, logos, signs or any print in his environment.
  a. With text of any sort.
  b. With numbers only.
Paper-pencil activities: includes writing or drawing on paper,
     chalkboard, or surfaces such as floor or walls, in which explicit
     teaching (#4) is not involved.
  a. With text: includes writing letters or words, circling or
     cutting out letters or words, and writing letters to
     relatives or friends.
  b. Without text: includes drawing, cutting and pasting, or
     number games.
Coloring in coloring books.
  a. With text: includes only those episodes in which the text
     is used or referred to by participant.
  b. Without text.
Observed literacy event: child observes another person engage
     in an event in which there is explicit use of written texts.

---

5 Note: Events #1a, 2a, 3a, 4a, 5, 6, 7a, 8a, 9a, and 10 by definition involve the use of written text.
They are grouped together as "learning events with text."

Figure 13.1
Percent of Time Children Spent Engaged in Specific Activities

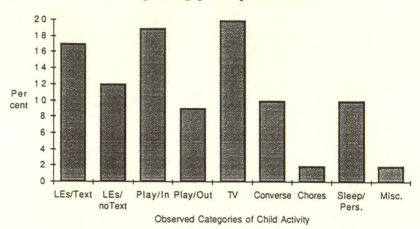

own literacy practices, and their contacts with the school. In addition, reported and observed printed materials of all types in the home were recorded on a checklist for each visit.

RESULTS

Activities and Learning Events of Latino Children

Figure 13.1 provides summary data on the full range of children's activities, giving an overall portrait of how children spent their time during home observation periods. Table 13.3 presents the incidence of learning events only, which constitute the first two categories in Figure 13.1.

Duration of literacy activities (i.e., learning events using some sort of written text) ranged from less than one minute to 101 minutes. Over half lasted less than six minutes, and 18 percent lasted less than two minutes, revealing a highly skewed distribution of observed events (mean = 8.2 min.; median = 4.5 min.; mode = 1 min. or less).

For reasons discussed above, the activities do not constitute a representative sampling of children's home learning experiences. In fact, these tables probably overestimate the incidence of learning events in children's lives, since most observations were conducted at times when many of these activities (e.g., doing or observing homework, playing school, reviewing school materials) were most likely to occur. Rather, Figure 13.1 and Table 13.3 illustrate the potential activities that children engage in and that the ecocultural niche will sustain.

Some aspects of activity settings, and hence some features of children's home literacy experiences, were similar across families. Several *personnel* and *task*

Table 13.3

Children's Participation in Learning Activities in Home Contexts

learning Activity (Observed/Participated)	Frequency	Per cent
Homework - with text	373	10.18%
Homework - without text	145	3.86%
School Mat. Review - w/ text	119	3.16%
School Mat. Review - w/out text	82	2.18%
Play School/Church - w/ text	115	3.06%
Play School/Church - w/out text	5	0.13%
Teaching - with text	425	11.30%
Teaching - without text	453	12.04%
Reading	318	8.46%
Literacy-related Games	105	2.79%
Environmental Print - w/text	218	5.80%
Environ. Print - numbers only	41	1.09%
Paper/pencil Activ. - w/ text	520	13.99%
Paper/pencil Act. - w/out text	426	11.35%
Coloring - with text	0	0.00%
Coloring - without text	264	7.26%
Observed Literacy Event	126	3.35%
TOTAL	3744	100.00%

Children ranged in frequency from 822 to 123 events
mean 374.4
SD: 221.6

attributes, as well as the larger cultural and personal *goals* underlying the activity settings, were quite consistent for the group of ten children as a whole. In contrast, other aspects of *personnel* and *task* did vary across families and activity settings, as did the *motives* and *scripts* that helped shape the activities. We are particularly interested in differences among activity-setting variables because of their presumed differential impact on the children's learning experiences and opportunities. We will first discuss those aspects of the activity settings that were relatively similar across the families.

Similarities in Literacy Activity Settings Across Cases

Personnel. In all ten study families, parents had at least some schooling and were sufficiently literate to enable them to assist their kindergarten children with work sent home from school. Further, except for Daniel, who was often alone or with a babysitter, all children had a parent or relative regularly available to help them with schoolwork or to engage them in learning activities. Dual-earner families, such as Freddy's, usually staggered their work schedules so that one parent was always home with the children. In Luis' family, his mother changed her work hours in order to be home with her young boys during the day. She then left them with their high-school-aged sister in the evenings.

In addition simply to being available, parents or relatives also monitored schoolwork, although with varying consistency and styles. For example, Luis' mother checked to see if he had brought work home; Jose's mother encouraged her son to work with his older brother; Fernando's mother drilled numbers and letters repeatedly; Carol's mother explained concepts from homework that her daughter did not appear to understand fully. We observed various instances where parents, upon a child's arrival from school, asked whether she or he had any homework.

In sum, the availability of parents competent to monitor children's completion of school tasks, and to assist with at least the level of academic work engaged in by their kindergarten children, was fairly uniform among our group of ten children, confirming previous findings among this population (Goldenberg 1987).

Goals. All parents expressed a deep belief in the value of education. "It is the best inheritance that a parent can give a child," said Daniel's mother. Paula's aunt, on her way to her evening adult education class, expressed the view that "no time that you spend in school is wasted time." Luis' mother, with a sixth-grade education herself, felt that with an education "one has the possibility of triumphing in life, of having a better future"; and Amalia's mother said simply, "Education is everything." These data again confirm our own previous findings and those of others (e.g., Delgado-Gaitan 1990).

This general belief in the importance of education is reflected in parents' monitoring of homework, at least at this initial stage of schooling when they feel they are competent to assist their children. Carol's father, who boasted of having two elementary school teachers and a municipal employee among his siblings, backed up his expressed desire that his daughters do well in school by purchasing books, flashcards, math exercise books, and an encyclopedia for the children. However, as in the case of Daniel, whose parents also purchased a child's encyclopedia and books for him, these books were never observed in use. They seemed to represent a commitment on the part of the family rather than an integral part of family activities. Thus, as in "Personnel," the belief in the value of education and the broad goal of school success were largely invariant in the sample.

Tasks. Just as families exhibited similarities in terms of personnel available and the educational goals for their children, they were also broadly similar in terms of types of tasks engaged in and materials used. All households participate, albeit marginally in some cases, in a literate society, and environmental print of some sort (labels, bills, ads, printed clothing, etc.) was observed in all homes.

On the other hand, few books or magazines were observed in any of the homes. In Jose and Freddy's homes, *no* adult books or magazines and only one children's book were ever observed. No children's books were observed in the homes of Nelly and Fernando. More than five adult books were not observed in any of the homes. This scarcity is probably due, at least in part, to the difficulty of obtaining commercial Spanish-language materials in an English-dominant society. Both the reading of stories and opportunities for children to observe adults engaging in literacy tasks were rare. While it would be incorrect to characterize homes in the present study as devoid of printed material, our overall impression is not one of homes infused with literacy or "filled with print," as Auerbach (1989) concludes about other inner-city households.

In each of the homes, the school had a major impact on the children's home literacy experiences, and as such was largely responsible for the consistency in types of tasks observed. Over 40 percent of all observed learning activities involved use of materials from school. In families such as Fernando's and Jose's, the flyers, calendars, homework, and booklets sent home by the school account for virtually all of the printed material in the home. Homework and homework-like drill initiated by parents were part of the literacy experience of all target children, and accounted for the majority of the learning activities in certain households. Paper and pencil activities reflecting activities taking place at school were also common. Indeed, several parents reported that they had waited to teach their child certain skills until the child went to school.

Variation in Literacy Activity Settings Across Cases

We now turn to the substantial variation found in the activity-setting dimensions of personnel, tasks, motives, and scripts. Each is discussed in turn, except for scripts, which vary as a function of other dimensions and are discussed in the context of each of those dimensions.

Personnel Variations—Parent Characteristics. Although all families had at least one adult available to interact with children in literacy activities or provide them with models of literacy use, there was great variability with respect to experiences, abilities, and beliefs about how children learn.

Parents' personal experience with education was one aspect of personnel that differentiated families. Even in this low-economic-status sample, parents' educational levels varied considerably, from one to twelve years of schooling. Variation in educational level also appears to be related to other potentially important dimensions of personnel characteristics.

There were four families in which neither parent went beyond elementary school (Fernando, José, Luis, Freddy). They are the same families in which neither parent reported using literacy on the job. This suggests either that their work requires few literacy skills or that they do not perceive or utilize opportunities for literacy that are present. Since we did not explicitly collect behavioral data on parents' workplace activities, either in or out of the home, we cannot discriminate between the two. In either case, what we can say is that in these four cases parents' work-related literacy is less salient than in the other families, and children have no opportunities to observe their parents engage in work-related literacy tasks. Moreover, parents' experiences with literacy are likely to be more limited, at least insofar as workplace literacy provides a range of experiences and opportunities not found elsewhere.

Parental education might also influence how parents perceive and help structure their children's learning. For example, Fernando's parents (both of whom stopped attending school at grade 4) grew up in rural Durango, where classes were initially held beneath a tree. Neither finished the elementary grades, and Fernando's father laughingly recalls hiding under a bridge instead of going to school. Fernando's parents were never observed teaching him learning strategies or showing him how to use his own experience to broaden his learning. Instead, they frequently engaged him in lengthy sessions of copying numbers and letters. On a rare occasion that Fernando initiated a question about a book from school, his mother simply shrugged and answered, "Who knows?"

The parents' goal that Fernando do well and succeed in school was not at issue. Both parents took great interest in his school and homework, and Fernando's mother was observed to follow up when the teacher recommended helping Fernando learn the numerals 1–10. The type of help his parents provided, however, and the scripts they used, placed enormous emphasis on repeating and practicing shapes, sounds, and words, without reference to meaning or to learning strategies beyond memorization and repetition.

In contrast, Alex's mother provided a learning strategy as he wrote a row of letter I's: "Every time you write a letter you should say to yourself 'I' so you learn it." Carol's mother carefully reviewed the girls' homework, demanding examples from their own experience beyond those in the exercises and fostering mastery of concepts behind the task, not merely its completion. Thus, parents' ethnolearning theories differentiated families and appear to be linked with the the parents' own school experience.

Nelly's mother, who went beyond elementary school in her hometown in Michoacan, which she described as "poor in money but rich in education," bolstered her daughter's education by actively assisting in her schoolwork in a way that was considerably different from Fernando's parents. For example, on one occasion she assisted her daughter in seeing a pattern, prompting her as she wrote numbers, "So how will 15 be? If 12 is a one and a two, and 13 is a one and a three, and 14 is a one and a four, then what is 15?" When Nelly wrote it correctly, her mother encouraged her: "Now why don't you say 15? Now comes 16. It's a one and a what?" While such scaffolding interactions, in which a parent assists a child to higher levels of performance, are not necessarily typical of the higher-educated parents, they were *never* observed in the homes of the parents with lower levels of education.

Further evidence that level of education influences the way parents interact with children (that is, the "script" of the activity) was seen when, after having Fernando do a lengthy number drill, his mother remarked to her husband in front of the child, "Nothing stays in his head." Similarly, Freddy's attempt to imitate his sister in writing to an uncle was discouraged by his father with the comment, "You only know how to write 'Freddy' anyhow," suggesting that such efforts by the child are are not appreciated and certainly not valued or nurtured. Parents with higher levels of education tended to view their children's efforts in a more positive light. Carol's mother (who reached the 9th grade in her native Guatemala) proudly reported that her daughter knew how to write her name before entering school, while Alex' mother (who reached the 9th grade in Mexico) initiated a review of homework with the encouragement, "I know my boy is very smart. Put your thinking cap on!"

Work pressures also affected the personnel in the home and how responsive parents were to engaging in learning activities with their children. After she began work in January, rising daily at 4:30 A.M., Alex's mother was less likely to sit down with her son and engage in the playful writing episodes that had characterized earlier visits. Paula lived with her mother and two aunts, all of whom worked outside of the home. Her mother reported that Paula has to find things, referring to learning activities, to keep busy by herself. When she wants someone to read with her, she must first "look to see who's in a good mood."

Personnel Variations—Child Characteristics. Auerbach (1989) criticizes the assumption, common to family literacy programs, that "the 'natural' direction of literacy learning is from parent to child." In our study, a great deal of variation was observed from family to family with respect to the amount of child initiation and structuring of learning events.

For example, both Luis and Paula initiated over 80 percent of the learning activities in which they were observed over the course of the year. However, since Luis exhibited little interest in reading and writing, he rarely initiated these activities, and they account for less than 4 percent of the time he was observed. Moreover, the great majority of learning events initiated by Luis involved coloring or drawing.

Particularly in homes where parents exhibited a laissez-faire attitude to children's learning and attempts at literacy, the degree of child initiation became a key factor in determining the frequency of literacy activities. Luis' mother did check to see if he had homework and looked on silently as he drew or colored, but she initiated only one learning event during the course of observation, and that was a homework assignment. Given Luis' low initiation rate, it is easy to understand why only 4 percent of the observed time was occupied with literacy events.

In contrast, Paula demonstrated great interest in literacy materials and activities. Her mother also demonstrated a fairly relaxed attitude toward early learning, due in part to work pressures described above; however, Paula was involved in text-related literacy activities 17 percent of the time she was observed. Typical, said her aunt laughing, was when Paula finished a drawing, disappeared into the bedroom for an envelope, and then raced to the kitchen to ask her mother to write her address on it. Paula's higher rate of engagement with literacy activities was almost entirely due to her clear interest in reading and writing and the frequency with which she initiated these activities. Although the personnel were available, the observed literacy activities most probably would not have taken place if Paula had not initiated them.

Similarly, Alex, who initiated 65 percent of the learning events in which he was engaged, was observed to recreate at home the activities that he had participated in at school. One afternoon, he drew sets of one, two, and three balls on the back of a school flyer, attached it to the door, and invited his mother to play a math game he had learned at school, saying, "Let's see who touches the number first." While declining to play, his mother called out numbers for him to touch.

Although the use of literacy skills in family life (for writing messages, making lists, jotting notes on a calendar, reading the newspaper, writing letters, paying bills, etc.) was not frequently observed, some children took advantage of print in their surroundings to mimic adult activities. For example, Fernando was intrigued by a stack of ads he had been given by a neighbor, and wrote his name and telephone number on the lines intended for this purpose on a coupon form. Using the voice of a "saleswoman," Nelly pretended to read the yellow pages of the telephone book, appropriately matching her "sales-pitch" to the content of the ads. By contrast, other children displayed only slight interest in initiating such activities, including Luis who even refused to join his brother in cutting letters out of the phone book.

Personnel Variations—Other Family Members. The family structure of the ten households observed varied from homes in which only nuclear family members resided to those that included grandparents, aunts and uncles, and even unrelated adults. Some of the nuclear families, such as Amalia's, Jose's, and Freddy's, are in such close proximity to and interaction with aunts, uncles, and cousins who live close by that they function as one extended household.

Four of the ten households contained elementary-school-aged children who could serve as literacy models for the younger child. For example, Nelly liked to work alongside her older brother as he did his homework. Once he asked her what word he was writing, moving to the letter level on seeing his question was too difficult for her. After she correctly identified a letter *U*, he pointed to others and had her repeat their names. In addition to including him in her activities, Freddy's eight-year-old sister took responsibility for organizing his papers and homework; as she reported, "when he has a lot of work, I help him, explain it to him, tell him to do it like this. He tells me, 'Will you help me, sis?' "

While the presence of an older, school-aged sibling can be a powerful incentive for a young child to engage in literacy and learning experiences, older children are not always positive models for learning behaviors. For example, over 40 percent of Carol's learning activities took place with her older sister. Yet on one occasion when her mother was occupied with the baby and Carol asked her sister what she should do on a particular page of homework, her sister glanced over without reading the instructions and explained the task in a way that did not correspond to the written directions. On occasions when Luis was cared for by his eleven-year-old sister, who was reported to be losing interest in school, no learning events were observed. Thus, the presence of a school-aged sibling in the home may produce different effects and does not necessarily indicate more frequent or effective learning activities.

Similarly, presence of adults other than parents did not necessarily increase the likelihood of learning activities. In Paula's case, an aunt read to her in English.

An uncle not only got Alex off to school after his mother started work, but also helped teach him concepts; on one occasion, he proudly showed a letter that he had helped Alex write to his grandmother. In contrast, relatives were often present in other households (such as Amalia's, Fernando's, and Nelly's), but they rarely engaged the children in learning activities or paid attention when children initiated them. In these cases, learning activity interactions tended to be exclusively "mother-child," "mother-sibling-child," or "sibling-child."

Task and Material Variations. As discussed earlier, children engaged in many of the same kinds of tasks from home to home, in large part because of the school's impact through sending homework activities and reading material (flyers, calendars, forms) to the homes. But just as school and families themselves generated consistently similar tasks, other societal institutions were responsible for notable variations in children's home literacy activities.

The role of the church in fostering literacy was evident in three homes. Amalia's family belonged to an evangelical church that placed a high value on Bible study and interpretation. Weekly Bible study sessions in the homes of different women of the church were also attended by children. Encouraged by their mothers to "play church," Amalia and her friend were observed reciting verses, singing, holding up the Bible as if reading, and giving verse numbers so others could mimic following along. In another case, Carol and her sister attended catechism classes, were read to from the Bible, and were encouraged to recite prayers and read from little children's Bibles their mother had purchased for them. In both families, reading is done not for the practice of literacy per se, but as a means of knowing and understanding a message, or, as Amalia's mother put it, "to learn more about and live according to the word of God."

Similarly, some parents had jobs requiring literacy skills that might be observed by their children, albeit rarely. Once, Amalia could not watch television in the bedroom because her father was writing a report there. Another time, Paula began filling out an application form inside her mother's Mary Kay magazine. Earlier she had observed her mother taking cosmetics orders over the telephone.

There was variation in the adult materials, religious materials, and child materials observed in the homes. Adult reading materials of any sort were not observed in three homes, while they were observed on four occasions or more in three homes. Similarly, children's reading materials (such as story books, magazines, and comics) were not observed in two homes, were present on one to three occasions in five homes, and were in evidence on more than four occasions in three homes. In some households there was little printed material except for environmental print and what was sent home by the school. In other homes, magazines and newspapers were occasionally observed, albeit infrequently. Ironically, children's books were rarely observed in the homes of David and Carol, where parents had purchased encyclopedias and other learning materials for their children.

Variation in Motives. As was discussed above, all parents shared the broad cultural goal of valuing and supporting the education of their children. Their more immediate motives for engaging in learning activities with their children varied, however, and did not always reflect this broad goal. For example, some parents read Bible stories to their children and taught them to recite verses for the purpose of learning more about the word of God. Some initiated drill activities in response to a teacher request that they assist their child at home. Others were observed to engage in learning activities for the purpose of entertaining the child.

Several of the families either lived in more dangerous parts of the community or were more worried about the dangers of drugs and crime than were others. These fears often led parents to keep children inside, which sometimes contributed to an increase in literacy and learning activities. Not wanting her daughter to play outside, Carol's mother added to her homework in order to keep her inside while her sister did her own homework. This helps explain why Carol was engaged in learning events of some sort during 49 percent of the time that she was observed.

An extreme example was that of Daniel, who was kept inside and often alone by parents who feared for his safety in a neighborhood of drug activity. His mother reported that her son preferred staying inside and studying to going outside, and observations revealed considerable exploration of literacy activities. He was observed to spend 37 percent of his time engaged in learning events. By contrast, Freddy's home had an enclosed driveway, and he was not kept inside or occupied with literacy activities. Thus, protection of children indoors may be a powerful factor motivating learning activities in some households, if not fostering literacy in and of itself.

The variation in motive for engaging in the learning activity was observed to affect the script—that is, how the activity was carried out. The majority of the literacy events, particularly those that were school-based, were dominated by attention to ''surface associations''—attention to letters, words, phrases, and their shapes or pronunciation, without reference to meaning (Goldenberg 1989). Evidence suggests that this was not due to these activities' being school-based necessarily, but rather to parents' own ethnolearning theories, which stress learning through drill and repetition. For example, Fernando's mother, when he would tire of copying a letter or number, exhorted him to ''continue until he knows it.'' Luis' mother expressed her satisfaction with the phonics materials sent home by the school, saying that they had been ''very helpful for her son because they had repeated things a lot.'' When parents engaged in activities with their children which *they* saw as learning experiences, these events took on the characteristics of repetition and drill, with little attention to the concept being practiced.

However, on the much less frequent occasions when parents engaged in activities for the purpose of entertainment, the content or message became the focus of the activity. One example occurred when Alex's mother engaged in pencil-and-paper play with her son, in an effort to keep him quiet and occupied while his father slept in the adjoining room. She extended a drawing activity to a map activity, by showing him where his house was in relation to the school and asking him to show how he walked to school. While Amalia's mother chatted with a neighbor, she entertained the daughters by showing them a pamphlet she had on baby nutrition, pointing to the pictures and showing them how they looked when they were little. Similarly, as noted previously, activities of a religious nature focused on the message of the text rather than on the form or decoding of it.

Ecocultural Factors Associated with Variations in Literacy Activities

A number of ecocultural niche factors influenced the activity settings in which children participate, contributing to observed variation from setting to setting and family to family.

Subsistence activities and work schedules of adults impact not only the personnel available to engage in learning activities with the children, but also their disposition to do this after a long day at work. A potentially significant role of subsistence activities in fostering literacy activities and opportunities for children was parents' modeling of work-related literacy skills in some of the homes. Similarly the religious involvement of three families also promoted the use and observation of literacy materials in the home. As mentioned, perceived dangers outside the home also impacted learning events within the home. In areas felt to be unsafe because of crime or traffic, parents were more likely to keep their children indoors and occupy them with paper and pencil activities. Families with safe outdoor play areas did not need to utilize such activities for the same purpose.

Variation in family structure created differing opportunities for children to interact with older siblings and other models for literacy and learning. Social support networks and extended family structures in some homes led some other adults to assist parents with childcare and to engage children in learning activities as well, although the presence of older siblings or other adults in the home in no way assured additional learning or literacy events for children.

Parents' home country and school experiences influence how they view the learning process and their role in it. Parents with higher levels of education were more likely to assist their children by teaching learning strategies, scaffolding children's interactions, and viewing their children's efforts at learning in a positive light. Parents with lower levels of education or lack of experience of success at being students themselves, while no less interested in their children's academic success, were less likely to attend to the concepts being practiced or to reinforce their children's learning attempts.

Taken as a whole, these data confirm the basic premise of ecocultural and activity theory. Culture and ecology manifest themselves in the lives of children through the activity settings that are created and sustained by their joint effects.

Table 13.4
Reading Achievement and Parent Literacy

	Child Name	Score	M Ed (years)	F Ed (years)	Mo.use literacy at work**	Fa. use literacy at work**	Home rdg mtrls score (1-6)†
High	Amalia	146	9	9	2	2	5
group	Paula	136	4	9*	2	1*	4
	Carol	109	9	6	2	2	3
Middle	Alex	83	9	2	1	0	5
group	Daniel	76	11	12	0	1	3
	Nelly	75	8	9	1	0	2
Low	Fernando	63	4	4	0	0	1
group	Freddy	59	6	4	0	0	1
	José	55	6	1	0	0	1
	Luis	53	6	3	0	0	2

Significance test for differences among high, middle, and low	K-W[1] H = 4.286	K-W H = 3.872	Chi-sq. = 15.333	Chi-sq. = 8.889	K-W H = 6.51
p= <	0.1	0.1	0.004	0.06	0.04

* aunt

** from parents' self reported use:
0 = none
1 = v. limited
2 = some

† Scores were assigned in three categories of literacy materials observed (or not observed) in the home: materials for adults; religious materials; child materials. In each category, families were scored 0 for not observed; 1 for observed 1-3 times; 2 for observed 4 or more times. Scores could range from 0 - 6.

[1] Kruskal-Wallis H

Moreover, variations in activity-setting characteristics will lead to differences in children's home literacy experiences and opportunities. Do these variations in home literacy experiences lead to differential school achievement?

Literacy Activity Variation and Achievement

Although this study did not focus on the correlation of home literacy experiences with children's reading achievement in school, we can report some limited data. At the end of the year, the ten children who participated in this study were tested using measures of Concepts about Print (Clay 1985; translated into Spanish for this study), oral story comprehension, metalinguistic production, sight word recognition, word writing, and phonic and decoding skills.[3] Forty-six other children from classrooms participating in a related study were also tested at the same time. Results of these tests for the ten children in our study appear in Column 2 (''Score'') of Table 13.4.

Grouping children into higher (scores over 100), middle (scores between 65 and 99), and lower achievers (scores below 64), we can observe that the four children who fell into the lower level group all had parents who had not gone beyond elementary school, who reported no use of literacy on their jobs, and who therefore were not observed by their children engaging in work-related literacy activities. Neither was religion observed to foster literacy activities or use of printed material in these homes. In fact, in only one of these families was reading material of any sort—except school provided—observed on more than three occasions over the course of the year.

By way of contrast, the families of children in the highest achieving group all had at least one adult in the home who had gone beyond an elementary school level of education. High scores on the materials scale indicate greater availability of materials that children could incorporate into their own literacy activities; adult, child, and religious materials observed in the homes were tabulated to create a "home reading materials" score (last column, Table 13.4). Furthermore, workplace or church, or both, impacted the literacy environment of all three of these homes by providing motives for literacy use and opportunities for children to see their parents model literate behaviors. These are the homes described earlier in which a father wrote reports on his maintenance jobs at home, a mother took telephone orders for cosmetics sales in the home, where women from the church met to read and discuss Bible lessons, and where children were read to from the Bible and encouraged to recite prayers and verses.

Families of children in the middle group exhibited some, but not all, characteristics of the higher group. Therefore, while no single characteristic could be used to predict a student's performance, the presence of a cluster of characteristics including parental levels of education and the impact of the church and the workplace were associated with higher levels of child achievement.

The achievement data for our ten children suggest a link between socioeconomic status and achievement, thus replicating a common finding. There is an important feature of these data, however, which brings us full circle back to Bloom's comment that "it is what parents *do* rather than their *status* that accounts for the learning development of their children" (Bloom 1981, p. 92). Although it is better-educated parents who provide more literacy experiences at home, it is not the parents' level of *education per se* that *determines* a child's educational achievement: The impact of parents' educational experiences on children is mediated through particular activity settings, such as the use of literacy in the workplace, the modeling of literacy behaviors at home, the viewing of incipient child literacy attempts in a positive and encouraging light, and the scaffolding of children's learning experiences. A child has a literacy experience because a more literate mother's reading skills combined with her religious convictions give rise to an activity setting in which literacy is used as a tool in goal-directed, joint activity. It is not who the mother is but what she does that determines the home literacy environment of her child.

DISCUSSION AND CONCLUSIONS

For individual Spanish-speaking children in our sample, everyday activities and the concomitant literacy experiences varied enormously. Associated with these variations in the literacy experiences were variations in ecocultural niche features. These included subsistence practices, division of labor, organizational involvement, and cultural knowledge.

These data indicate that studies of emergent literacy in this population must take account of the variations within the group: it is necessary to have detailed information at the level of the individual family concerning specific niche features and the activity settings to which they give rise. In this way the specific mediating linkages between children's experience and their development can be identified and subjected to empirical test.

Our data confirm White's (1982) important conclusion: *Being poor itself does not create reading problems.* The data also suggest extending White's conclusion to include "being Spanish-speaking and Latino itself does not mean an absence of emergent literacy experiences." Frequency and variety of child literacy experiences depended on a family's ecocultural niche, and the activity settings the niche scaffolded. By looking for specific empirical links among ecocultural features, activity settings, and children's literacy experiences, we can avoid "stereotyping" entire categories of families based on packed variables such as socioeconomic status or ethnic group membership.

There is yet another way to view our data. Families are not passive respondents to environmental forces. In spite of significant niche constraints, including limited education, some of the families take action to create contexts that provided their children with significant literacy development opportunities. While they may not have the number and variety of options available to them as do other groups in the United States, some Latino families in our sample were observed to play an active role in shaping their children's learning experiences. They followed through on the monitoring of homework and on teacher suggestions for helping children at home; they attended parent meetings at school, and purchased instructional materials for their children to use at home. Parents were also observed to alter work schedules, enroll in English classes, and pursue job training courses—all in an effort to improve their situation and that of their children. Economic and other ecological constraints are resistant to social and personal maneuvers, but not entirely so. Nor are cultural beliefs and values always a straitjacket. They can also be flexible tools that families can bend and utilize to solve problems of adaptation.

All Spanish-speaking families in low-income areas cannot be viewed the same, in respect to the kinds of literacy experiences they create for their children. Despite the burdens to which they must adapt, some of the families are managing to create contexts that do foster improved learning and performance. Identifying ecocultural and activity-setting variations in these households can provide, in our view, a useful basis for understanding educational problems of children and for advising schools how to confront them adequately.

NOTES

1. In three of the four participating classrooms, all contacted parents (seven) agreed to participate in the study. The parents of one child could not be contacted because the family did not have a telephone. In the fourth classroom, the parents of nine children were contacted in order to obtain the remaining three subjects. Children in this classroom could not be included due to conflicting parents' work schedules or to our inability to establish contact with parents. Two children initially included were discontinued—one because of midyear special education placement, the other because the family went to Mexico for an extended period and various family members became ill for long periods upon their return. One child's parents could not be contacted because there was no telephone in the home.

2. Children do of course learn from other events as well, such as watching TV, listening to conversations, and playing with others, but we use the term "learning events" to refer to those activities identified in these tables, most of which involve written elements of some sort or, alternatively, oral attempts at teaching or learning.

3. Scores of the ten sample children ranged from 53 to 146 (mean = 85.5; s.d. = 33.6), and from 24 to 196 for the entire sample (N = 56; mean = 85.5; s.d. = 41.2). (For a full description of the procedure, see Goldenberg 1990).

REFERENCES

Anderson, A. B. and Stokes, S. J. (1984). "Social and Institutional Influences on the Development and Practice of Literacy." H. Goelman, A. Oberg, and F. Smith (Eds.), In *Awakening to Literacy*, pp. 24–37. Portsmouth, NH: Heinemann.

Arias, M. B. (1986). "The Context of Education for Hispanic Students: An Overview." *American Journal of Education*, 95: 26–57.

Auerbach, E. (1989). "Toward a Social-Contextual Approach to Family Literacy." *Harvard Educational Review*, 59: 165–181.

Bloom, B. (1981). "The Effect of the Home Environment on Children's School Achievement." B. Bloom (Ed.), In *All our children learning*. New York: McGraw-Hill.

Bruner, J. S. (1962). Preface to L. S. Vygotsky, *Thought and Language*. Cambridge, MA: MIT Press.

Bruner, J. S. (1973). "Organization of Early Skilled Action." *Child Development*, 44: 1–11.

Bruner, J. (1983). *Child's Talk: Learning to Use Language*. New York: W. W. Norton.

Bruner, J. S. (1984). "Vygotsky's Zone of Proximal Development: The Hidden Agenda." B. Rogott and J. V. Wertsch (Eds.), In *Children's learning in the "Zone of Proximal Development."* San Francisco: Jossey-Bass.

Clay, M. (1985). *The Early Detection of Reading Difficulties*, 3rd ed. Portsmouth, NH: Heinemann.

Cole, M. (1985). "The Zone of Proximal Development: Where Culture and Cognition Create Each Other." J. Wertsch (Ed.), In *Culture, Communication, and Cognition*, pp. 146–161. New York: Cambridge University Press.

CTB/McGraw-Hill (1982). *CTBS: Comprehensive Test of Basic Skills Forms U and V, Norms Book, Grades K-3*. Monterey, CA: CTB/McGraw-Hill.

CTB/McGraw-Hill (1988). *SABE: Spanish Assessment of Basic Education, Technical Report*. Monterey, CA: CTB/McGraw-Hill.

Delgado-Gaitan, C. (1990). *Literacy for Empowerment*. New York: The Falmer Press.

Feitelson, D. and Goldstein, Z. (1986). "Patterns of Book Ownership and Reading to Young Children in Israeli School-Oriented and Non-School Oriented Families." *The Reading Teacher*, 39:924–930.

Fillmore, L. W. (1981). "Cultural Perspectives on Second Language Learning." *TESL Reporter* 14(3):23–31.

Gallimore, R., Weisner, T. S. Kaufman, S. Z. and Bernheimer, L. P. (1989). "The Social Construction of Ecocultural Niches: Family Accommodation of Developmentally Delayed Children." *American Journal of Mental Retardation*, 94(3): 216–230.

Goldenberg, C. (1987). "Low-Income Latino Parents' Contributions to Their First-Grade Children's Word-Recognition Skills." *Anthropology and Education Quarterly*, 18:149–179.

Goldenberg, C. (1989a). "The Home Literacy Experiences of Low-Income Hispanic Kindergarten Children." Paper presented at the annual meeting of the American Educational Research Association, March, San Francisco.

Goldenberg, C. (1989b). "Language Use in Two Home Literacy Events: The Effect of Activity Setting on Spanish-Speaking Parents Language." Unpublished manuscript.

Goldenberg, C. (1990). "Literacy Instruction for Spanish-Speaking Kindergartners." *Language Arts*, 67:590–598.

Haycock, K. and Navarro, S. (1988). *Unfinished Business: Fulfilling Our Children's Promise*. Oakland, CA: The Achievement Council.

Hess, R. D. and Holloway, S. (1984). "Family and School as Educational Institutions." R. D. Parke (Ed.), In *Review of Child Development Research, 7: The family*, pp. 179–333. Chicago: University of Chicago Press.

Leont'ev, A. N. (1981). "The Problem of Activity in Psychology." J. V. Wertsch (Ed.), In *The Concept of Activity in Soviet Psychology*, pp. 37–71. Armonk, NY: Sharpe.

LeVine, R. (1977). "Child Rearing as Cultural Adaptation." P. Leiderman, S. Tulkin, and A. Rosenfeld (Eds.), In *Culture and Infancy*. pp. 15–27. New York: Academic Press.

Mason, J. M. and Allen, J. (1986). "A Review of Emergent Literacy with Implications for Research and Practice in Reading." *Review of Research in Education*, 13:3–48.

Minick, N. J. (1985). "L. S. Vygotsky and Soviet Activity Theory: New Perspectives on the Relationship between Mind and Society." Unpublished doctoral dissertation, Northwestern University.

Minick, N. (1987). "Implications of Vygotsky's Theories for Dynamic Assessment." In C. S. Lidz (Ed.), *Dynamic Assessment: An Interactional Approach to Evaluating Learning Potential*, pp. 116–140. New York: Gilford Press.

Munroe, Ruth, Munroe, Robert and Whiting, B. (Eds.) (1981). *Handbook of Cross-Cultural Human Development*. New York: Garland Press.

Ogbu, J. (1981). "Origins of Human Competence: A Cultural-Ecological Perspective." *Child Development*, 52:413–429.

Orfield, G. (1986). "Hispanic Education: Challenges, Research, and Policies." *American Journal of Educational Press*, 95:1–25.

Rogoff, B. (1990). *Apprenticeship in Thinking: Cognitive Development in Social Context.* Oxford: Oxford University Press.

Rogoff, B. and Lave, J. (Eds.). (1984). "Everyday Cognition: Its Development in Social Contexts." Cambridge, MA: Harvard University Press.

Super, C. and Harkness, S. (Eds.). (1980). *Anthropological Perspectives on Child Development: New Directions for Child Development*, No. 8. San Francisco: Jossey-Bass.

Super, C. and Harkness, S. (1986). "The Developmental Niche: A Conceptualization at the Interface of Child and Culture." *International Journal of Behavior Development*, 9:1–25.

Taylor, D. and Dorsey-Gaines, C. (1988). *Growing Up Literate: Learning from Inner City Families.* Portsmouth, NH: Heinemann.

Teale, W. H. (1986). "Home Background and Young Children's Literacy Development." In W. H. Teale and E. Sulzby (Eds.), *Emergent Literacy: Writing and Reading*, pp. 173–206. Norwood, NJ: Ablex.

Teale, W. H., & Sulzby, E. (Eds.). (1986). *Emergent Literacy: Writing and Reading.* Norwood, NJ: Ablex.

Tharp, R. G. and Gallimore, R. (1988). *Rousing Minds to Life: Teaching, Learning, and Schooling in Social Context.* Cambridge: Cambridge University Press.

U.S. Department of Commerce (1988). *The Hispanic Population in the United States: March 1988 Advance Report.* Bureau of the Census Current Population Reports, Series P-20, No. 431. Washington, DC: U.S. Government Printing Office.

Vygotsky, L. S. (1978). *Mind in Society: The Development of Higher Psychological Processes.* M. Cole, V. John-Steiner, S. Scribner, & E. Souberman (Eds. and Trans.). Cambridge, MA: Harvard University Press.

Weisner, T. S. (1984). "Ecocultural Niches of Middle Childhood: A Cross-Cultural Perspective." W. A. Collins (Ed.), In *Development during Middle Childhood: The Years from Six to Twelve*, pp. 335–369. Washington, DC: National Academy of Sciences.

Weisner, T. S. and Gallimore, R. (1985). "The Convergence of Ecocultural and Activity Theory." Paper read at the annual meetings of the American Anthropological Association, Washington, DC.

Weisner, T. S., Gallimore, R., and Jordan, C. (1988). "Unpackaging Cultural Effects on Classroom Learning: Hawaiian Peer Assistance and Child-Generated Activity." *Anthropology and Education Quarterly* 19:327–353.

Wells, G. (1985). "Preschool Literacy-Related Activities and Success in School." D. R. Olson, N. Torrance, and A. Hildyard (Eds.), In *Literacy, Language, and Learning: The Nature and Consequences of Reading and Writing*, pp. 299–255. Cambridge: Cambridge University Press.

Wertsch, J. V. (1981). *The Concept of Activity in Soviet Psychology.* New York: M. E. Sharpe.

Wertsch, J. V. (1985). *Vygotsky and the Social Formation of Mind.* Cambridge, MA: Harvard University Press.

Wertsch, J. V., Minick, N., & Arns, F. A. (1984). "The Creation of Context in Joint Problem-Solving." B. Rogoff and J. Lav. (Eds.), In *Everyday Cognition: Its Development in Social Contexts*, pp. 151–171. Cambridge: Harvard University Press.

White, K. R. (1982). "The Relation between Socioeconomic Status and Academic Achievement." *Psychological Bulletin*, 91:461–481.

Whiting, B. (1976). "The Problem of the Packaged Variable." In K. Riegel and S. Meachan (Eds.), *The Developing Individual in a Changing World: Historical and Cultural Issues*, Vol. 1. The Hague: Mouton.

Whiting, B. (1980). "Cultural and Social Behavior: A Model for the Development of Social Behavior." *Ethos*, 8:95–116.

Whiting, B. and Edwards, C. (1988). *Children of Different Worlds: The Formation of Social Behavior.* Cambridge, MA: Harvard University Press.

Whiting, B. & Whiting, J. (1975). *Children of Six Cultures.* Cambridge, MA: Harvard University Press.

Chapter 14

Culture, Class, and Race: Three Variables of Decision Making in Schools

Lenore M. Parker

INTRODUCTION

For as long as I can remember I've been fascinated by how people make decisions. A large part of this fascination is wondering why, when presented with the same information, different people make different decisions. Not only decisions about intervention, but about the person, the situation, and the problem. This interest was piqued more when reading Robert Rosenthal and Aaron Jacobsen's study on the "self-fulling prophecy" in education.[1]

In this study, classroom teachers were informed that certain students had high IQs and others had low IQs. Through the year those students labeled as high IQ had higher grades and made more progress than those labeled with low IQs. The twist was that Rosenthal and Jacobsen switched the groups when reporting to the teachers. Specifically, the children Rosenthal and Jacobsen reported had high IQs were children with lower IQs, while those reported as children with low IQs really had the higher IQs. This research reinforces the belief that people become what we believe they will become, or, as Rosenthal and Jacobsen labeled it, the "self-fulling prophecy."

The whole idea of the self-fulfilling prophecy was intriguing and led to two decades of research about the labeling effect and its influence on educational and counseling philosophies. Other researchers have investigated teacher expectations concerning student attractiveness of good and poor students,[2] teacher expectations of reading performance,[3] the child's socioeconomic status and teacher expectations,[4] counselor feelings toward clients and the effectiveness of change,[5] and the gender of students and teacher expectations.[6]

While these studies support the concept of the self-fulfilling prophecy, what was it about those teachers that influenced their perception of those children, which appears to result in the expected behavior or performance of the child? Rosenthal in collaboration with Monica Harris asked the question: ''What are the personality characteristics related to the expector's ability to bias others in the direction of their expectancy?''[7] This study looked at the labeling effect from two perspectives: the counselor characteristics associated with the labeling of clients, and client characteristics associated with conforming to counselor labeling. Harris and Rosenthal found that counselor personality characteristics associated most strongly with the labeling of clients are dominance, Machiavellianism, internal locus of control, need for achievement, persuasiblity, and authoritarianism.

While these findings were important and though provoking they didn't necessarily explain how people make decisions and what comprises the decision-making process. Throughout my professional and academic career, I've kept going back to Rosenthal and Jacobsen's study, intensely fascinated with exploring how beliefs and attitudes influence practice decisions.

During my doctoral education I became interested in welfare dependency. My particular interest was in the negative attitudes and beliefs of the general population and professionals toward recipients of public assistance. I remembered growing up and my father talking about poor his family was and how he wore the same pair of athletic shoes throughout high school because they didn't have money to buy new shoes. My father ended the story with pride by saying, ''no matter how poor we were we never went on welfare.'' As I began teaching, this sentiment was echoed by graduate students. When talking about clients living in poverty many would say, ''why don't they get a job instead of relying on public assistance''; ''their house is such a mess, why don't they clean it—don't they think cleanliness is important,'' and ''why do they keep having babies when they can't afford to support them.'' This led to my dissertation, ''The Influence of Public Child Welfare Workers' Attitude Towards the Poor on Practice Decisions.''[8]

The following vignette was provided for public child welfare workers' in the states of New York and Virginia.

> The S family came to the attention of the Department of Social Services as the result of a call from the local hospital. The S's had brought their daughter, Elizabeth, into the emergency room with her shoulder pulled out of its socket. The hospital referred the case to the Department of Social Service as was standard operating procedure in this type of case. The Department of Social Service has no prior record related to the S's. According to the S's they had taken Elizabeth for a walk through the park. Each parent had an arm and Elizabeth asked to ''be like a swing,'' so the S's lifted Elizabeth off the ground by her hands and began to swing her back and forth. As a result, Elizabeth's arm came out its socket. The S's, Roger and Laura, have been married for five years. Roger is 25 years old, Laura is 24 years old, and Elizabeth is four years old. Elizabeth, according to the S's, is a difficult child. She goes into a temper tantrum when she does not get her way. When she goes into a tantrum she falls on the floor, kicks her feet, and

screams. According to the S's Roger leaves the room when Elizabeth goes into a tantrum. Laura, on the other hand, tries to soothe Elizabeth by telling her that everything will be okay and she should not kick and scream. After about 10 minutes, Laura also leaves the room where Elizabeth is having a tantrum. Shortly thereafter, Elizabeth stops having a tantrum and usually begins playing with her toys. While they report they argue at times, Roger and Laura report that they get along well. They appear to have a stable marriage.[9]

Because I was interested in how attitude toward the poor influenced practice decisions, four socioeconomic conditions were specified with regard to the vignette: (1) a family who had been welfare dependent for two years, (2) a working poor family, (3) a middle-class family, and (4) an upper-middle-class family. While there was much consistency about the identified problem, there were some surprising responses. Several respondents noted that the father in the poor family had a substance abuse problem, several reported that the father in the upper-class family was so consumed with work he had no time to love and support his family. Several reported that the mother in the working poor family should get a job rather than stay home with her daughter, and one reported that the daughter had temper tantrums because she was epileptic.

Where did these different perspectives come from? How could educated and professionally trained people make unexplainable decisions? How did they read some of the information into the cases? Aren't there some basic professional guidelines for decision-making? Isn't that why decision-making trees are developed to ensure more consistent decisions and interventions? These questions keep returning regardless of the project I work on, the class I teach, or the student I supervise in fieldwork. This chapter is an attempt to explain this phenomenon from a theoretical perspective by looking at the literature on decision making, culture, class, and race.

DECISION-MAKING THEORY

Decision-making, according to Irwin Bross, is the process of making a choice between two or more alternative courses of action.[10] More specifically, in order for a decision to be made, three conditions must be met: ''(1) there are two or more alternative courses of action possible with only one that can be taken; (2) the process of making a decision will select a single course of action to carry out; and (3) the choice of the action must accomplish a designated purpose.''[11] Bross goes on to explain that there are five components that create the decision-making process (see Figure 14.1): data, a predicting system, a value system, decision criteria, and the recommendation. The predicting system determines the probability of any given outcome. In this phase, the decision maker searches for stable characteristics that persist over time, and can be used to help predict the likelihood of a particular course of action producing an anticipated outcome. The predicting system is based on *experience*. The value system is *intuitive* and

Figure 14.1
Bross' Decision Components

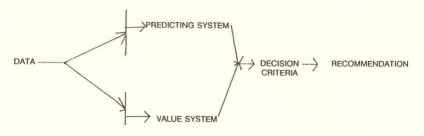

concerned with the desirability of the outcome. This component allows the decision maker to view each alternative as good, bad, or indifferent.

James Bieri (et al.) discusses both decision making and judgment when presenting the information theory model.[12] According to Bieri, the decision-making process includes input, a mediating structure, and output. There are three conditions that influence the decision-making process: value (attractiveness of the alternatives); risk (costs of error); and feedback (availability of information about the outcome of a decision). This process of decision making can be seen in Figure 14.2 and is similar to Bross' model if Bieri's mediating structure is interpreted as Bross' predicting and value systems.

Bieri goes a step further than Bross and discusses the judgment process. He says that a judgment occurs

> when an individual assigns one of a set of stimuli to one of two or more response categories. These response categories are usually well defined for the judge and bear a more or less direct relation to the stimuli being judged in that the task requires a fairly immediate perceptual discrimination. When the assignment of a stimulus to a category involves a consideration by the judge of value, preference, or outcome of each response alternative, the judgement task assumes more of the characteristics of *decision-making*.[13]

Bieri therefore includes the concept of judgment as a part of the decision-making process. At the moment the decision maker is choosing between two or more alternative actions, he or she is making a judgment about which alternative is best. In fact, judgment becomes the mediating structure Bieri describes in the information processing model of decision making (see Figure 14.3).

The judgment process, according to Bieri, includes the stimulus, the characteristics of the "transmitter of information," situational variables, and the output.[14] Within his conceptual framework, the transmitter of information is the judge, or the person making the decision. Characteristics of the judge influencing judgment include personal characteristics, professional characteristics, theoretical commitment, and level of experience. Situational variables that influence the

Figure 14.2
Bieri's Decision-Making Process

INPUT ------$\rangle$ MEDIATING STRUCTURE ------$\rangle$OUTPUT

judgment process include agency environment and interpersonal factors between the client and the clinician.

Although there is not much difference between Bross' and Bieri's theories of decision making, Bross clearly does not address the characteristics of the person making the decision. While he discusses the predicting system and the values system, both are viewed from a rational framework and do not take into account the professional or situational characteristics that may have an influence on the decision. Bieri does discuss these factors when talking about the transmitter of information, or the decision maker, and situational variables within the judgment process.

CULTURE, CLASS, AND RACE

What characteristics can be included in Bieri's "transmitter of information" or decision-maker aspect of the mediating structure? While professional characteristics, such as education and training, are important, as well as the individual's theoretical framework and level of experience, it seems that personal characteristics must be taken into account in discussion of the decision maker. This is even more apparent given the different decisions professionals make about students and clients regardless of professional and theoretical similarities presented in this discussion. In the example from my dissertation, it is interesting to note that there was no statistically significant difference within the sample based on educational level, gender, and age. Despite the similarities in personal characteristics, the definition of the problem, its seriousness, and plans for intervention were different. It seems that the most important personal characteristics influencing decision making are culture, class, and race.

Culture

According to Paul Pederson, behavior has no meaning until you add the context.[15] He notes that the context is culture. But what is culture? The *Social Work Dictionary* defines culture as "the customs, habits, skills, technology, arts, science, and religious and political behavior of a group of people in a specific time period."[16] Because of the broad definition of culture, it includes ethnographic, demographic, status, and affiliation groups. In training, Pederson reports that we are all a part of about a thousand cultures. For instance, I'm in the culture of women because of my gender, academia because of my status as an assistant professor, and middle class because of my salary.

Inherent in culture are the concepts of class and ethnicity. A major dilemma

Figure 14.3
Bieri's Information Processing Model of Decision Making

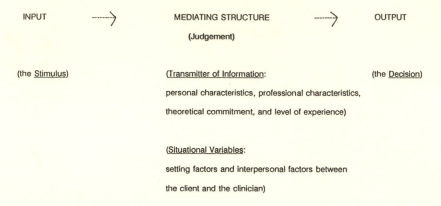

INPUT   ----->   MEDIATING STRUCTURE   ----->   OUTPUT

(Judgement)

(the <u>Stimulus</u>)   (<u>Transmitter of Information</u>:   (the <u>Decision</u>)

personal characteristics, professional characteristics,

theoretical commitment, and level of experience)

(<u>Situational Variables</u>:

setting factors and interpersonal factors between

the client and the clinician)

today is the focus on culture as a separate reality, or as a "thing unto itself."[17] To understand culture we must also understand class and race.

Class

Class, in the context of this discussion, can also be called social class. Social class is a person's self-perceived rank or status in society (typically a combination of social and economic factors, which result in a relative rank in a hierarchy of prestige).[18] The distinction between social class and socioeconomic status is the addition of social factors.

According to Donna Langston,

> as a result of the class you are born into and raised in, class is your understanding of the world and where you fit in; it's composed of ideas, behavior, attitudes, values, and language; class is how you think, feel, act, look, dress, talk, move, walk; class is what stores you shop at, restaurants you eat in; class is the schools you attend, the education you attain; class is the very jobs you will work at throughout your adult life. Class even determines when we marry and become mothers.[19]

For example, a crack dealer may make $150,000 a year and consider himself upper class from a socioeconomic perspective. When asked his social class, he may say lower class because he lives in government-subsidized housing and has only a sixth-grade education. At the same time, a women making $18,000 per year may consider herself lower class socioeconomically. However because she grew up in a wealthy family and has a college education from a major university she may identify herself as upper class when asked to report her social class. In this vein, social class is all-encompassing as well as socially constructed, influencing our perceptions of the world and available options, not only for ourselves but others.

Race

Racial identity, according to Janet Helms, is "a sense of group or collective identity based on one's perception he or she shares a common racial heritage with a particular racial group."[20] At times the concepts of race and ethnicity are used interchangeably. But how is race different than ethnicity? Racial groups, according to Oliver Cox, are distinguished by their physical characteristics.[21] Based on this definition, racial groups in the United States would include black Americans, Asian Americans, Native Americans, Mexican Americans, and white Americans. Ethnic groups, while they may also be considered racial groups, share a cultural and social history passed from one generation to the next rather than Cox's distinguishing characteristic of physical characteristics.[22] Examples of ethnic groups include African Americans, European-Americans, Jewish Americans, Korean Americans, and South Americans.

One important aspect of race is the formation of racial identity. The literature describes two primary models of racial identity formation: W. E. Cross model of black racial identity formation[23] and Helms' model of white racial identity formation.[24] While Cross' model deals specifically with blacks, identity formation occurs along similar lines for the majority of oppressed groups. Both processes, if resolved successfully, result in a positive sense of racial identity not only for the specific person but for encounters with people from other racial groups.

Black Racial Identity Formation. There are five stages in Cross' model: preencounter, encounter, immersion/emersion, internalization, and internalization-commitment. These stages are in no way meant to be considered as linear steps that proceed on a specific schedule or sequentially. Beverly Tatum suggests that black racial identity formation is more like a spiral, where "a person may move from one stage to the next, only to revisit a new stage as the result of a new encounter experience."[25]

White Racial Identity Formation. Helms' model identifies six stages where people "abandon racism and develop a nonracist White identity"[26]: contact, disintegration, reintegration, pseudo-independent, immersion/emersion, and autonomy.

ATTITUDE

Culture, class, and race influences all that we do. In this discussion it is clear that they act as filters for our perceptions, as well as our behavior. But how does that happen? From the literature on attitude and attitude formation, it appears that culture, class, and race also add a context for our beliefs about people,

Figure 14.4
Rokeach's Model of Attitude Formation

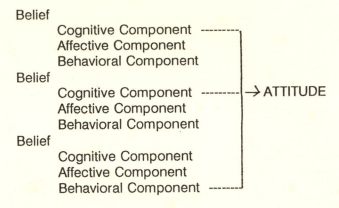

events, and the world. By looking at the literature of attitude, a clearer picture of this interaction between culture, class, and race may be developed.

Bieri and Bross note that one piece of the judgment process is attitude.[27] In this section, Milton Rokeach's attitude theory will be presented along with the way attitudes are developed and perpetuated. What is an attitude? According to Rokeach an attitude is "a relatively enduring organization of beliefs around an object or situation predisposing one to respond in some preferential manner."[28] He continues by saying that an attitude is a frame of reference. It provides a basis for induction and deduction, organizes knowledge, has implications for the real world, and changes in the face of new information or knowledge.[29]

Attitudes consist of beliefs and beliefs are made up of cognitive, affective, and behavioral components. The cognitive component is the knowledge about what is "good or bad, true or false, desirable or undesirable."[30] The affective component consists of the "arousing affect of varying intensity about the object of the belief or other objects."[31] All attitudes lead to some kind of action, according to Rokeach, and these actions make up the behavioral component of beliefs. The kind of action is determined by the content of the belief (see Figure 14.4).

While the delineation between the cognitive, affective, and behavioral components of a belief is clearly seen in Figure 14.4 and can be discussed from a theoretical perspective, it becomes almost impossible to isolate these components. Therefore, in most analyses of attitudes and beliefs, these components are not teased out to determine which is the most important. Attitudes are typically measured by asking people to respond favorably or unfavorably to a list of beliefs. The total score or picture that is painted by looking at the totality of a person's beliefs about a certain subject, group, or whatever amounts to their attitude toward that subject or group.

Bernice Boehm concurs by saying that beliefs and attitudes include thinking, feeling, behaving, and interacting with others.[32] Boehm also says that attitudes are our likes and dislikes. "They are our affinities for and aversions to situations, objects, persons, groups, or any other identifiable aspects of our environment, including abstract ideas and social policies."[33]

Because attitudes are a result of beliefs, most discussions about the development of attitudes stem from information about the development of beliefs. According to Katherine Levine and Arito Lightburn, beliefs are developed from personal experience.[34] These experiences include those an individual has directly perceived or felt, as well as experiences from others who are viewed as knowledgeable or in positions of authority. Ramon Rhine says that people learn attitudes the same way they learn different concepts, over a period of time and through their experiences.[35] He gives the following example about how people learn concepts and attitudes:

> The child learns the concept of cow because his parents and others point to objects in the field or in pictures and call them by that name. He learns that color alone is not the key to cow-ness, but that it is helpful. All black objects are not called cow, but green objects are never called by that name. The child soon learns to discriminate between cows and other objects as he learns that cow-ness is a feature of not one stimulus pattern but of a whole class of patterns.
>
> The child learns about people in much the same manner. He discovers that one dimension of [black-ness] is dark skin, but that a deep suntan does not make one [black]. He gradually learns that [black-ness] involves other dimensions such as facial characteristics and hair properties. This learning eventually enables him to make fairly accurate discriminations between [blacks] and other persons. So far, the child has a concept of [blacks] but not an attitude, because an attitude involves an evaluative dimension. Suppose, however, he has some unpleasant personal experiences with [blacks] or receives adverse information about them from his parents. Then the child's concept might be based on the dimensions, "dark skin, kinky hair, thick lips, speaks with a drawl, and bad." Since an evaluative dimension now appears in the concept, he has acquired an attitude.[36]

Once the evaluative piece occurs, the belief or concept has become an attitude. Rokeach defines the evaluative process as the cognitive component of a belief or the knowledge about what is good or bad.[37]

In discussing the formation and perpetuation of attitudes, Leonard Doob states that "the learning, retention, and decline of an attitude are no different from the learning of a skill, a piece of prose, or a set of nonsense syllables; and they must also involve the problems of perception and motivation."[38]

According to Boehm, attitudes perpetuate themselves because of social influences.[39] Social influences include the mass media, interpersonal influences (people influencing other people), social norms, reference groups, and reference

Figure 14.5
Parker's Model of the Influence of Culture, Class, and Race on Decision-making

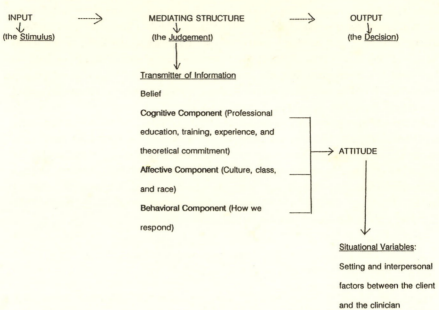

groups in conflict. For instance, if you have a negative attitude toward those living in poverty, you are more likely to continue that attitude if Tom Brokaw interviews former President Reagan who calls people on public assistance "cadillac driving welfare queens," or if your boss says that people living in poverty are lazy, or if society believes that only those people who overcome adversity are worthwhile, or if all of your friends believe the same as you.

THE PROFESSIONAL AS A DECISION MAKER

Decision Making as a Dynamic Process

How does all this fit together? Does it begin to answer the questions posed in the beginning of this chapter. Where do these different perspectives of clients and issues come from? How can educated and professionally trained people make unexplainable decisions? and How do they read some of the information into cases? Bieri's model of decision making plays an important role in answering these questions, particularly his concept of the mediating structure. Given the literature discussed on culture, class, race, and attitude a modification of this model can be made to clarify the mediating structure (see Figure 14.5).

The "transmitter of information" is the professional. The attitude(s) of the professional is the filter for which judgments are made. According to Rokeach, attitudes are comprised of cognitive components, affective components, and behavioral components. It appears that the cognitive component includes professional education, training, experience, and theoretical commitment; while the affective component includes the professional's culture, class, and race; and the behavioral component is how we respond to the belief in terms of our cognitive and affective components. Attitudes become the filter through which we look at situational variables, including the setting and interpersonal factors between the client and the clinician or the student and the teacher. This mediating structure, then, filters the input and results in the decision.

The reason that predicting how professionals make decisions and what decisions they make is difficult is because all professionals have their own mediating structure. Until what comprises each professional's mediating structure can be understood, predicting decisions and standardizing the decision-making process will be difficult if not impossible and may result in either blaming the professionals for lack of skill or blaming the clients for responses that are predictable given the decision-making process of the professional.

Professional as Peanut Butter and Jelly Sandwiches: An Analogy

Through this look at the theoretical aspects of decision making, I've decided that a perfect analogy for this dynamic process is a peanut butter and jelly sandwich. We're born with a bottom piece of bread, which consists of aspects of who we are that are unchangeable, like race and sexual orientation. As we grow up, peanut butter is spread on our bread. The peanut butter is our class, the various cultures we belong to, our experiences, our interpretation of our experiences, societal norms and expectations, and our attitudes.

When we decide to become professionals within the educational field, whether as teachers or social workers, our professional training becomes the jelly placed on top of our peanut butter. Through our reading, practice experiences, and integration of theory and practice, some of the jelly mixes with the peanut butter. Some stays separate. Graduation or certification is the top piece of bread. Sometimes the top piece of bread is already heavy with personal expectations of life as a professional, college loans to pay back, and familial expectations. The weight begins to push the peanut butter and jelly together. Again, some mixes well but some comes out of the sides. Sometimes only peanut butter comes out, sometimes only jelly, but sometimes both peanut butter and jelly come out of the sides of the sandwich. Whatever comes out of the sides is the part of decision making that cannot be predicted or channeled through a decision-making tree. In fact, in many instances what comes out of the sandwich determines how we interpret the person, situation, or problem. So, from the beginning who we are, in terms of our culture, class, and race influences all that we do. Our professional and educational training impacts our decision making, but no matter how hard we try, sometimes some of our peanut butter is going to stay inside the sandwich and the jelly is going to come out of the sides because it acts as a filter for everything we do, say, and believe.

SUMMARY AND CONCLUSIONS

So what does all this mean? Basically, decision making is a dynamic rather than a linear process. It means recognizing that people, no matter what level of training, make decisions based on much more than the facts of the case. Their own culture, class, race, and attitudes are important ingredients to understanding decision making. In fact, by looking only at professional standards about decision making we ignore the impact of the person making the decision on the actual decision. This results in a focus on the child, youth, or family that is experiencing the problem and gives an excuse to blame the victim for the their plight.[40] I hope this discussion of the influence of culture, class, and race raises strong concerns about ignoring ourselves when making decisions that affect peoples' lives.

Implications for the Fields of Education and Social Work

Where do we go from here? How can we minimize the influence of our own culture, class, and race on our decision making? I think the first place to begin is in the recognition and acceptance of its impact. Second, we can provide safe places for students and professionals to talk about and explore what pieces of their own background may "spill out."

Supervision. In terms of supervision, an environment should be constructed that allows both the worker and the supervisor to discuss their respective beliefs and attitudes about certain client groups and issues. It would help if the environment was free of judgment and focused on helping workers recognize their beliefs and attitudes and how they influence their decisions about clients.

In addition, case review provides an opportunity to begin to discuss how teachers and social workers perceive their clients. But again, it is important to develop a safe and nonjudgmental environmental where professionals are free to discuss their attitudes without being ridiculed and told they are wrong. The key is recognition because only then can change occur.

Education. The place to begin to impact how the culture, class, race, and attitudes of professionals impact their decision making is within the educational system—not only for professional education, but as an ongoing process from the beginning of the formal educational process. In many instances, universities and colleges are beginning to require courses in multiculturalism, ethnicity, and to discuss the issues of racism and classism. Many of these courses deal with knowledge about specific groups. While this focus is important, it must be taken to the level of self-awareness. In terms of race, educators must be prepared to help students struggle with their own racial identity formation to move them through the stages to develop a healthy identity. Academicians must also recognize their own culture, class, race, and attitude and how that affects not only their teaching, but responses to students.

Training. On-going professional training is an important adjunct to professional education. Using teachers and social workers' real life examples of how they make decisions and what about themselves "spills" over the decision-making process is a key training need. Typically training deals with skill building and special topics related to issues that professional face. While this is important, taking a close look at how we identify what skills are needed or special projects are addressed can provide clues for our own biases.

Difficulties in Helping Professionals Look at their Decision-Making Process

Sounds easy? It's difficult to realize and accept that who you are in terms of your culture, class, race, and attitudes influences what you do as a professional. Some of the difficulties can be considered "sources of resistance."[41] While Tatum discusses them specifically in terms of racism and racial identity formation, it seems that these difficulties are inherent in learning about and looking at our own issues with culture, class, race, and attitude:

1. Race is considered a taboo topic for discussion, especially in racially mixed settings.
2. Many students, regardless of racial-group membership, have been socialized to think of the United States as a just society.
3. Many students, particularly white students, initially deny any personal prejudice, recognizing the impact of racism on other people's lives, but failing to acknowledge the impact on their own.

Tatum goes on to discuss strategies for reducing these resistances. While her strategies are targeted for the classroom, they are adaptable to supervision (both group and individual), as well as ongoing training. These strategies are

1. the creation of a safe classroom atmosphere by establishing clear guidelines for discussion;
2. the creation of opportunities for self-generated knowledge;
3. the provision of an appropriate developmental model that students can use as a framework for understanding their own process; and
4. the exploration of strategies to empower students as change agents.[42]

Conclusion

Despite our best intentions of being clear about the influence of our attitudes, culture, class, and race on our decision making, we have to stay open to the inevitability of a "spill." I remember living in Manhattan several years back and getting off the bus in my neighborhood in Greenwich Village. A girl of about eight years old was walking down the street with her mother and baby sister. The girl wore dirty clothes, the mothers' hair was disheveled, and the baby sister was crying. The young girl stopped me and asked if I could help. Thinking she wanted directions, I asked what I could do to help. She asked me for money. I shook my head and walked away, mumbling under my breath, "how could that mother teach that child to beg?" I was appalled with myself. Where did that come from? What was I thinking? I began to explore the attitudes I had about parenting and responsibility, the middle-class work ethnic that had been instilled in me since I was born, and the father that was proud that no matter how poor they were as a child his family never asked for help. Instead of being harsh on myself, I began to understand and to look at the situation from other perspectives: the young girl's, as well as from my professional education, training, and theoretical framework. Once I understood and moved past my own personal issues around culture, class, race, and attitude to focus on the young girl's situation and my professional education and training in education and social work I could help, not only the young girl and her family, but myself.

NOTES

1. Robert Rosenthal and Aaron Jacobsen, "Self-Fulfilling Prophecies in Behavioral Research and Everyday Life," *Claremont College Reading Conference 32nd Yearbook.* February 1968.

2. Jordan Rich, "Effects of Childrens' Physical Attractiveness on Teachers' Evaluations," *Journal of Educational Psychology*, October 1975: 599–609.

3. Samuel Weintraub, "Summary of Investigations Relating to Reading," *Reading Research Quarterly*, Winter 1969: 131–647.

4. Dale G. Harvey and Gerald T. Slatin, "The Relationship between Childs' SES and Teacher Expectations: A Test of the Middle Class Bias Hypothesis," *Social Forces*, 54(1) (1975): 140–159.

5. Richard Sharf and J. B. Bishop, "Counselor Feelings toward Clients as Related to Intake Judgements and Outcome Variables," *Journal of Counseling Psychology*, May 1979: 267–269.

6. Linda H. Schlosser, and Bob Algozzine, "Sex, Behavior, and Teacher Expectancies," *Journal of Experimental Education*, Spring 1980: 231–236.

7. Monica J. Harris and Robert Rosenthal, "Counselor and Client Personality as Determinants of Counselor Expectancy Effects," *Journal of Personality and Social Psychology*, 50(2) (1986): 362–369.

8. Lenore Parker, "The Influence of Public Child Welfare Workers' Attitude Towards the Poor on Practice Decisions," unpublished Doctoral Dissertation, Fordham University, 1991.

9. Ibid., pp. 62–63.

10. Irwin D. J. Bross, *Design for Decision* (New York: The Free Press, 1965).

11. Ibid., pp. 19–20.

12. James Bieri, Alvin L. Atkins, Scott Briar, Robin Lobeck Leaman, Henry Miller,

and Tony Tripodi, *Clinical and Social Judgement: The Discrimination and Behavioral Information* (New York: John Wiley, 1966).

13. Ibid., p. 5.

14. Ibid.

15. Paul Pederson, "Mediating Multi-Cultural Conflicts," Workshop presentation at California State University, Fullerton, 1993.

16. Robert L. Barker, *The Social Work Dictionary* (Silver Springs, MD: National Association of Social Workers, 1987), p. 33.

17. Stephen Steinberg, *The Ethnic Myth* (Boston: Beacon Press, 1989).

18. Barker, *The Social Work Dictionary.*

19. Donna Langston, "Tired of Playing Monopoly?" in Margaret L. Anderson and Patricia Hill Collins (eds.), *Race, Class, and Gender* (Belmont, CA: Wadsworth Press, 1992), p. 112.

20. Janet Helms, *Black and White Racial Identity: Theory, Research, and Practice* (Westport, CT: Greenwood Press, 1990), p. 3.

21. Oliver C. Cox, *Caste, Class, and Race* (Garden City, NY: Doubleday, 1978).

22. Joe R. Feagin, *Racial and Ethnic Relations* (Englewood Cliffs, NJ: Prentice Hall, 1989).

23. W. E. Cross, Jr. "The Negro to Black Conversion Experience: Toward a Psychology of Black Liberation," *Black World,* 20(9) (1971).

24. Helms, *Black and White Racial Identity.*

25. Beverly Daniel Tatum, "Talking about Race, Learning and Racism: The Application of Racial Identity Development Theory in the Classroom," *Harvard Educational Review,* 62(1) (1992): 12.

26. Helms, *Black and White Racial Identity,* p. 13.

27. Bieri et al., *Clinical and Social Judgement*; Bross, *Design for Decision.*

28. Milton Rokeach, *Beliefs, Attitudes, and Values: A Theory of Organization and Change* (San Francisco: Jossey-Bass, 1968), p. 112.

29. Ibid., p. 131.

30. Ibid., p. 140.

31. Ibid., p. 141.

32. Bernice Boehm, "An Assessment of Family Adequacy in Protective Cases," *Child Welfare,* January 1990: 10–16.

33. Ibid., p. 14.

34. Katherine Grody Levine and Anita Lightburn, "Belief Systems and Social Work Practice," *Social Casework: Journal of Contemporary Social Work,* March 1989: 139–145.

35. Ramon J. Rhine, "A Concept-Formation Approach to Attitude Acquisition," in Martin Fishbein (Ed.), *Attitude Theory and Measurement* (New York: John Wiley, 1958).

36. Ibid., p. 383.

37. Rokeach, *Beliefs, Attitudes, and Values.*

38. Leonard W. Doob, "The Behavior of Attitudes," in Feishbein, *Attitude Theory and Measurement,* p. 38.

39. Bernice Boehm, "The Community and the Social Agency Define Neglect," *Child Welfare,* November 161–168.

40. William Ryan, *Blaming the Victim* (New York: Vintage Books, 1976).

41. Tatum, "Talking about Race, Learning about Racism," p. 5.

42. Ibid., p. 18.

Selected Bibliography

Alexander, Jeffrey C. (1983). *The Classical Attempt at Theoretical Synthesis: Max Weber.* Berkeley: University of California Press.

Altenbaugh, Richard (1987). "Teachers and the Workplace." In *Urban Education,* 21 (January): 365–389.

Altenbaugh, Richard J. (Ed.) (1992). *The Teacher's Voice: A Social History of Teaching in Twentieth Century America.* London: Falmer Press.

Altenbaugh, Richard J. (1993). "Families, Children, Schools, and the Workplace." In Stanley W. Rothstein (Ed.), *Handbook of Schooling in Urban America.* Westport, CT: Greenwood Press.

Ashton, Patricia T. and Webb, Rodman B. (1986). *Making a Difference: Teachers' Sense of Efficacy and Student Achievement.* New York: Longman.

Ashton-Warner, Sylvia (1963). *Teacher.* New York: Simon and Schuster.

Association for Supervision and Curriculum Development Handbook (1992). "Foreign Language Principles." Alexandria, VA: ASCD.

Banfield, Edward, and Wilson, James Q. (1963). *City Politics.* Cambridge, MA: Harvard University Press.

Banks, Cherry A. McGee (1993). "Restructuring Schools for Equity—What We Have Learned in Two Decades." *Phi Delta Kappan* 9 (43) (September):42–48.

Banks, James. (1989). "Integrating the Curriculum with Ethnic Content: Approaches and Guidelines." In James and Cherry A. McGee Banks (Eds.), *Multicultural Education: Issues and Perspectives,* 1st ed. Boston: Allyn and Bacon.

Banks, James (1988). *Multiethnic Education: Theory and Practice,* 2nd ed. Boston: Allyn and Bacon.

Banks, James (1993). "Multicultural Education: Historical Development, Dimensions and Practice." In Linda Darling-Hammond (Ed.), *Review of Research in Education.* Washington, DC: American Educational Research Association.

Becher, Tony and Maclure, Stuart (1978). *The Politics of Curriculum Change.* London: Hutchinson.

Becker, Howard S. (1962). "Social Class Variations in the Teacher-Pupil Relationship." *Journal of Educational Sociology*, 25 (April): 451–465.

Becker, Howard S. (1970). "Schools and Systems of Social Status." In Howard S. Becker, (Ed.), *Sociological Work*. Chicago: Aldine.

Bendix, Reinhard (1958). *Max Weber: An Intellectual Portrait*. New York: Doubleday.

Benedict, Ruth (1949). "Continuities and Discontinuities in Cultural Conditioning." In Patrick Mullahy (Ed.), *A Study of Interpersonal Relations*. New York: Hermitage Press.

Benton, Ted (1984). *The Rise and Fall of Structural Marxism*. New York: St. Martin's Press.

Bernstein, Basil (1960). "Language and Social Class." *British Journal of Sociology*, 2: 271–276.

Bernstein, Basil (1982). "Codes, Modalities and the Process of Cultural Reproduction: A Model." In Michale W. Apple (Ed.), *Cultural and Economic Reproduction in Education: Essays on Class, Ideology and the State*. London: Routledge.

Bernstein, B. (1990). *The Structuring of Pedagogic Discourse* Volume IV: *Class, Codes and Control*. London: Routledge.

Blanck, Gertrude and Rubin (1974). *Ego Psychology: Theory and Practice*. New York: Columbia University Press.

Blauner, Robert. (1972). *Racial Oppression in America*. New York: Harper and Row.

Bourdieu, Pierre (1971). "Systems of Education and Systems of Thought." In Edward Hopper (Ed.), *Readings in the Theory of Educational Systems*. London: Hucthinson.

Bourdieu, Pierre (1973). "Cultural Reproduction and Social Reproduction." In Richard Brown (Ed.), *Knowledge, Education, and Cultural Change*, London: Tavistock.

Bourdieu, Pierre (1977). *Outline of a Theory of Practice*. Translated by Richard Nice. Cambridge: Cambridge University Press.

Bourdieu, Pierre (1986). *Distinction: A Social Critique of Judgement of Taste*. Translated by Richard Nice. London: Routledge.

Bourdieu, Pierre and Passerson, Jean-Claude (1979). *The Inheritors: French Students and Their Relation to Culture*. Chicago: University of Chicago Press.

Bourdieu, Pierre and Passerson, Jean-Claude (1976). *Reproduction in Education, Society and Culture*. Beverly Hills: Sage Publications.

Bowles, Samuel and Gintis, Herbert (1976). *Schooling in Capitalist America: Educational Reform and the Contradictions of Economic Life*. New York: Basic Books.

Boyer, E. L. (1983). *High School: A Report on Secondary Education in America*. New York: Harper and Row.

Braverman, H. (1974). *Labor and Monopoly Capital*. New York: Monthly Review Press.

Brophy, James E. and Good, T. L. (1974). *Teacher-Student Relationship*. New York: Holt, Rinehart & Winston.

Callahan, Raymond E. (1960). *An Introduction to Education in American Society*. New York: Knopf.

Callahan, Raymond E. (1963). *Education and the Cult of Efficiency*. Chicago: University of Chicago Press.

Cohen, Sol. (1963). *Progressives and Urban School Reform: The Public Education Association of New York: 1895–1954*. New York: Teachers College, Columbia University.

Coleman, J. S., Campbell, E., Hobson, C., McPartland, J., Mood, A., Weinfield, F., and York, R. (1966). *Equality of Educational Opportunity.* Washington, DC: U.S. Government Printing Office.

Cosin, Bernard R. (Ed.) (1972). *Education: Structure and Society.* Harmondsworth: Penguin.

Cox, Oliver Cromwell (1970). *Caste, Class and Race: A Study in Social Dynamics.* New York: Modern Reader Paperbacks.

Craft, M. (1974). "Talent, Family Values and Education in Ireland." In John Eggleston (Ed.), *Contemporary Research in the Sociology of Education.* London: Methuen.

Cremin, Lawrence (1961). *Transformation of the School.* New York: Knopf.

Cremin, Lawrence (1977). *Traditions of American Education.* New York: Basic Books.

Cremin, Lawrence (1980). *American Education: The National Experience, 1783–1876.* New York: Harper and Row.

Cubberley, Ellwood P. (1916). *The Portland Survey: A Textbook on City School Administration.* New York: World Book Company.

Cubberley, Ellwood P. (1920). *The History of Education.* Cambridge, MA: Houghton Mifflin.

Cubberley, Ellwood P. (1919). *Public Education in the United States.* Cambridge, MA: Houghton Mifflin.

Cummins, John (1986). "Empowering Minority Students: A Framework for Intervention." *Harvard Educational Review,* 56: 18–36.

Darder, Antonia (1991). *Culture and Power in the Classroom: A Critical Foundation for Bicultural Education.* Westport, CT: Bergin & Garvey.

Dreeben, Robert (1970). *The Nature of Teaching.* Glenview, IL: Scott, Foresman.

Durkheim, Emile (1956). *Education and Sociology.* New York: The Fress Press.

Durkheim, Emile (1960). "On Anomie." In C. Wright Mills, (Ed.), *Images of Man: The Classical Tradition in Sociological Thinking.* New York: George Braziller.

Durkheim, Emile (1961). *Moral Education: A Study in the Theory and Application of the Sociology of Education.* Translated by Everett K. Wilson and Herman Schnurer. New York: The Free Press.

Durkheim, Emile (1964). *The Division of Labor in Society.* Translated by George Simpson. New York: The Free Press.

Edwards, Newton and Richey, Harman (1963). *The School in the American Social Order.* Boston: Houghton Mifflin.

Eggleston, John (1973). "Decision-making on the School Curriculum: A Conflict Model." *Sociology,* 7.

Eggleston, John (1977). *The Sociology of School Curriculum.* London: Tavistock.

Fernandez, John (1993). *The Diversity Advantage.* Lexington, MA: Lexington Books.

Freire, Paulo (1973). *The Pedagogy of the Oppressed.* New York: Seabury Press.

Freud, Sigmund (1961). *Civilization and Its Discontents.* Translated by James Strachey. New York: W. W. Norton.

Freud, Sigmund (1965). *The Interpretation of Dreams.* Translated by James Strachey. New York: Avon Books.

Freud, Sigmund (1977). *Introductory Lectures on Psychoanalysis.* Translated and Edited by James Strachey. New York: W. W. Norton.

Freud, Sigmund (1989). *The Ego and the Id.* New York: W. W. Norton.

Fuchs, Estelle (1969). *Teachers Talk: Views From Inside City Schools.* Garden City, Doubleday.

Fuchs, Estelle (1973). "How Teachers Learn to Help Children Fail." In Norman K. Denzin (Ed.), *Children and Their Caretakers.* New Brunswick, NJ: Transaction Books.

Goffman, Erving (1961). *Asylums: Essays on the Social Situation of Mental Patients and Other Inmates.* New York: Doubleday-Anchor.

Goodlad, John I. (1984). *A Place Called School: Prospects for the Future.* New York: McGraw-Hill.

Graham, Patricia A. (1974). *Community and Class in American Education, 1865–1918.* New York: John Wiley.

Greer, Colin (1970). *Cobweb Attitudes.* New York: Teachers College Press.

Greer, Colin (1972). *The Great School Legend.* New York: Basic Books.

Guess, R. (1981). *The Idea of a Critical Theory.* Cambridge, MA: Harvard University Press.

Harrington, Michael (1962). *The Other America: Poverty in the United States.* New York: Macmillan.

Heath, Shirley Brice (1986). "Sociocultural Contexts of Language Development." In *Beyond Language: Social and Cultural Factors in Schooling Language Minority Students.* Los Angeles: Evaluation, Dissemination and Evaluation Center, California State University.

Heath, Shirley Brice (1983). *Ways With Words.* New York: Cambridge University Press.

Honig, William (1991). *Remedying the Shortage of Teachers for Limited-English-Proficient Students.* Sacramento: California Department of Education.

Hyman, Harold H. (1954). "The Value System of Different Classes." In Reinhard Bendix, and Seymour Lipset (Eds.), *Class, Status and Power.* London: Routledge and Kegan Paul.

Irvine, Jacqueline J. (1991). *Black Students and School Failure: Policies, Practices, and Prescriptions.* Westport, CT: Greenwood Press.

Jersild, Arthur T. (1955). *When Teachers Face Themselves.* New York: Teachers College Press.

Johnson, Donald (1981). "Althusser's Fate." In *London Review of Books.* April 16–May 6 Issue: 13–15.

Johnson, David (1981). *Reaching Out: Interpersonal Effectiveness and Self-Actualization.* Englewood Cliffs, NJ: Prentice-Hall.

Kaestle, Carl F. (1983). *Pillars of the Republic: Common Schools and American Society, 1780–1860.* New York: Hill and Wang.

Katz, Michael (1968). *The Irony of Early School Reform: Educational Innovation in Mid-Nineteenth Century Massachusetts.* Boston: Beacon Press.

Katz, Michael B. (1975). *Class, Bureaucracy, and Schools: The Illusion of Educational Change in America.* New York: Praeger.

Katz, Michael B. (1976). *A History of Compulsory Education Laws.* Bloomington, IN: The Phi Delta Kappa Educational Foundation.

Katznelson, Ira (1981). *City Teachers: Urban Politics and the Patterning of Class in the United States.* New York: Pantheon.

Katznelson, Ira and Weir, Margaret (1985). *Schooling for All: Class, Race, and the Decline of the Democratic Ideal.* New York: Basic Books.

Kojeve, Alexandre (1969). *Introduction to the Reading of Hegel.* Edited by Allan Bloom, translated by James H. Nichols, Jr. New York: Basic Books.

Kozol, Jonathan (1991). *Savage Inequalities: Children in America's Schools.* New York: Crown.

Lacan, Jacques (1989). *Speech and Language in Psychoanalysis.* Translated by Anthony Wilden. Baltimore: Johns Hopkins University Press.

Lacan, Jacques (1991). *The Seminar of Jacques Lacan.* Edited by Jacques-Alain Miller, translated by Sylvia Tomaselli. New York: W. W. Norton.

Laing, R. D. (1965). *The Divided Self.* Harmondsworth: Pelican Books.

Laquer, Thomas W. (1976). "Working Class Demand and the Growth of English Elementary Education." In Lawrence Stone (Ed.), *Schooling and Society: Studies in the History of Education.* Baltimore: Johns Hopkins University Press.

Lazerson, Marvin (1971). *Origins of the Urban School: Public Education in Massachusetts, 1870–1915.* Cambridge, MA: Harvard University Press.

Lazerson, Marvin (1973). "Revisionism and American Educational History." *Harvard Educational Review*, 43.

Lazerson, Marvin and Grubb, W. Norton (1974). *American Education and Vocationalism: A Documentary History, 1870–1970.* New York: Teachers College Press.

Lightfoot, Sara Lawrence (1978). *Worlds Apart: Relationships Between Families and Schools.* New York: Basic Books.

Lightfoot, Sara Lawrence (1983). *The Good High School: Portraits of Character and Culture.* New York: Basic Books.

Litwack, Leon (1973). "Education: Separate and Unequal." In Michael B. Katz (Ed.), *Education in American History: Readings on the Social Issues.* New York: Praeger Publishers.

Lortie, D. C. (1975). *Schoolteacher: A Sociological Study.* Chicago: University of Chicago Press.

Lukes, Steven (1972). *Emile Durkheim: His Life and Work.* New York: Harper and Row.

Lutz, Frank W. and Merz, Carol (1992). *The Politics of School/Community Relations.* New York: Teachers College Press.

Lynd, Robert S. and Lynd, Harriet M. (1937). *Middletown in Transition.* New York: Harcourt Brace.

Mahler, M. S. (1963). "Thoughts About Development and Individuation." In Heinz Hartman (Ed.), *The Psychoanalytic Study of the Child.* New York: International Universities Press.

Mannheim, Karl and Stewart, W.A.C. (1962). *An Introduction to the Sociology of Education.* London: Routledge and Kegan Paul.

Nasaw, David (1979). *Schooled to Order: A Social History of Public Schooling in the United States.* New York: Oxford University Press.

Oakes, Jeanne (1990). *Multiplying Inequalities: The Effects of Race, Social Class, and Tracking on Opportunities to Learn Mathematics and Science.* Santa Monica, CA: The Rand Corporation.

Ogbu, John U. and Fordham, Signithia (1986). "Black Students and the Burden of 'Acting White.' " *The Urban Review: Issues and Ideas in Public Education*, 18 (3); 176–206.

Ogbu, John (1978). *Minority Education and Caste.* New York: Academic Press.

Oxford, Rebecca (1990). *Language Learning Strategies.* Boston: Heinle and Heinle.

Parsons, Talcott (1951). *The Social System.* New York: The Free Press.

Parsons, Talcott (1961). "The School as a Social System." In A. H. Halsey, J. Floud, and C. A. Anderson (Eds.), *Education, Economy and Society*. Glencoe, IL: The Free Press.

Peterson, Paul (1985). *The Politics of School Reform 1870–1940*. Chicago: University of Chicago Press.

Ravitch, Diane (1974). *The Great School Wars*. New York: Basic Books.

Ravitch, Diane (1983). *The Troubled Crusade: American Education 1945–1980*. New York: Basic Books.

Rice, Joseph M. (1893). *The Public School System of the United States*. New York: The Century Company.

Rist, Ray (1973). *The Urban School: A Factory for Failure*. Cambridge, MA: The MIT Press.

Rist, Ray (1978). *The Invisible Children: School Integration in American Society*. Cambridge, MA: Harvard University Press.

Rose, Peter I. (1990). *They and We: Racial and Ethnic Relations in the United States*. New York: McGraw-Hill.

Rothstein, Stanley William (1979). "Orientations: First Impressions in an Urban Junior High School." *Urban Education*, 14 (1): 91–116.

Rothstein, Stanley W. (1991). *Identity and Ideology: Sociocultural Theories of Schooling*. Westport, CT: Greenwood Press.

Rothstein, Stanley W. (1993). *The Voice of the Other: Language as Illusion in the Formation of the Self*. Westport, CT: Praeger.

Rothstein, Stanley W. (1993). "A Short History of Urban Education." In Stanley W. Rothstein (Ed.), *Handbook of Schooling in Urban America*. Westport, CT: Greenwood Press.

Rothstein, Stanley W. (1994). *Schooling the Poor*. Westport, CT: Bergin & Garvey.

Sarason, Seymour (1983). *Schooling in America: Scapegoat and Salvation*. New York: The Free Press.

Seidler V. J. (1980). *One Dimensional Marxism*. London: Allison and Busby.

Sergiovanni, Thomas J. and Starratt, Robert J. (1988). *Supervision: Human Perspectives*. New York: McGraw-Hill.

Shakeshaft, Charol (1993). "Meeting the Needs of Girls in Urban Schools." In Stanley William Rothstein (Ed.), *Handbook of Schooling in Urban America*. Westport, CT: Greenwood Press.

Simmel, Georg (1950). *The Sociology of Georg Simmel*. Translated by Kurt H. Wolff. New York: The Free Press.

Smith, Steven (1984). *Reading Althusser: An Essay on Structural Marxism*. Ithaca, NY: Cornell University Press.

Stein, Maurice (1960). *The Eclipse of Community*. New York: Harper and Row.

Stinchcombe, A. L. (1969). "Environment: The Cumulation of Effects Is Yet to be Understood." *Harvard Educational Review*, 39: 511–572.

Tonnies, Ferdinand (1957). *Community and Society*. New York: Harper and Row.

Tyack, David (1967). *Turning Points in American Educational History*. New York: John Wiley.

Tyack, David (1974). *The One Best System: A History of American Urban Education*. Cambridge, MA: Harvard University Press.

Vidich, Arthur and Bensman, Joseph (1968). *Small Town in Mass Society: Class, Power and Religion in a Rural Community*. Princeton NJ: Princeton University Press.

Waller, Willard (1961). *The Sociology of Teaching*. New York: Russell and Russell.

Waller, Willard (1962). "What Teaching Does to Teachers." In Maurice R. Stein, Arthur J. Vidich, and David Manning White (Eds.), *Identity and Anxiety: Survival of the Person in Mass Society*. Glencoe, IL: The Free Press.

Warwick, David (1974). "Ideologies, Integration and Conflicts of Meaning." In M. Flude and J. Ahier (Eds.), *Educability, Schools and Ideology*. London: Croom Helm.

Webb, Rodman B. and Sherman, Robert R. (1989). *Schooling and Society*, 2nd ed. New York: Macmillan.

Weber, Max (1958). *Protestant Ethic and the Spirit of Capitalism*. New York: Charles Scribner's Sons.

Weeres, Joseph G. (1993). "The Organizational Structure of Urban Educational Systems: Bureaucratic Practices in Mass Societies." In Stanley W. Rothstein (Ed.), *Handbook of Schooling in Urban America*. Westport, CT: Greenwood Press, pp. 113–130.

White, Dana (1969). "Education in the Turn-of-the-Century City: The Search for Control." *Urban Education*, 4 (July): 170–172.

Whitty, Geoff (1985). *Sociology and School Knowledge: Curriculum Theory, Research and Politics*. London: Methuen.

Wilson, John (1991). "Power, Paranoia, and Education." *Interchange: A Quarterly Review of Education*, 22 (33): 43–54.

Winnicott, D. W. (1953). "Transitional Objects and Transitional Phenomena." *International Journal of Psychoanalysis*, 34: 89–97.

Wirt, Frederick and Kirst, Michael (1982). *Schools in Conflict: Politics of Education*. Berkeley, CA: McCutchan.

Index

About the Contributors

RICHARD J. ALTENBAUGH is a noted educational historian on the faculty of Slippery Rock University in Pennsylvania. His most recent book, *The Teacher's Voice*, is becoming one of the most widely read and respected oral histories of the teaching experience over the past half century.

CAROL BARNES is a professor and chairperson of the Department of Elementary and Bilingual Education at California State University, Fullerton. She is a noted authority in the field of teacher preparation for diverse student populations.

WALTER F. BECKMAN is the chairperson and professor of the Graduate Department of Educational Administration at California State University, Fullerton. He is an expert in educational law and assessment processes in selecting and training school administrators.

DAVID ELI DREW is a professor of Education and Executive Management at Claremont Graduate School. He is a widely respected researcher and theorist who has specialized in the management of scientists and the assessment of science education. Previously, he was a senior researcher at the Rand Corporation, and is now a member of the National Academy of Science/National Research Council. He has authored four books and numerous articles and monographs.

ANDREW E. DUBIN is a professor of educational administration at San Francisco State University and an expert in providing supportive settings for special needs children.

RONALD GALLIMORE is a professor at the University of California at Los Angeles who specializes in the problems associated with schooling the disadvantaged students in urban schools. He and James Loucky were awarded the 1993 Grawemeyer Award in Education for *Rousing Minds to Life: Teaching, Learning and Schooling in Social Context.*

WACIRA GETHAIGA is a professor in African Ethnic Studies at California State University, Fullerton.

CLAUDE GOLDENBERG is assistant research psychologist at UCLA. His specializations include early literacy development amongst Hispanic children.

LAURANCE IANNACCONE is a noted political scientist who has written many books and referred articles about the politics of school boards. He is a professor at the University of California at Santa Barbara.

MIKYONG KIM-GOH is a clinical social worker and assistant professor in the Human Services Program at California State University, Fullerton. Her research interests include minority mental health and service delivery issues.

JAMES LOUCKY is an associate professor of Anthropology and the director of International Studies at Western Washington University. He is continuing his research on education of immigrant children.

FRANK W. LUTZ is a distinguished and widely read political scientist who specializes in problems of governance and the politics of school boards. He is the director of the Center for Policy Studies and Research in Elementary and Secondary Education at East Texas State University.

MOUGO NYAGGAH is a professor in the History Department at California State University, Fullerton. His interests include historical perspectives on the African-American experience in the United States.

LENORE M. PARKER is an assistant professor in the Human Services Program at California State University, Fullerton.

LESLIE REESE was on the faculty at UCLA. She is currently doing research in the psychology of learning.

JOHN RIVERA is a graduate of the doctoral program in Educational Administration at Claremont Graduate School.

STANLEY WILLIAM ROTHSTEIN is a professor of educational administration at California State University, Fullerton. He is a social critic who uses multidisciplinary approaches to probe the nature of schooling in mass society. His most recent books are *Schooling the Poor* (Bergin & Garvey, 1994) and *Handbook of Schooling in Urban America* (Greenwood, 1993).

DANIEL G. SOLORZANO is an assistant professor in the Division of Social Sciences and Comparative Education at the UCLA Graduate School of Education. He is also a Scholar in Educational Policy for the Tomas Rivera Center for Policy Studies. His work centers upon minority education in the United States and the Chicana and Chicano experience in the Southwestern United States.

JOSEPH G. WEERES is a professor in the Graduate Department of Educational Administration at Claremont Graduate School and a respected authority on the problems associated with institutional change.

CARMEN ZUNIGA-HILL is a professor of education in the Department of Elementary and Bilingual Education at California State University, Fullerton. She is a noted authority in the field of teacher preparation for diverse student populations.